THE COMPLETE BOOK
OF MANAGEMENT

THE COMPLETE BOOK
OF MANAGEMENT

Donald Grunewald

and

Sol Shaviro

Mellen Studies in Business
Volume 10

The Edwin Mellen Press
Lewiston•Queenston•Lampeter

Library of Congress Cataloging-in-Publication Data

Grunewald, Donald.
  The complete book of management / Donald Grunewald and Sol
Shaviro.
    p. cm.-- (Mellen studies in business ; 10)
  ISBN 0-7734-8469-8 (hardcover)
  1. Management. I. Shaviro, Sol. II. Title. III. Series:
HD31.G774 1998
658--dc21   98-9240
                                                                  CIP

This is volume 10 in the continuing series
Mellen Studies in Business
Volume 10 ISBN 0-7734-8469-8
MSB Series ISBN 0-88946-152-X

A CIP catalog record for this book is available from the British Library.

The Edwin Mellen Press   The Edwin Mellen Press
        Box 450   Box 67
   Lewiston, New York   Queenston, Ontario
  USA 14092-0450   CANADA L0S 1L0

The Edwin Mellen Press, Ltd.
Lampeter, Ceredigion, Wales
UNITED KINGDOM SA48 8LT

Printed in the United States of America

THE COMPLETE BOOK OF MANAGEMENT

Table of Contents

PREFACE

This book is about the practice of the profession of management. It has often been said that management is getting things done through people. Management also involves appropriate use of other resources, such as materials and money, to get things accomplished effectively. This book is designed to help both the practitioner of management and the student of management who hopes to be a practitioner of management in the future.

Both authors of this text have taught courses in management for many years at the college and graduate school levels. They have also had considerable experience in management of organizations in the real world as chief executive officers and other senior officers in organizations.

This book provides a survey of management knowledge. The authors believe that a study of management functions and processes will help managers become more effective as managers.

This book has benefited from the encouragement and advice of many persons. The authors take full responsibility for what has been written and any errors. We do wish to acknowledge all who have helped us complete this text. We wish to acknowledge the support of our colleges. Special thanks goes to the administration and faculty of both Touro College and Iona College for their helpful advice and support. We wish to thank the staff at The Edwin Mellen Press for their assistance in the publication process. Thanks go to Judie Szuets, who typed the final draft of this manuscript, and the word processing staff at Iona College for all their help in earlier drafts of the manuscript.

Finally, we wish to thank our families for all their assistance and support.

This book is dedicated to our families and to all who work or aspire to work in the profession of management.

Donald Grunewald
Sol Shavior

January 1, 1998

1

Introduction: The Nature of Management

Good managers don't sleep too much; they have no time. Management is an ever continuing, highly demanding, never relenting, ruthlessly stressful, but a greatly rewarding occupation. It offers consummate prizes to the winners: money, power, honor, a sense of accomplishment. For the losers, the inefficient, the ineffectual, and the unfortunate, the penalty is bankruptcy or being fired.

Management is important on many levels. For the firm, it spells the difference between success and failure, profit and bankruptcy. For the nation, it propels us to economic growth or slows us to stagnation or decline. Economists often ignore management, but those who are more perceptive acknowledge poor management as one of the causes of poor economic growth. There was a time when American management was the paragon of the world. Not so today. The troubles of the American auto and small appliance industries, when compared to those of Japan, may be traced, in part, to comparatively better management in Japan.

This does not imply that all management in the United States is poor, but rather that some industries have lost their superiority temporarily. The reasons have to do with the difficulties of management in an ever changing environment. The business stage on which the manager performs is demanding and dynamic. Cues are not clear. Directions are ever shifting. The manager as player on this stage must deal with constant change, intense competition, vague uncertainties, public regulations, formidable challenges, consumer questions, union demands, vendor failures, and a fickle public.

Competition has been likened to the Darwinian evolutionary struggle in which only the fittest survive. The failure rate among new business firms is extremely high. But even giant firms, conglomerates, multinationals, and monopolies, supposedly insulated from competition, do not perform in a Garden of Eden. Even in these mighty arenas, the struggle for survival persists.

Perhaps it is this challenge which justifies the substantial rewards that successful managers receive and vindicates those who choose to study management. Like seekers of the Holy Grail, managers set their sights high. Top business managers enjoy earnings of millions of dollars a year. Even less stellar performers in giant firms may earn salaries, bonuses, and other benefits in six figures.

Managers are needed to enable organizations to reach their objectives. The U.S. 3rd Army could not have smashed through the German lines without a general like Patton. Annie Hall could not have been produced without Woody Allen. The Model T would not have appeared without Henry Ford.

Managers are needed to choose among various goals, sometimes contradictory. Should a firm sacrifice quality for short-run profits? Should a new product be introduced if it makes an old staple obsolete? Should a firm jeopardize a secure market for the uncertainties of new markets?

Managers must deal with constant change. New technologies make old procedures archaic. New products replace old. New competition invades safe harbors. New consumer preferences demand fresh ideas. New regulations prevent old practices.

Managers are needed to meet repeated crises. Strikes, threats of hostile takeovers, loss of top personnel, dwindling sales, rising costs, and foreign competition must be dealt with, not just on rare occasions, but as a routine element of management.

On a daily basis, managers are needed to reach goals effectively and efficiently. And managers are needed simply to keep an enterprise moving. Someone has to see to it that the plant is open, that employees come to work, that supplies are available, that activities are ongoing. This may seem self-evident, yet it is urgent. It is the manager who brings order out of chaos, and assures that the little, discrete requirements of complex activities are achieved.

For the welfare of society, managers are needed for progress, growth, and economic welfare. Such high purposes are not always achieved. Critics of modern management have pointed to cases of diseconomies, antisocial behavior, selfish activities, dishonesty, and the destruction of the environment. Surely no realistic appraisal of society would deny these charges. Yet it is often forgotten, in the zeal of the reformers, that capitalist firms, led by managers, have also helped achieve an abundant and ever growing standard of living. The management profession is indispensable to modern society.

MANAGEMENT DEFINED

Management has been defined in various ways. Some writers say management is what managers do, or is what makes organizations perform. Others refer to the functions of management, and argue that management is the activity which includes functions such as planning, organizing, leading, motivating, directing, staffing, influencing, and controlling. Some writers discuss management as a process of decision making and engaging in other activities to achieve the goals of an organization. Still others discuss the use of human and material resources as the core of management. Many insist that management must be efficient and effective, and include these conditions in their definition.

We offer our own version: *Management is the dynamic process, in a formal, purposive organization, of using human and material resources cooperatively, effectively, and efficiently, to reach organizational objectives.*

THE MANAGER vs. THE ENTREPRENEUR

The separation of ownership and control in large corporations is well known. The top officers and directors may own only a small percentage of the shares of common stock in a very large firm with aggregate shares valued at hundreds of millions of dollars. Since ownership in most of these firms is widespread, ownership of a small percent of the outstanding stock may be sufficient for the board members to maintain control of the firm. So it is that the chief officers and directors are more nearly characterized as managers than as owners. In other cases, the owner is the entrepreneur who created the firm, and he may be filling both roles — that of owner and manager.

The manager must be contrasted with the entrepreneur. In smaller organizations, the top person may be both; indeed, he or she usually is. Many firms, including the largest, were initially organized by entrepreneurs who continued as managers, even after shares of common stock in the firm became widely owned. Despite numerous examples of individuals in dual roles, it is clear that the roles are different. The entrepreneur is the risk taker, the innovator, the profit maximizer, the person with the vision to start a new enterprise and to instigate change. His motive is to earn a profit. The entrepreneur is the man who established the corner stationery store; he is also John D. Rockefeller, who created the world's largest energy corporation. On the other hand, the manager is the analytic planner, the rational organizer, the thoughtful motivator, the skilled supervisor, the vigilant controller, and the reasonable administrator. He or she is the person who assures that the firm is properly operated. If the manager happens to have an ownership interest, he or she is motivated to earn a profit in that separate role, but as a manager he or she earns a salary.

In many cases, particularly for successful small firms, the entrepreneur may go on to become an excellent manager. Of the small firms that fail, the reason may be that the entrepreneur was a superior risk taker and innovator, but a poor manager. In large firms, it is essential that eventually the pure entrepreneur give way to the professional manager.

A striking example is General Motors. Ernest Dale has written about the role of William C. Durant, the brilliant founder of GM, and Alfred P. Sloan, his successor. Durant was the intuitive innovator whose genius created the giant automobile firm. But Durant's hasty decision making and his management by intuition eventually brought General Motors to the verge of bankruptcy. The firm had become too large and complex to be managed as a one-man operation. His successor, Sloan, brought in a team of professional managers, and introduced a systematic, rational approach to decision making. The entrepreneur had been replaced by the manager, and GM went on to win great fortunes.

VARIETIES OF MANAGEMENT

It is argued that the principles of management are universal, but their application is different in parts of the world where the business environment is dissimilar. A student of management cannot apply American school learning in Nigeria or Japan exactly as he or she would in the United States; in each nation the singular environment poses distinct problems and demands particular solutions.

The understanding of management is made difficult by the variety of management types. The chairperson of the board of a giant multinational conglomerate has a different job than the manager of a supermarket. This variety must be explored. Management can be classified by the level at which it takes place. We generally discuss managers as top level, middle level, and line managers.

Types

Managers can be classified by the types of organizations they manage. Organizations have been classified (see Amitai Etzioni, *Modern Organizations*, Englewood Cliffs, N.J., Prentice-Hall, 1964) as coercive, utilitarian, and normative. An example of a coercive organization is the Army where orders must be obeyed without question. A utilitarian organization is the regular business firm in which success requires harmony and order. A normative organization may be a religious institution where faith causes people to conform. It should be obvious that the job of the manager of each of these organizations — the general, the president, and the priest — is different in many ways. However, it should not be forgotten that there are similarities too. The general must make value judgments, and the businessman must include ethics in decision making. The priest must have a business head to operate a large institution, and may have to lay down the law without equivocation when the occasion demands. Yet even if management principles are universal, the differences must be explored.

A major difference between types of management is found in firms with differing goals. The manager of a government agency must be more concerned with the purpose of the agency, sometimes without regard to costs. An example is the action of an officer during time of war. While the administrator of a university must be deeply concerned with cost, he or she cannot neglect quality. The public administrator and the manager of a nonprofit firm have different parameters of action than the director of a firm whose main concern is profit.

The size of the firm also dictates differences in management style as well as duties and responsibilities. We generally direct attention to the management of large institutions. We will discuss small business management in a separate chapter.

While experts agree on the universality of management principles, those who hire managers for firms in specific industries usually ignore such arguments —read the help wanted ads. The conventional wisdom of those who do the hiring is that the new employee must have experience in the particular industry for which he or she is being hired.

This narrow approach is not followed without reason. In our complex world, a tremendous amount of particular knowledge is needed. An employer seldom is willing to hire a high level manager who must spend a long period learning, and who cannot make good decisions until he or she knows the industry.

It must be obvious that the manager of an old, stable industry needs different skills than the manager of a firm in a new, expanding field. A textile firm may be occasionally concerned with new technology and new materials, but an electronics firm must live with innovation as a primary concern.

The environment affects management style. Firms which burn coal have environmental concerns not considered important a few years ago. Drug companies must be responsive to health considerations. All these factors affect the kind of management needed.

Management style depends on the operation. An autocratic manager is needed during a time of crisis, as in wartime. Participative management may be sensible when dealing with professionals, such as research scientists. This loose approach to discipline and control would make no sense in running a crew digging a ditch.

A distinction can be made between the specialist and the generalist. In some industries or institutions, specialized knowledge is critical. Usually the middle manager, particularly in an industry depending on new technology, must be a specialist, while the top manager may be a generalist. This is because the top manager must deal with all the problems facing a firm, from legal to financial to technical to marketing to personnel to organizational. At times the nature of the organization demands specialization, as in the armed forces where officers must have unique information about their field of activity. We are unwilling to entrust combat decisions to laymen, though generals and admirals have been known to move into private industry without problem.

Another distinction can be made between the managers of domestic firms and the managers of multinationals, or firms with substantial operations overseas. Most important for those who deal with or in foreign nations is an understanding of the culture and the laws of these nations.

Some differences are real, some are semantic. We make invidious comparison between business management and public administration. The image created may be the petty businessman standing alongside the great statesman. Administration has a grander sound than management, and so we reserve the word "administration" for the affairs of state. In this case, the sound may be more important than the meaning. Public administration may involve petty management, as with the operation of a small town tax collector. Private business management may involve major issues affecting the welfare of the nation. Such is the case of firms in the steel, auto, airline, or communications industries facing foreign competition.

MANAGEMENT SKILLS: THE GOOD MANAGER

Distinctions between entrepreneurship and management do not suggest that the manager should not be an innovator. A firm in the business world is not like an ice cube in a frozen lake; it is more like a wave in the ocean. The manager faces continuous flux, movement, change. He must respond creatively. He must be open-minded, sensitive, adaptable to change, ready to meet new challenges from unaccustomed technology and competition.

The manager must be rational, yet have good instincts. Few people, if any, are entirely rational. Decisions should be based on a careful analysis of the facts that are available. Yet precise facts are not always obtainable; herein lies the difficulty. Facing uncertainty, where statistical parameters cannot be determined, takes the intuitive skill of an entrepreneur. On the other hand, rational management skills are needed in facing risk, where the parameters of action can be stated with some degree of mathematical certainty. The factors to be considered are so complex and so numerous that at times intuitive reactions may be as good as rational decisions.

This lack of certainty, however, does not give license to irrational, preconceived, impetuous decisions. Because of dangers which lie along perilous roads, it is all the more important for the manager to use reason and logic to identify those features of which he or she has reasonable knowledge. We will find, in this imperfect world, that not all managers are rational; on the other hand, we may find that not all problems can be solved with pure reason. Some firms are so blessed with computer capabilities, so overwhelmed by data, that they are unable to digest the facts and choose among alternatives. The truth is that management is in part science and in part art. The middle course is hard to find.

One reason for the difficulty in choosing the reasonable way is the complexity of modern management. Firms may have hundreds of thousands of employees, engage in dozens of distinct industries, deal with a plethora of laws and regulations, operate in widespread territories across the United States and foreign nations. The problems are varied and include financial, personnel, technological, marketing, legal, and engineering. Decisions involve different people and different groups with varied interests. The objectives may be short-term or long-term. Nor do the decisions present themselves singly, in orderly sequence. The good manager must be a juggler as well as a logician.

Good managers need special skills. Most authorities have delineated three categories of skills needed by managers: conceptual, interpersonal, and technical. Conceptual skills, including analytic and diagnostic abilities, are most important to senior administrators. Technical skills are the specific tools of a discipline, such as the particular knowledge of the accountant, the engineer, or the attorney. These skills are usually of greatest importance to those lower on the management pyramid. Interpersonal, or human relations skills, are needed by all, especially today when the study of human relations is considered one of the chief ingredients of the management soup.

Another skill, usually neglected, is the ability to fight, to push, to drive on under difficulties, to work with strength and fervor. More than in most professions, the prime requisites of management are determination, power, energy, vigor, resolution, and motivation. Management is not for the gentle, the weak, and the irresolute.

MANAGEMENT UNDER ADVERSITY: A HERCULEAN TASK

The Roman Emperor, Marcus Aurelius, must have been a knowledgeable manager; he told us that life is a battle. The experienced manager is surely a veteran of many battles in which only the fittest survive. Some people cannot take the stress of such adversity. For those, management is not the best choice. For others, adversity stimulates the adrenal glands, and provides the challenge that the driving, aggressive manager needs.

The nature of management, particularly in a competitive environment, is one of decision making under stress, facing difficulties and dangers. Often, the time for careful analysis is lacking. The manager may have to make a decision in an instant on a matter of major profit or impending bankruptcy. And if such cataclysmic events do not come regularly, smaller issues cause stress daily.

We will examine a number of battlefields which demand special attention, such as a strike, a hostile takeover, an impending bankruptcy. However, other ordeals may cause ulcers. A strong competitor may invade your territory. A new technological invention may make your plant or your product obsolete. A crazed individual may lace your product with poison. A racketeer may invade your operation. Management is only for the tough, and good management under adversity is the mandate for survival.

THE ENVIRONMENT, SOCIAL RESPONSIBILITY, AND ETHICS

To the management scribe, environment means more than the natural world of air, water, and earth. The environment in which managers operate is the system of customs, laws, habits, and the institutions which exist all around us. The environment of a business includes the extent of competition, the technology of the industry, the infrastructure of the economy, perceptions of the public, the banking system, the concept of law and order. The environment of management today involves not only big government, but organized labor and alert consumers. A fact of life in management is the increasing frequency of lawsuits by vendors, unions, consumers, stockholders, and the public. The manager cannot ignore these forces.

A problem receiving increasing attention these days involves questions of ethics. Ethical perceptions are part of the environment and vary in different parts of the world. Business persons operating in some foreign nations may be faced with painful choices, such as paying bribes or losing business. Though we cannot make certain that all managers will follow ethical precepts, at least we can discuss the problems explicitly. It is important to instill ethical concepts in management ideology.

In the "good old days," the good guys and some not so good had the freedom to make management decisions as they saw fit. These were the early days of the industrial revolution when child labor was unrestricted, when hours of work exceeded 16 a day, when sanitation and safety in the work place were unknown. Radical theories arose, in part as a response to the misery of the early industrial revolution. It is to the credit of our democratic capitalist society that the response was an improvement in the standard of living and reforms in the conditions of work.

Today, many managers deplore the restraints on their freedom of action imposed by labor unions and government regulation. Though these historic developments were a response to early excesses by some businessmen, most managers believe that business profitability has been endangered more than necessary. The management profession has been involved in political action to prevent excessive regulation. We discuss such activity in this text as an integral part of management strategy necessary for survival. However, a student of management should understand that we will never return to the days of unbridled freedom by managers and entrepreneurs. A good manager must be prepared to deal with the environment as it is, with laws, rules and regulations, countervailing forces, restraints and parameters, and limitations to free management decisions. The manager must fight against unreasonable regulation, not tilt against windmills.

Discussion of government regulations inevitably brings us to the subject of the physical environment. Without doubt, business firms have contributed to the pollution of our water supply and the air we breathe. In the past, managers failed to take action to prevent pollution, not because they were wicked, unconcerned individuals, but because of the facts of economic behavior. No one business can clean up the air alone. Why should one landlord increase expenses to reduce smoke if millions of other landlords do not? Action by all landlords is needed, and public regulation has been the manner in which concerted action has been achieved. Thus, managers must operate within the parameters of government regulation.

CHANGING VIEWS OF MANAGEMENT

No discipline remains fixed for all time. Our views of management have changed with our understanding of human nature, with learning from experience, with changes in public perception of right and wrong.

Earlier management was authoritarian. Modern management is more aware that human beings cannot be treated as robots. Older management practices were simplistic. Modern views are made complex by many considerations. Today we discuss human relations, systems, contingencies. The growth of management thought is part of the dynamic history of all human thought.

In the next chapter we will discuss changing beliefs about the principles of management. However, a few broad strokes may be drawn here. Early management thought was formal, sometimes called "scientific," following the fixed notions of the early management preacher, Frederick Taylor. Later theory, especially following Elton Mayo, was concerned with human relations. At a still later date, management theory became involved with more sophisticated analysis, including behavioral research, decision technology, mathematical approaches, and increased attention to social systems and the environment.

One approach of particular importance is systems analysis, a holistic approach which emphasizes an integration of all facets of an enterprise, and considers the organization as an open system, interacting with the external environment. Another important view is the contingency approach which denies that there are panaceas, or simple universal guidelines, and insists that organizations operate under varying conditions and respond in different ways to different situations.

CAREERS: THE NEED FOR BETTER MANAGERS

Different people study management for different reasons. Some think it provides an easy route to advancement. Others believe that management knowledge will make them better managers. Some nonmanagement personnel may want to pursue a career in management. For those, we point out that the field of management is an excellent choice.

Good management is badly needed. The quality of management must be raised for the sake of individual business firms and for the sake of the American economy. But business leaders need not resort to exhortation. The rewards of management speak for themselves.

2

History of
Management Thought

Behold the angels! In their ranks you can find clear evidence of organizational structure and hierarchy. In their stations you can find clear assignment of function.

Various descriptions of the organization of angels can be found in the Apocrypha and elsewhere. At the head of the angelic hosts is Metatron, also known as Enoch. Then come the seven (sometimes listed as four) archangels: Uriel, Raphael, Raquel, Michael, Sariel, Gabriel, and Jarahmeed. Some writings refer to seven ranks of angels, though Maimonides lists 10 ranks. The heavenly hosts are said to be divided into 12 mazzalots, each with 30 armies of angels. Each army has 30 camps, each camp has 30 cohorts, each cohort has 30 corps, each corps has 365,000 myriads, and each myriad has 10,000 angels. However, in later writings, countless angels seem to exist, possibly beyond the hierarchical listing.

The angels have functions, the main one to mediate between God and man. Related functions are intercession; that is, pleading for individuals before God and performing specific missions, such as leading the Israelites out of bondage in Egypt. Angels are assigned duties representing particular persons, or presiding over clouds, hail, light, and so on.

IN THE BEGINNING . . .

Out of the darkness of early history come glimmerings of civilization. Civilization itself implies the development of social and political entities, or the organization of people into persistent units. In the description of early civilization, we talk of the structure of groups as families, tribes, clans, bands, and larger associations, often with functions assigned to various members, and with leaders, priests, and common people arranged in hierarchies. This is the substance of management. Management was not discussed in these early times as an abstract idea, a special consideration, or even as a general notion. There was no subject known as management. However, management did exist. It was practiced by rational individuals, attempting to improve their lot by organizing their resources in some reasonable way.

This notion of management as a rational process is the reason we do not go back to the practices of ants and bees in the discussion of the genesis of management. At first glance, a colony of bees seems to be an exemplar of management structure, with different members of the colony assigned particular duties in a complex society. However, the organizational structure of the bees, or of the ants, seems to be a matter of instinctive behavioral patterns rather than rational choice. We turn, then, to human examples.

There is evidence in Paleolithic times of humans living in small communities, equipped with tools and weapons, engaging in organized, systematic, communal hunts and ritual ceremonies. A community, of course, is a social organization, a rudimentary administrative unit and so we presume management practices can be traced back to Paleolithic times. Neolithic sites show traces of permanent settlement, agriculture, and the production of goods such as clay pots and cloth. Jericho was fortified by 6000 B.C. with walls and a ditch, towers, and buildings of packed stone inside. Management was important in those days.

The earliest evidence of management expertise in a more advanced civilization has been found in the plain of Sumeria, in the southern part of the land later known as Mesopotamia, an area leading to the Persian Gulf. In the years between 3900 B.C. and 3500 B.C., settlements in Sumeria show the development of cities and complex irrigation projects in the valley of the Tigris and Euphrates Rivers. The Sumerians were skilled in pottery and working with copper, gold, and silver. They also developed cuneiform writing, made use of seals which attest to ownership, and used numbers in business transactions.

It is supposed that the irrigation ditches in Sumeria did not spring up overnight, but that Sumerian civilization and management practice may go back to 10,000 B.C. Thus the canals and cities developed slowly along with organizational structures. The Sumerians assumed the land was owned by the gods; in fact, the land was administered by the priests and worked by thousands of persons. William H. McNiell says in *The Rise of the West* (Chicago: University of Chicago Press, 1963, p. 33) the priests "regularly served as managers, planners and coordinators of the massed human effort..." Later (p. 36) he notes the "Priestly control ... permitted the proliferation of administrative and craft specialists. . . ."

In later years Sumeria and Akkadia, to the north, were united by the military conquests of Sargon and the nation of Mesopotamia was formed. Hammurabi founded Babylonia, the capital of Mesopotamia, perhaps about 1700 B.C. Under Hammurabi, there are clear signs of bureaucracy. Royal officials served the Amorite ruler throughout the land. Central records were maintained with the names and responsibilities of thousands of officials. The cuneiform writings were expanded with the needs of communication in the vast bureaucracy.

An important indication of the role of administration was the Code of Hammurabi, recorded in cuneiform writing and listing rules applied to property, real estate, business, trade, agriculture, purchases, sales, contracts, and leases.

Organizational structure was also known to the Hebrews. The most striking early reference to organization can be seen in the Old Testament. In Exodus 18:13–26, Jethro observes Moses judging the people "from the morning unto the evening." He tells Moses, "Thou wilt surely wear away," and counsels that Moses should teach the people ordinances and laws, and moreover, that they should create an organization, by choosing from the people men "to be rulers of thousands, and rulers of hundreds, rulers of fifties, and rulers of tens."

Ancient Egypt, too, stands as evidence of early management skill of the highest order. It is estimated that each of the great pyramids was built by at least 100,000 slaves working for two decades or more. The great pyramid at Khufu, built in 2600 B.C. of six million tons of stone, and standing 481 feet high was so accurately engineered that the base does not vary in elevation by more than one-half inch.

The military power of the Egyptians, the complex irrigation projects for control of the annual floods of the Nile, the huge bureaucracy of the Pharaoh and their extensive foreign trade are all evidence of their administrative skill.

India, too, shows signs of early hierarchical structure. The caste system developed in the Indus valley as early as 2000 B.C. While the caste system was a means of repression, it was also a device for segregating the different functions of members of society, such as worship, warfare, crafts, or agriculture. Two cities, 350 miles apart on the Indus River — Mohenjodano and Herappa — covered about one square mile each. With baked brick houses in a regular layout, capacious granaries, and citadels (possibly the homes of priests), there must have been a strong central government and centralized administration.

In China, civilization first appeared along the Yellow River about 1500 B.C. During the Shang Dynasty (1500 to 1027 B.C.), we find evidence of fortified towns, the manufacture of bronze, writing, the growing of wheat, and the use of horse and chariot. Later, construction of the Great Wall is proof of the exceptional administrative capabilities of the Chinese.

We seek evidence of management not only in tribal activities, but in central government functions. The early story of American Indians, as the Iroquois, does not enter most accounts. Yet the long houses of the Iroquois were used by tribal councils to govern by agreement among elders, perhaps a forerunner of participatory management.

Authoritarian management can be found in the Andes of South America. William Howells (*Back of History*, Garden City, New York: Doubleday & Company, 1954) argues that the Incas invented totalitarianism. The Incas put laborers under a foreman in groups of 10, organized 10 such groups into a "tribe," and created four great divisions of the empire. They regimented life to the point of dictating what the common people could own. At the head of the empire was a single ruler with absolute power. Hierarchical structure and organization seem to have developed independently in many parts of the world.

The development of management practices accelerated as the world became more complex, more advanced, and (perhaps) more civilized. The Greeks seem to have discouraged professional administration and reserved management practices for the home. The Romans, however, advanced the art of management, especially in the administration of their vast empire and in the conduct of their armies. One of the great examples of central administrative control can be found in the organization of the Catholic Church. The Catholic Church made use of advanced management techniques, not only in hierarchy, but also of specialized functions and the use of staff.

Military organizations have also made use of hierarchy and staff organization. The Crusades, the construction of great cities and grand cathedrals, as well as the development of trade were all evidence of skilled management.

Evidence of management practice is not confirmation of explicit management thought. Only recently have specific treatises been written on the subject of management. Early examples of management writing are few; an exception is the work of Luca Pacioli, published in 1494, on double entry bookkeeping.

Niccolo Macchiavelli, a practicing statesman, lost power in 1512 and turned to writing about the actual practice of rulers. His work, primarily on the great affairs of state, reflects on administration. He suggested four principles for administrators to follow: reliance on mass consent, cohesiveness in organization, leadership, and the necessity of survival by any means.

In England, in the years of the early Industrial Revolution, management practices were carried out in an environment of laissez-faire; the factory owners were free to organize their plants as they pleased to maximize profit. Factory standards were incredibly poor by today's precepts, with long hours of work by women and children and extremely poor sanitation. Yet efficiency was not ignored. In the Soho foundry in Great Britain, the sons of James Watt, inventor of the steam engine, engaged in forecasting and planning, the use of power equipment in place of labor, the standardization of parts, cost controls, and work flow.

An early example of humane management was found in the New Lanark mill purchased by Robert Owen in 1800. Owen instituted a number of reforms. He astonished his fellow mill owners by refusing to hire children under 10 years of age, sending them to school instead. His factories were clean, his workers well treated. Remarkably, his profits were high.

Management discussion increased in the 1800s. Charles Babbage (1782–1871), the English mathematician who invented a calculating machine, a forerunner to the computer, discussed the division of labor in production and prepared guidelines to compare the value of machine processes to human operations.

An important contribution to management theory was made by Max Weber (1864–1920), the German sociologist who developed the idea of bureaucracy. The word "bureaucracy" today represents excessive formalism and red tape in large organizations. Weber used the term to mean an organized approach to public administration in place of the personal, loose, irregular, unsystematic administration found in the German States at the time he wrote. Weber urged that officials be given regular official duties in a fixed hierarchy. He argued for a consistent system of rules to be followed in all cases and that officials be appointed and promoted for their knowledge and ability, and not as a reward for friendship with the ruler.

FREDERICK TAYLOR AND SCIENTIFIC MANAGEMENT

Frederick Taylor (1856–1915) is known as the "father of scientific management." His is the example of a Horatio Alger story, rising from an apprentice patternmaker and machinist to chief engineer of the Midvale Steel Company. His greatest contribution to management was the development of time and motion studies to "scientifically" determine how much a worker should produce in a "fair day's work." While others contributed to this kind of study, Taylor popularized it, especially in his extensive testimony before the U.S. Congress.

Perhaps the best known example of scientific management was the pig iron experiment which Taylor conducted at the Bethlehem Steel Company as a consultant in 1899. Taylor had long been convinced that workers "soldiered" (loafed) on the job; they tried to look busy though actually doing little work, like soldiers in a peacetime army. Moreover, Taylor believed there was only one best way to do a job and increase productivity. The key was to determine, by careful observation, how much work was possible for the efficient worker, specifically by timing each small motion made in the work process.

At the Bethlehem plant, a gang of about 75 men moved 92 pound pig irons from a field where the iron was stored to railroad cars nearby. Each man moved 12½ tons a day on average. Taylor reasoned that with periods of rest between handling the pigs, a man should be able to move 47 to 48 tons a day. His first step was to select a subject for the experiment. After watching the gang work, Taylor selected four possibilities. One was "a little Pennsylvania Dutchman who had been observed to trot back home for a mile or so after his work in the evening, about as fresh as he was when he came trotting down for work in the morning" (Frederick Winslow Taylor, *The Principles of Scientific Management*, New York: Harper & Row, Publishers, 1947, p. 43).

Taylor then reports a conversation with the man, to whom he gave the pseudonym Schmidt. After asking Schmidt if he was "a high priced man" willing to earn $1.85 a day instead of the customary $1.15, he told Schmidt, "Well, if you are a high priced man you will do exactly as this man (the foreman) tells you tomorrow, from morning till night. When he tells you to pick up a pig and walk, you pick it up and you walk, . . . and when he tells you to sit down and rest, you sit down . . . and what's more, no back talk." (Ibid, pp. 45, 46.)

By the end of the day, Schmidt had moved 47½ tons. He kept up the pace for three years, during which time other men were trained to match his accomplishment.

Taylor claims that he was opposed to exploitation, and noted that Schmidt earned pay at a rate 60 percent higher than formerly. He does not remind us that production rose 400 percent.

Other examples of the work of Taylor are instructive. In one experiment he pointed out that workers traditionally used their own shovels to shovel coal. There was no standard size for a shovel, though the types of coal varied; some coal was compact and heavy, some light and porous. Taylor suggested "that a first-class man would do a biggest day's work with a shovel load of about 21 pounds . . . for example, this man would shovel a larger tonnage of coal with a 21–pound load than with a 24–pound load or than with an 18–pound load on his shovel." (Ibid, p. 65.) He convinced Bethlehem to provide eight to 10 types of shovels, each appropriate to the type of material.

The essence of the approach pioneered by Taylor was to determine by time and motion studies the amount of work that could be accomplished. He argued that previously management had been unable to compare actual work done with any standard so that discipline had been arbitrary. He believed that exact knowledge of how much work could be done would eliminate arbitrary rule and create harmony. This would lead to a new attitude on the part of labor and management. He suggested that the division of the returns from production were less important than an increase in production, i.e., we should not argue about how to cut up the pie but how to make a larger pie. Workers would accept the fairness of a wage determined by scientific experiment and observation, and fewer strikes would be the result.

The work of Taylor is still followed widely today, despite the advent of schools of management which stress psychological factors and human relations as well as efficiency. Yet there are doubters who say some firms follow the ideas about efficiency without the doctrine of fairness. For one thing, Taylor has been accused of patronizing workers. In his *Principles* (Ibid, p. 59) he discusses men like Schmidt, saying, "the very first requirements for a man who is fit to handle pig iron as a regular occupation is that he shall be so stupid and so phlegmatic that he more nearly resembles in his mental makeup the ox than any other type." In his earlier work, *Shop Management*, (New York: Harper & Row, Publishers, 1947, p. 98) he argues that workers should be relieved of planning and clerical work, and further that "All brain work should be removed from the shop and centered in the planning . . . department." Of course, this refers to management as much as to workers.

Another sample of his attitude is gleaned from what he calls "An amusing instance . . ." (Ibid, p. 73). He recalls that the manager of a plant "tried several modifications of day and piece working an unsuccessful attempt to get children who were engaged in sorting over the very small screws to do a fair day's work. He finally met with great success by assigning to each child a fair day's task and allowing him to go home and play as soon as the task was done. Each child's playtime was his own and highly prized while the greater part of his wages went to his parents."

It is no surprise that labor was opposed to Taylor, though many managers were also opposed, believing their prerogatives were being taken away. Under Taylorism, the work details were set by planners, and the only remaining job of the foreman was to see that the work was carried out as predetermined.

Taylor believed that a military type of organization, with one man taking orders from one boss, did not belong in a shop. He suggested a type of functional management, with workers coming in contact with eight different bosses, "Four of these bosses are in the planning room . . . [and] Four others are in the shop." The idea is that each boss has a specialized function and deals with workers in carrying out that particular function only. Examples are speed bosses who monitor the efficiency of work, quality inspectors, and repair bosses who supervise care and maintenance of machines. The suggestions are not widely followed since they create a heavy load of supervisory help, but may be the precursors of matrix management with multiple management control.

Fundamentally, Taylor pioneered efforts to measure work scientifically and set rigorous standards for productivity. In addition, he tried to establish a philosophy of labor–management cooperation. He was correct in suggesting that modern industrial output was based on harmony and cooperation, but naive in his expectation that conflict between labor and management could be overcome by paying what he judged to be a fair day's pay for a fair day's work.

Yet we must not judge Taylor in the context of current beliefs and understanding. He was not heartless about child labor. In his time, child labor was common. He did not despise workers, but merely assumed mental brilliance was not needed to move pig iron. He had no acquaintance with an industry in which workers were required to master advanced technology. He preached harmony between labor and management and urged that labor share the benefits of improved productivity. The problem lay in deciding what was a fair division. In

Marxist Russia, the communist leaders admired and copied many of Taylor's ideas in an attempt to raise productivity. Taylor advanced the practice of management to a new level of competence. His shortcomings can be forgotten in view of his achievements.

THE FOLLOWERS

Henry L. Gantt (1861–1919) worked with Taylor at Midvale and Bethlehem Steel. He is best known for the Gantt chart which schedules the progress of work in production.

He also worked out a refinement of the bonus pay system developed by Taylor. Instead of a simple differential pay rate for high and low producers, he proposed a minimum wage for all work, plus a bonus for workers and their supervisors when output passed a minimum level.

Frank Gilbreth (1868–1924) and Lillian Gilbreth (1878–1972) were a husband and wife team, mostly known for their contribution to time and motion studies. They perfected the technique of using a camera with a large clock in the background to determine the "one best way" of performing a job.

Frank Gilbreth started work as a bricklayer but soon became interested in finding a way to increase productivity. He observed that bricklayers wasted motion in laying brick and devised a way to eliminate the waste. He designed scaffolding and bins for the mortar and brick so that the bricklayer could reach the materials standing still. The bricklayer was required to reach for the brick with one hand and the mortar with the other at the same time, using exactly the right amount of mortar to minimize the quantity of excess mortar which had to be wiped away. The exact mix of mortar was specified to assure the best consistency. As a result, an average bricklayer was able to increase output from about 120 bricks per hour to 350.

Gilbreth was so immersed in his vision of efficiency that he carried his methods home. He taught his 12 children how to take baths with the fewest number of motions. He even tried to shave with two razors at a time, but failed because he could not coordinate the movements of his hands. His bricklaying experiments were more successful.

Gilbreth classified the specific motions workers used into a few basic motions which he named "therbligs" (Gilbreth spelled backwards with the "th" transposed). A therblig might be a motion such as reaching, grasping, or positioning a brick. He then tried to eliminate waste motions, such as taking a step to reach a brick or wiping off excess mortar that should not have been put on the brick in the first place.

Lillian Gilbreth is interesting in her own right. One of the few women in management, she encountered prejudice from her male peers. Her doctoral dissertation on psychology was published on the condition that the author be listed as L.M. Gilbreth, hiding the fact that the author was a woman. She added an understanding of the human side of the worker to the doctrine of efficiency, including such subjects as morale and the monotony of much work.

Henri Fayol (1841–1925) was a French engineer and geologist who first systematized general organizational theory. While Taylor and his followers had concentrated on efficiency in the plant, Foyol was concerned with the broad principles that governed all management. In 1916 he published his great work, *General and Industrial Management*, reflecting his experience as an industrialist with a mining company. Unfortunately, his work was not generally known in North America until 1949.

Fayol classified management into six operations: technical (manufacturing), commercial (buying and selling), financial, security (protection), accounting, and administrative. His major contribution concerned administration, listing 14 general principles:

1. Division of work (specialization for efficiency)
2. Authority and responsibility (authority is the right to command and responsibility implies accountability)

3. Discipline (organization required obedience)

4. Unity of command (one man, one boss)

5. Unity of management (a common goal for the organization)

6. Subordination of individual interest to the common good (organizational interests before personal ones)

7. Remuneration of staff (must be fair)

8. Centralization (but depending on the situation)

9. Hierarchy (scalar chain of command)

10. Order (a place for everything and everything in its place)

11. Equity (fairness, achieved by kindness and justice)

12. Stability of staff (high turnover is detrimental)

13. Initiative (at all levels of the hierarchy)

14. Esprit de corps (harmony and teamwork)

Fayol warned against slavishly following the principles. It would not be wise for communications between persons in different departments to go up the ladder to a common supervisor and then down to the intended recipient, as implied by Principle 9. Instead. Fayol advocated a "gangplank," or direct link between the persons involved.

While the concepts of Fayol were not known in North America until recent times, their importance is undeniable. The concept of the general subject matter of administration is the basis of all textbooks on management. Of particular importance is the discussion of the functions of management, including planning, organizing, commanding (leading), coordinating, and controlling. These functions, with only small variations, are still accepted as basic to an understanding of management today.

THE HUMAN RELATIONS APPROACH

The scientific management approach assumed worker–management cooperation. Taylor believed that a fair day's pay for a fair day's work would assure harmony, but harmony did not exist in most industries. Certainly the Marxists stressed conflict between workers and capitalists. Union members argued about the meaning of a "fair day's pay" and perceived a "fair day's work" as a speed-up. Strikes and other labor unrest were common. The purely mechanical approach to productivity and efficiency was not an unbridled success. Managers, as well as psychologists, began to worry about worker motivation. The human side of management became a topic of interest.

We remember Robert Owen who became a wealthy mill owner despite the introduction of decent working conditions in his factories. Hugo Munsterberg (1863–1916) was more consciously involved in the human side of management. He is known as the father of industrial psychology, applying psychological principles to management. In his book, *Psychology and Industrial Efficiency* (Boston: Houghton Mifflin Company, 1913), he discussed how industry might find the best person for a position, put into effect the best psychological conditions for effective work, and obtain the best results.

As noted earlier, Lillian Gilbreth was a pioneer in personnel management. Another woman who contributed to management theory was Mary Parker Follet (1868–1933) who argued that leadership came from the superior knowledge of the manager, not merely from his or her position of formal authority. She stated what she called the "law of the situation"; that is, that authority arises from the situation rather than from hierarchy.

THE HAWTHORNE STUDIES, MAYO, AND HUMAN RELATIONS

The human relations schools of management emerged from a series of experiments on the effect of illumination on productivity. A higher level of illumination than had been previously possible was made available with the development of advanced electric lights and General Electric wanted to promote its use.

GE funded a series of tests to show better lighting meant higher productivity.

One study, lasting three years, started in the Hawthorne plant of the Western Electric Company in Cicero, a suburb of Chicago. In one of the most interesting of the experiments, a number of female operators were moved to a separate room where their output could be monitored. Lighting was slowly increased from 24 foot candles to as high as 70. Not surprisingly, output rose dramatically, but there did not seem to be a consistent pattern between specific changes in illumination and particular changes in output. Finally, the assistant manager tried another experiment, reducing illumination to 0.06 foot candles, approximately the amount of light on a moonlit night. Output continued to rise as illumination decreased, and showed only a very small drop when the moonlight level was reached.

There was no direct correlation between productivity and light; some other factor was at work. Elton Mayo, a Harvard University professor was consulted. He sent two of his associates, Fritz Roethlisberger and William Dickson to investigate, and a new series of experiments were begun.

Six girls, each about 16 years old, were moved to a test room to assemble electric relays. Despite their age, they were experienced operators. An observer kept records in a pleasant, friendly atmosphere. Thirteen test periods were organized between 1927 and 1929, during which working conditions were changed. Rest periods of different duration and timing were tried, variations were made in the way defective relays were handled, and the workday was reduced. The twelfth test period, lasting 12 weeks, was crucial. The girls were returned to a full workday with no breaks. During the test, total weekly output rose, though hourly output of four of the workers dropped slightly. One conclusion seemed evident; there was no simple correlation between conditions and productivity.

The Hawthorne studies are associated with Elton Mayo though he took no direct part in the experiments except for visits to the plant on two occasions. Even the detailed reports were done by his associates. However, Mayo is credited with the analysis of the results; it is his interpretation which is acclaimed.

He argued that productivity rose because of the relaxed atmosphere in the test room and because of the attention paid to the young workers. More generally, the operating factors were psychological and behavioral. The workers felt important; they were being treated as human beings, not just as workers.

Arguments have been made about the specific conclusions reached by Mayo. For example, he attributed the increased output to management style. Others believe that economic factors, incentives, and the quality of work life contributed to the results. For a while, writers on management used the Hawthorne experiments to demonstrate the superiority of the human relations approach to the teachings of scientific management. Thus, Elton Mayo is associated with the new human relations school. Surely, the Hawthorne experiments demonstrated that complex factors were involved in worker motivation and productivity and not merely technical studies of time and motion. However, another conclusion might be that both approaches are important and a synthesis is needed.

MODERN DEVELOPMENTS

Our understanding of how to manage does not stand still. New developments might be expected and have come as our ideas about the world have changed. Many factors are at work in the reshaping of management theory.

Our grasp of scientific method has improved, our view of the world expanded. Our notions of the rights of workers, women, and minorities has affected management practices. The impact of the environment on management decisions is significant today. Unions play a role managers cannot ignore. Government regulations are more invasive than in previous times. Professional management has replaced entrepreneurial management in giant firms and financial management seems to eclipse professional management, at least in conglomerates and takeover targets. In the United States, top managers are more often lawyers or financiers than engineers and management technicians. The result is a more complex and more sophisticated approach to management.

By the end of World War II, a number of psychologists and sociologists were busy in the field of management. Abraham Maslow suggested there was a sequence, or hierarchy, of human needs affecting motivation on the job. Douglas McGregor introduced *Theory X* and *Theory Y*. Chris Argyris found that the demands of an organization were often incongruous with the needs of the individual and proposed job enrichment. Rensis Likert discussed types of management systems based on management concern for people or for output, suggesting worker participation in management. Frederick Herzberg examined factors which motivate, including satisfiers and dissatisfiers. Earlier theory appeared simplistic and an attempt to use management to manipulate workers.

With increasing sophistication, we see a movement from a simplistic human relations approach to the more scientific behavioral schools of management. The new strategy relies on broad fields of knowledge, including not only psychology and sociology, but anthropology, economics, the health sciences, and political science. Management specialists discuss individuals and their interrelationships, group behavior, and organizational behavior as it affects the management of the organization.

QUANTITATIVE SCHOOLS

The Scientific Management School tried to use scientific observation of work to improve productivity. While the lessons of that school were important, many writers have expressed doubt that the studies of Taylor and others were truly scientific. The inquiries were narrow and based on the prejudices and preconceptions of the observers. "Scientific Management" refers to Taylor and his followers. "Management Science," on the other hand, has a different meaning.

During World War II, planners in Great Britain, confronting a superior German war machine with limited resources, looked for the best way to use their strength. The difficulty of allocating scarce resources was essentially an administrative problem. It was solved by the use of mathematical models. Herein began the use of management science, also known as operations research.

In essence, management science involves the creation of a model of reality, in which factors are quantified, then solving the model with mathematical tools. A model, like a map, is an oversimplification of the real world, but one which is amenable to analysis. Extraneous factors are eliminated so that the essentials can be examined.

Some writers refer to management science as the analysis of management problems with mathematical tools. Operations research is sometimes considered the application of management science to practical situations. For example, a firm with a large inventory may use math to determine the best time to reorder supplies, balancing the cost of holding inventory with the difficulties which arise if needed parts are missing. Since large quantities of information are often needed, most models are computer-based and use management information systems.

Conventional wisdom holds that the purpose of business is to maximize profit. Unfortunately, determining the exact output or combination of resources needed to maximize profit is difficult to determine. Computer-based models can give answers not otherwise available to managers.

MANAGEMENT PROCESS THEORY

While management science is a modern development, the views of the Management Process School are essentially an outgrowth of the classical administrative theories which started with Henri Fayol and his concept of separate management functions. The modern emphasis on function is as a series of activities that are closely interrelated, rather than discrete tasks.

Fayol originally suggest five functions of management: planning, organizing, commanding, coordinating, and controlling. Luther Gulick and Lyndall F. Urwick, writers on public administration, expanded the list to include planning, organizing, staffing, directing, coordinating, reporting, and budgeting. They contained the list in the awkward acronym POSDCORB. Modern writers cannot agree on a proper list so that diverse books on management contain slightly different lists, usually close to the Fayol version and always including planning, organizing, and controlling. Fayol's "commanding" is replaced variously by directing, leading, influencing, or motivating. A fifth function found in many texts is staffing, but others include staffing in one of the other categories. Ultimately, the specific list is unimportant since all the activities of management are included; the differences are merely classification.

While the management process approach is not as modern as the quantitative schools with their computers and complex mathematical formulae, it does permit an orderly, methodical, systematic study of management based on interrelated activities. The job of the manager can be seen as a process in which closely related functions are carried out continuously. The separation of functions is partly artificial and the management process school acknowledges their inseparability in practice. However, breaking down interrelated activities into a number of components makes for better understanding. As a practical matter, most writers of management texts accept the management process classification as the basis of their exposition.

SYSTEMS THEORY

Systems theory is among the newest and oldest approaches to management. The economist, Kenneth Boulding, was one of the first to discuss general systems theory as it applies to economics, and therefore to the business world, in an article published in 1971. ("General Systems Theory — A Skeleton of Science," in P.P. Schoderbek, ed., *Management Systems*, 2nd Ed., New York: John Wiley & Sons,

Inc.). However, good managers have applied systems concepts, perhaps unconsciously, from the beginning of management.

Systems theory is based on the understanding that all elements of an organization and its environment are closely interconnected. The various parts affect each other; they are not discrete, independent units. Production affects sales. Sales depend on quality. Quality depends on financing. Financing responds to public perceptions. The public is influenced by the product.

A system is defined as an entity, a whole, a collection, a set composed of components or parts or elements which function interdependently for a common purpose. A living being is a unique entity composed of heart, lungs, brain, plus circulatory, muscular, and skeletal subsystems. Every organization, as a system, is a unified, purposeful assemblage of associated subdivisions. The system can be divided into subsystems, each of which can be viewed as a system in its own right. A business firm is a system, while the various departments, including production, marketing, finance, and so on, are subsystems.

Systems can be closed or open. A closed system is self-sufficient. An open system is affected by the environment. An example of a closed system is hard to find. It has been suggested that a battery-operated watch is a closed system, but a new battery must be installed at certain times and it operates effectively only after the correct time is set by an entity outside the watch. A manufacturing firm can be viewed as operating within the walls of a plant, but it gathers raw materials from the outside, sells a product outside, and operates within rules and laws established outside. A monastery is more self-sufficient than a college. Openness is a matter of degree.

Other concepts are associated with system analysis — one is that of synergy, defined as the combined action of the parts so that the total effect is greater than the sum of the parts.

An early version of the systems concept can be found in the writings of Chester I. Barnard (1886–1961), formerly president of New Jersey Bell. Barnard considered organizations as cooperative systems, with communications as the link between the purpose of the organization and the willingness of individuals to serve.

While good managers always understood instinctively the relationship between departments and between the firm and the outside world, some management authors ignored the obvious in their special pleading. This is certainly true of the early advocates of scientific management and human relations.

Systems theory does not give the manager a hard rule about how to act. In contrast, a time and motion study can lead to a specific action. However, the importance of systems theory should not be ignored. Too often individual departments act as if they are independent. A sales department has been known to accept orders which the production department cannot produce in time. Or a production department has been known to establish output goals without determining if the product can be sold. Or a foreman has been known to enforce a speed-up without regard to quality. Or a purchasing department has been known to outsource a component without considering the probable union response.

The lesson of the systems approach is for managers to be aware of the ramifications of their actions on others. It is a matter of sensitivity to the environment. It is a function of managers to coordinate their activities with others.

But there is another benefit of systems thinking. For years, writers have tried to integrate the various schools of management theory; systems theory is a vehicle for this integration. It permits the combination of scientific management and behavioral management theory since both are needed for good management. The quantitative approach need not rule out the management process approach. Systems theory also leads us to another school of thought, contingency theory.

CONTINGENCY OR SITUATIONAL THEORY

Many managers have always understood that the particular techniques of management depend on the situation. Even a nonauthoritarian manager will tighten control in a crisis. An administrator who believes in participatory management will act autocratically during a battle in wartime. Giving leeway in work assignments is more sensible when dealing with research scientists than with ditch diggers. Yet in the past, most authors of particular management schools wrote as if their proscriptions were the only, best way to manage. Taylor believed scientific management would reveal the one, best way to do a job. The contingency approach holds that there is no single, universal approach to management which is appropriate at all times. Situational management is sometimes considered a more extreme form of the idea that the situation should determine management style. Contingency management does not hold that the general principles of management are invalid. It considers alternative choices of management style and the effective manager chooses the most appropriate method.

Contingency management follows directly from the systems approach. It implies that there are many variables in management, many interests to be considered. A rational strategy is to do research to determine the best course of action in a particular situation. The idea of contingency management is not new. It is the obvious principle that technical or humanistic, quantitative or intuitive, autocratic or participative management are alternative possibilities which should be applied as appropriate, depending on the conditions of the organization. We see contingency management as the latest step in the tendency of management experts to combine older theories in a new synthesis.

3

Planning

The creation of the world is the prime example of long-range planning. As a first step, the environment was surveyed and found to be a void. Then a set of objectives was established, with a clear, seven-day timetable. The objectives were implemented according to a schedule: light, the first day, then the firmament, dry earth, and vegetable life. Later steps included the creation of animals, and finally man. The work was evaluated and found to be very good. But as with all things in a dynamic environment, change took place and imperfections crept into the world.

Planning is a pervasive human activity. It is practiced by the entrepreneur starting a new firm, by the general preparing for battle, by the tourist scheduling a trip, by the cook arranging a banquet, by the carpenter building a house, by the farmer planting a crop, and by the teenager getting dressed for her first date.

Yet planning is not ubiquitous. There is the drifter of Western lore who rides from town to town as the wind blows. There is the steel executive who failed to invest in modern furnaces to match the post-war German plants.

Planning, in the generic sense, is merely an informal activity of thoughtful people. As discussed in management texts and business circles, planning has a more specific meaning. It is a formal, systematic, rational process, at least in theory. (In due time we will see why this is not necessarily true in all cases.) Unlike the drifter, the planner knows where he wants to go and prepares a careful written document delineating the steps.

DEFINITIONS OF PLANNING

Planning is a management function best understood as part of a systems approach to management. It deals with the future, but a future which will be here soon enough. There are many definitions of planning, but they all amount to the same thing. Planning is a predetermined course of action to reach established objectives. It is a formalized process to reach goals. It is a way for organizations to get where they want to go. It is a methodical procedure of formulating objectives, developing alternative strategies to achieve the objectives, and choosing the preferred strategy. It is the methodical development of programs aimed at desired results.

We suggest the following formulation: *Planning is a systematic process of choosing alternative routes to reach predetermined goals.*

While planning has been practiced from the start of civilization, it is only in fairly recent times that it has been formally discussed.

WHY PLAN?

First, because the world is dynamic, complex, uncertain, changeable, and without planning we may lose our way. Second, our resources are limited and our wants are unlimited; without planning we may waste those scarce resources. Third, in this world of uncertainty and scarcity, planning helps clarify questions, forces consideration of objectives, reveals the total picture, and focuses attention on relevant facts. Last, planning makes success more likely because it promotes control and discloses accountability.

Under the simpler conditions of backward, agrarian societies, intuitive planning had a better chance of success than in the modern, industrial world. In the complexity of industrial enterprises intuition will not suffice. Consider the innumerable steps needed to produce a new model of an automobile.

Starting with the concept of the kind a car, we must produce a series of designs, a detailed engineering blueprint, a marketing survey, and a budget.

Equipment must be ordered and put in place, a material inventory accumulated, workers hired, contracts made with suppliers of parts, a marketing venture must be started, dealers contacted for distribution, and a host of other functions too numerous to list here. This process could not be completed efficiently without formal, detailed planning, perhaps supported by PERT diagrams, timetables, budgets, standards, rules, accounting and marketing procedures, specific objectives, subunit plans, and evaluation techniques.

As we have noted, the two major factors which justify planning are uncertainty and scarcity.

Uncertainty

We find it difficult to succeed in business because we live in a complex world, characterized by change, uncertainty, and conflict. Multiproduct firms do not have a clear, unambiguous road to profit maximization. Multiple goals are not only difficult to balance; they may be in conflict with one another. Multinational firms are buffeted by varied winds. New products are constantly emerging; old products fade away. Competition may be capricious, spasmodic, turbulent, erratic. Customer loyalty may be fickle. Government regulations may change. The economic climate and business health vary in irregular cycles. This causes uncertainty.

Scarcity

Perhaps the most distinctive feature of any economy in this world is the scarcity of resources. We suffer from insatiable wants and limited means. The principle of opportunity cost teaches us that the cost of any choice is the alternative which must be given up. With limited means, if we acquire one asset, we sacrifice another. If a nation produces more guns, it may have to produce less butter. If we consume more beef, pork sales may drop. If we drink more tea, we may drink less coffee. If we make one product, we may not have the resources or time to produce another. We must make choices, abandoning some alternatives in order to enjoy others. This is scarcity.

Facing the twin obstacles of uncertainty and scarcity, the process of choosing rationally among alternatives requires a formal method. If we are to deal successfully with uncertainty and scarcity, we must be thorough, rational, and systematic.

But there are other reasons for formal planning. Too often, we are not sure about the questions to ask when deciding on a course of action. In a firm with too little time and a feverish pace, should we be concerned about competition, new products, cost reduction, financial resources, or government regulation as a first priority? Or are there other questions which should be asked first? The planning process itself, starting with a systematic exploration of the environment, is likely to crystallize the problems which firms face. In practice of planning, the relevant questions are likely to come to the fore.

It is common for the manager to concentrate on the immediate problems and to neglect other more urgent, though less timely, troubles. How do you deal with fresh, powerful competition just emerging when cash flow problems command your attention? How do you respond to new government regulations or union demands when your productivity is slipping badly? Current problems are likely to monopolize attention, diverting thought from other matters which may have a greater impact in the long run. Planning forces management to deal with the whole span of issues.

It is common for the manager to focus on his particular field of expertise. The executive officer who rose from the ranks as a marketing manager is likely to worry about marketing activities; the former engineer will be concerned with efficient manufacturing; the financier may regard capitalization as primary. Planning puts all these issues together. It reveals the total scene, balancing the various elements in a unified whole.

Planning discloses accountability. Various persons are responsible for the success of different aspects of a complex operation. However, in the rush of daily activity, it is not always clear who is responsible for what. The plan, by explicit statement, makes responsibility obvious.

Everyone knows that control is essential. But control is not possible unless you know what you hope to achieve. What process do you want to regulate? What outcome should you monitor? Is the purpose of control to achieve speed or quality? Do you want to reduce costs or keep customers? Planning permits rational control. Indeed, it makes control possible, since the very notion of control includes a clear idea of what results you want to achieve.

BARRIERS TO PLANNING

Planning is no panacea. It is not the solution to all problems. Some old-time entrepreneurial managers prefer the intuitive approach. Planning is difficult. Thorough planning is expensive and time-consuming. Some devotees to planning may forget that the plan is not an inflexible instrument to be followed slavishly. Some managers fear planning because it exposes them to evaluation. Moreover, some planning may be done poorly so that it may have been better not to plan.

Examples of poor planning are as common as they are unfortunate. U.S. auto manufacturers assumed Americans were wedded forever to big, gas guzzling cars. They did not plan for the entry of the high quality, small Japanese car. But tastes did change. Americans, pressed by rising gasoline prices, opted for the more efficient Japanese cars, and welcomed the excellent quality of the Japanese product.

It may be argued that no one could have known with absolute certainty of the impending market changes, but signs were everywhere. The U.S. auto manufacturers had no contingency plans for the Japanese invasion. Planning alone might not have kept the Japanese out, but GM, Ford, and Chrysler undoubtedly made the entry of Japanese cars easier.

Of course, many American firms plan, and plan well. When we discuss the advantages of planning, we will assume that the process is carried out with intelligence. When we argue that planning is essential, we will mean good planning.

TYPES OF PLANNING

Planning has been classified into many categories. There are long-range plans and short-range plans, as well as intermediate plans which can be discussed as a separate category. There are standing plans, amounting to ongoing procedures, which can be contrasted to single-use plans for a one-time, specific purpose. We sometimes hear of aggregate, comprehensive planning for the entire business enterprise as compared to partial, functional planning for specific departments, such as marketing, production, research, and so on.

Strategic vs. Tactical Plans

The most common distinction is between strategic planning and tactical planning. This contrasting pair is also known as long-range planning and short-range planning, or grand planning and operational planning. Strategic planning, however, is more than long-range in scope. It is comprehensive, integrated, holistic, and aimed at the achievement not only of specific, narrow objectives, but of the broadest goals of the firm. Strategic planning is a grand plan which often includes the more limited operational, or tactical, plans as parts. While lower level objectives must be consistent with the higher level mission of an organization, strategic plans are not mere aggregates of operational plans. They are more clearly concerned with the future, with a sense of direction, and with the achievement of the mission or purpose of the firm.

Tactical or operational plans are narrow, specific, and based on particular objectives. While strategic plans focus on comprehensive design, tactical plans focus on concrete results. While strategic planning is typically the province of entrepreneurs, tactical planning is managerial. While strategic planning may be concerned with uncertainty, operational planning deals with risk. Strategic planning deals with unstructured problems, and with broad, subjective alternatives. Tactical planning deals with quantifiable goals, and narrow, specific choices. Strategic planning deals with corporate aims, while tactical planning deals with departmental and functional aims.

Planning may be centralized or decentralized, or it may combine both types. A strategic plan may be drawn up by a planning staff responsible only to the chief executive officer. Tactical planning is often a function of various departments or subunits of the firm. Modern planning is considered a centralized responsibility, but is carried out by the combined efforts of all levels of management.

Standing vs. Single-use Plans

Another classification of plans includes standing plans and single-use plans. Standing plans are usually policies, general guides, procedures, or rules of a permanent nature. A single-use plan is an individual program, a particular project, or a budget for a specific period.

Examples of single-use plans are generally operational, dealing with matters such as forecasts, specific plans for capitalization of a new process, a proposal for the development of a new product, or a particular research project. In a strategic plan, standing and single-use operational plans may be subsections. Consideration of retrenchment, growth, consolidation, ethical standards, or the acquisition of new businesses are more likely found in strategic plans.

Contingency Plans

A special type of plan is the contingency plan. This may be a single-use plan held in abeyance for an emergency. A firm may have a plan prepared in case of a strike by employees, or an impending hostile takeover attempt. A firm with severe financial problems may prepare a plan for major changes if conditions fail to improve and bankruptcy looms. Or a firm may prepare plans for action if the national economic picture changes. For example, a construction firm may stockpile construction plans and hold a marketing plan in reserve in case mortgage interest rates should drop. The point is not to wait for opportunities or dangers, but to prepare in advance.

NATURE OF PLANNING

To define planning as choosing alternative routes to predetermined goals is straightforward. It appears a logical exercise in decision making. But it really isn't so simple! We can look at planning from two points of view: (1) as a rational process, or (2) as the subjective behavior of opinionated human beings. Formal planning is assumed to be a process which is sequential, systematic, rational, future-oriented, incremental, pervasive, and purposive in nature. But it isn't always so!

Rational Planning

Planning is not a finished product or a department; it is an activity, an ongoing effort, a process. The process consists of a sequence of small events following an orderly pattern. There is a method to the process, moving from step to step, from research to possibilities, from alternatives to choices, from implementation to evaluation, from judgment to modification. The process is repeated in a cycle of goal, alternatives, choice, action, evaluation, adjustment, new goals, and new alternatives.

In theory, planning is a rational exercise which replaces intuition in preparing for the future. The process follows a clear set of guidelines or steps, described later in this chapter. What is important is to note that there is a routine approach, fairly well accepted by all planners (with only occasional modifications which do not change the basic principles), based on the concept of a plan as a rational process.

The planning process is a pervasive element at all levels of management. Frederick Taylor considered planning a separate activity of special staff members. Today, we believe that to be successful, a plan must be the creation of persons at all levels of management. Top executives spend a great deal of time on planning. Middle managers spend less time on planning duties, but planning is still important to them. Even foremen plan, though they spend less time in planning activities than do managers higher in the organization.

Planning as Subjective Behavior

Unfortunately, the story of planning does not end here. There are other aspects of planning neglected by this neat view of the planning process. Planning is not only rational. It is also dynamic, complex, political, contradictory, and subject to change, uncertainty, and ambiguity. Planning is judgmental, not computational. It is based on opinions, not merely on facts; planners evaluate facts. They may believe they are acting logically, but cannot shake off the system of values and beliefs of their society.

Planning, and strategic planning in particular, is carried out by many participants. It should not be the work of a single chief executive officer or by a planner in seclusion. Successful plans are the work of managers at all levels; in some firms, low level workers are included in the planning process to assure that the plan, when completed, will be understood and supported. One consequence of this diversity of participants is that planning is the product of people with disparate interests and diverse benefits arising from each of the alternatives. There is no one correct plan; different plans have different results which affect different people in different ways.

Planning, unless imposed from above, involves negotiation and bargaining. In many cases, the negotiation may be coercive, since it is often carried out by participants with unequal power. In any event, it reflects the views of the parties involved, and not some absolute, predetermined perfection.

Planning is affected by the broad environment, not merely the particular physical setting. It is affected by laws, customs, prevailing standards, historic conditions, political considerations, competition, the state of the economy, existing contracts, public perceptions, and the internal and external situation.

Limitations to Rationality

We argue that planning is rational. It would be better to say that planning *should* be rational, even if so only from the viewpoint of one actor in the game. Not all actors are rational. A chief executive officer may force through a plan which ultimately could harm the interests of the firm. This may be due to illogical thinking, or to the absence of relevant information, or because of the vagaries of life in this world of uncertainty. As a corollary to uncertainty in choosing goals, we may have multiple goals, some of which may be contradictory, such as improving quality while cutting costs. If both cannot be achieved, which is the rational goal?

In another example, a marketing survey may suggest a new product will sell well, while a financial survey may reveal excessive costs. The action a firm may undertake may have complex results, some which are desirable and some which are not. A number of small firms entered the field of robotics with high hopes, but their success lured giant firms into the industry. The smaller firms could not compete and their plans failed. It is not clear that the original plans were irrational.

Nor is profit always a clear guide for planners. An entrepreneur does not choose between gargantuan profits and devastating losses. Profits may be borderline or delayed. In such cases, the planning decision may rest on intuition rather than rational calculation.

Moreover, since we are faced with continuous change, our fortunes change with time. A plan may have good prospects in the long-term, but undesirable consequences in the short-term. Examples are not difficult to find. A move which reduces costs may also lose customers. A reduction in price may increase sales, but attract competition. A new product may be successful in itself, but may reduce sales of other products sold by the same firm. A new activity may produce profits, but use up cash.

STEPS IN PLANNING

Since planning, in theory, is essentially rational, despite the aberrations caused by human error and environmental change, it is possible to outline a series of steps to be taken by planners. The steps are the same in strategic and tactical planning, though we may have broader concerns in strategic planning. Following specific steps may help avoid irrationality.

There are many versions of the steps that may be taken in the planning process, but the differences are in details, not in substance. In all cases, planning moves from the basic purpose, or mission, to goals and objectives, to alternative strategies and activities, to choosing activities, to implementation, and, finally, to evaluation and review.

Differences among steps listed by various planners often have to do with specifications about how to reach particular steps. Goals are not picked at random from a box of possibilities. They are determined by custom, the perceptions of management, the history and resources of the firm, the shape of the environment, and an evaluation of future prospects. Since some steps take place simultaneously, it is possible to reverse the order of these steps.

Despite possible variations, we suggest the following as a reasonable series of the steps required in a rational planning process:

1. Develop mission statement and statement of goals.
2. Analyze the external environment and internal resources.
3. Outline specific objectives and alternative activities to achieve the objectives.
4. Choose desired objectives and activities.
5. Develop detailed activities and related documents, including an activity narrative, timetables, budget, and performance evaluation measures.
6. Implement.
7. Evaluate and report.
8. Revise plan, if necessary.

The simple listing of steps hides a number of complications. First of all, many inputs are needed to carry out the steps. For example, the mission can be developed only after extensive research into the outside environment and internal resources. The mission is listed as the first step because most managers are sure they know the purpose of the firm. After Step 2, the research step, the mission statement should be reconsidered. Indeed, continual feedback is a necessary ingredient of all planning. It is sometimes called *cybernetics*.

Cybernetics

A complication of the planning process is that there must be a continual feedback of information so that corrective action can be taken, if necessary. When a system is designed to be self-regulating, we call it a cybernetic system. An example is a thermostat on a heating system which tells the boiler to turn on when the temperature is too low, and to turn off when the temperature is too high.

The planning process is a cybernetic system. At every stage of the process, information is developed which should be fed back to correct actions carried out in earlier steps. For example, the development of activities may raise difficulties which might serve as a warning that some of the goals and objectives are unrealistic. Evaluation reports often suggest revision of plans.

DEFINITIONS

A prerequisite to an understanding of the planning process is an agreement on the terms used. Unfortunately, planning terms are used in a variety of ways. While the meaning of mission is widely accepted, there is disagreement over the terms "goals" and "objectives." Goals may be defined as broader than objectives, or as parts of objectives. We define the terms as follows.

Mission

The ultimate purpose of the firm in the long-run. For example, a firm may exist in order to earn maximum profits consistent with ethical standards. The mission is the most abstract statement of what a firm wants to accomplish. It has the widest focus of attention and deals with matters such as the broad financial situation, environmental concerns, long-term profitability, the suitability of the output of the firm, and the very survival of the institution. It deals with the purpose of the entire corporation. It is often published and is sometimes used for public relations purposes.

In practice, the mission statement may be a true reflection of the purpose of the firm, or it may be a public relations ploy. For planning purposes, of course it should be realistic. For a business firm, earning a fair profit appears more reasonable as the mission than unselfish service to the public. The mission of a railroad may be to earn reasonable profits by the efficient operation of trains, or it may be to provide full transportation services. The mission of a publisher may be to publish the finest quality textbooks, consistent with demand by colleges. The mission of a college may be to provide the highest level of education, perhaps in a particular discipline, or to provide education for disadvantaged persons.

Goals

Goals are subdivisions of the mission. Consistent with the mission, goals are broad statements of the targets towards which a firm must move in order to achieve the mission. Goals are less abstract than the mission statement. They focus on slightly narrower aspects of the firm, such as the particular goods and services to be provided. They often deal with the subunits of a firm, rather than the whole firm itself. They are less likely to be published, and used for public relations, unless they are the goals of a major unit of a firm which does its own advertising. They often deal with the medium-term.

The goals of a railroad may include providing freight service from New York to Boston. The goal of a publisher may be to enter the field of management textbooks. The goal of a college may be to expand course offerings in international business.

Objectives

The narrowest of the aims, objectives are specific and quantifiable. They are subdivisions of goals. They are never abstract. They focus on particular activities and results desired. They are never published. They usually deal with small subunits of the firm. They are invariably short-run.

The objective of a railroad company may be to improve on-time arrivals in the New York/Boston division by eight percent within six months. The objective of a steel producer may be to reduce the cost of sheet steel by four percent by May 1, 1999. The objective of a publisher may be to issue a textbook in organic chemistry in time for the next college semester in sufficient numbers to satisfy the demand of colleges in the United States. A college may have an objective to increase average class size in the business department from 15 to 20 by the next semester.

ANALYSIS OF STEPS IN PLANNING

Step 1: Develop mission statement and statement of goals.

Mission

The development of the mission statement is anything but straightforward. Indeed, many plans fail because the mission of the firm is taken for granted. An example, often cited in management texts, is the railroad's mission. Many railroads assumed, without question, that their mission was to run a railroad. They made little effort to counter the development of trucks, and they lost a lot of business as a result. The proper mission of the railroads was not merely to run a railroad, but to provide transportation. With this mission, it is reasonable for railroad companies to purchase trucking firms operating at major terminals to supplement the trains.

Defining a mission is a difficult business because it requires an Olympic view of the world. It demands that we step back from the daily rush of events and from our concern with pressing problems. It requires an innovative, inquiring, irreverent, entrepreneurial mind. And it may require unusual courage, especially if major change is needed.

In a more practical sense, defining the mission, as well as the goals of the firm, requires much research. It is critical that the outside environment and the internal structure and resources be analyzed. In actual practice, the preparation of a statement of the mission and goals takes place at the same time as Step 2, in which the environment and the internal resources are analyzed. However, after Step 2 is completed, the planner should probably return to reconsideration of the mission and goal.

Even before the documents outlining outside environmental factors and internal resources have been prepared, the actual writing of the mission statement can begin. The mission statement typically is less than a page long. Before the statement is accepted, it should be widely circulated. Comments of all interested parties should be received and studied.

The mission often tends to be couched in lofty terms. This is not necessarily wrong. However, it is important that it be realistic. Don't seek to make the best radio in the world if you plan to sell it at low prices. Don't expect to win a market share not consistent with your financial and marketing resources. Lofty does not mean unrealistic.

You must always be alert to the possibility that your mission may have to be revised in the future. This may be disturbing to those who believe that the mission of the firm, the ultimate purpose for which the firm was organized, should be sacred. Indeed, it is desirable to have a formal, fixed purpose in mind which tempers all future activities. However, in a complex, dynamic, and changeable world, management must always be prepared to renew, revise, review, reconsider, and revolutionize.

Murray Lincoln, for many years a vice president of the Farm Bureau Insurance Companies (now Nationwide) referred to himself as the "Vice President in charge of Revolution." Changing the mission may seem like a revolution, but should not be avoided.

Goals

After comments on the mission statement have been analyzed and the statement is accepted as policy, planners can move on to the statement of goals.

The statement of goals follows directly from the mission statement; each of the goals must help fulfill the mission. If the mission includes several purposes, each separate purpose should lead to a series of related goals. Goals differ from the mission in that they are more specific. For example, if the mission of a railroad company is to offer transportation, goals may include extending delivery of cargo by truck from train terminals to customers. The mission of a manufacturing firm may include the production of portable radios; the goals might include the extension of the range of portable models that are offered from the cheapest to the most expensive. A college might include service to the disadvantaged in its mission; the goals might include the expansion of remedial courses in math. A publisher may aim at supplying management texts of high quality, and then divide this broad purpose into goals specifying the publication of texts in specialized fields of management.

There may be a large number of goals, some of which may contradict other goals. A reduction in costs of production coupled with an increase in quality may be an example. Earning a maximum profit may not be consistent with expanding into a new market. The management should not necessarily shy away from contradictory goals. In the first case, a compromise might be reached which permits some cost reduction and better quality. In the second case, the profit maximization may be a long-term aim, despite short-run losses. In general, contradictory goals should be avoided, but only after careful consideration.

Step 2: Analyze the external environment and internal resources.

The shape of the environment is a primary consideration. We start with the entire economy and ask about future prospects. Is the economy of the nation, or the entire world, entering a period of prosperity or recession? Are there major political changes which may affect world conditions? What are prospects for war or peace, hostility or détente? What are prospects for international trade? What is the climate for business? What is happening to interest rates, taxes, government spending, tariffs, the money supply?

We then turn to the industry or industries in which the firm operates, and ask whether conditions are getting better or worse. What are trends in competition? What is happening to foreign competition? What changes are expected in the composition of the industry, its location, the size of plants, the introduction of new techniques, labor relations, the cost and availability of supplies, transportation? Are new products threatening to change demand for the products of the firm? Is legislation expected that may affect your industry? This is especially important in industries that are regulated by a government agency, and in industries sensitive to public concerns about the physical environment. Perhaps there are new developments that may suggest the firm is in the wrong business. Maybe there are better opportunities elsewhere. Here is the opportunity to ask if the old mission is viable, or if a new approach is needed.

An inward look is also needed. It may bode well to ask whether the firm is strong enough to support the mission or goals. Does the firm have a table of organization capable of meeting the challenges of mission achievement? Does the firm have the internal resources which are necessary, including management, finances, facilities, marketing ability, research capabilities, skilled labor?

A railroad company may well ask if it has the financial strength it needs to acquire trucking companies to move cargo from the railroad terminal to the final destination. A publisher may well ask if it has the skilled editors and marketing specialists to succeed in expanding its offerings. A college may question the space available for expansion.

Documents should be prepared outlining the findings explicitly. A stronger U.S. dollar may cast a shadow on hopes to market a new product overseas. An improvement in relations with Russia may be a disaster for defense industries. New products may point to doom for old industries. Research into external and internal factors is not for scholarly understanding; it is aimed directly at the suitability of the mission and goals and should lead to confirmation or reconsideration.

Step 3: Outline specific objectives and alternative activities.

Objectives and activities are linked together in one step because they are so closely related. Indeed, the activity is merely a more detailed statement of the objective and how to carry it out.

The objectives, as defined here, are the narrowest aims of a firm. They are concise, clear, specific, and quantifiable. They are always stated within tight time frames. While the mission and goals must be attainable, this quality is most important and verifiable in the case of objectives, usually in the short-term.

Objectives can best be illustrated by examples. The objective of a radio manufacturing firm may be to start manufacturing a specific new model at the rate of 500 a day by September 1, 1999. The objective of a railroad company may be to have 20 new, five ton trucks operating from the Des Moines terminal by June 30, 1999. The objective of the publisher may be to have 5,000 copies of the new introductory textbook on chemistry available for the fall 1999 semester. The objective of the college may be to have the new course in marketing management offered in the fall 1999 semester, serving at least 20 students.

Objectives are easy to monitor. On September 1, 1999 is the firm producing 500 radios a week? The answer is unambiguous; it is either yes or no.

The activity is implied in the objective. Some planners may wish to expand a little on the formal objective, fleshing in some details by outlining activities. More important, there may be more than one way to achieve an objective. Thus, several activities may be listed as alternative paths to the objective.

For example, a radio manufacturer may have several different locations for the production of the radio; the activity may be a little different at each of the locations because of different resources available at each location. The railroad company may consider leasing or purchasing trucks in order to achieve the objective of having a certain number of trucks available at a site by a certain day.

In a sense, setting objectives is identical to developing alternative activities. The activities must be parallel to the objectives. Each activity is aimed at the achievement of an objective. If, for any reason, it does not seem possible to succeed in completing a particular activity, the objective on which it is based should be dropped or changed. Of course, this cybernetic approach is essential to the planning process.

It may not be possible to prepare alternative activities for each objective. In some cases, there may be only one way to accomplish the objective. In other cases, there may be various approaches. Is it best to transfer existing resources to the new production, or should new resources be acquired? Such a question may be resolved by reference to other goals, such as those which deal with the availability of funds, or the existence of other objectives which use the limited resources of the firm.

The development of activities may make clear the conflict that exists between various objectives. Again we note that in due time some of the objectives may have to be changed.

Step 4: Choose objectives and activities.

In a practical sense, planners probably make choices in the very act of listing the objectives. There may be a tendency to omit objectives which are not preferred. We list the act of choosing because it is so important.

However, there is a second reason for listing this choice as an individual step. Listing objectives may be a function of lower level staff, but choosing objectives is in the province of top management. While the planning documents associated with the objectives and related activities may be centrally determined, the actual writing of specific objectives and activities is usually the function of technical staff individuals or members of the department directly affected. This is done because the department directly involved is most expert in the narrower view required for specifying objectives or activities in a quantifiable fashion. The lower level department is best qualified to state numbers, dates, and realistic production possibilities.

However, the lower level planners may not see the problems of conflict among activities, or how they fit into the broad scene. This step provides the time to accept, reject, or delay some of the proposed activities. This is the time to commit resources. This is the opportunity to review the future, not as an ideal, beautiful public relations dream, but as a sound, practical, credible program of action.

To choose is to decide. The activity of making decisions is important. We devote an entire chapter to decision making.

> **Step 5: Develop detailed activity and related documents, including an activity narrative, timetable, budget, and performance evaluation measures.**

Activity Narrative

The activities may be detailed in a narrative which outlines the specific resources — financial, physical, and personal — which must be committed. The activity narrative starts with a statement of what is to be done.

If a radio is to be produced, a general description of the radio is made, supported by detailed engineering plans. The location of the plant, the equipment needed, the specific individuals responsible, the labor force needed, the materials required, and the commitment of all resources necessary must be indicated. Moreover, the activity narrative specifies the production process, especially if different from normal. In short, the activity narrative is a statement of what is to be done, how, and by whom.

Timetable (Milestones)

At this juncture, timetables are developed. We refer to the timetables as milestones. These are particular dates by which certain operations must be completed, listed in a separate document. They are necessary for control. How the timetable was prepared is of some importance. Elsewhere in this text we discuss PERT and CPM, methods of charting the time of completion of projects, and determining the fastest way to reach that point. A PERT chart may be included to assure the reliability of the time estimates.

There are other parts of the activity narrative that must be completed. One such essential element is the budget.

Activity Budgets

Budgets are an essential management tool. They must be included in an activity narrative. Of course, there are difficulties in assigning costs to a specific activity, particularly overhead costs, but the work must be done. The budget, or financial projection, is not merely a listing of expected costs, albeit organized into logical categories. There should be supporting documentation, showing how the figures were obtained, and why they should be believed.

For example, if a supervisor is to spend only part of his time in a particular activity, the budget should show his full salary, the percentage of time to be spent on the project, and the cost assigned to the project. If raw materials are to be purchased, some proof of the cost should be submitted, perhaps by reference to contracts, sources of supply, or market prices.

Alternatives may be developed for the use of equipment. Should the firm acquire an expensive machine which requires little labor, or a cheaper machine which requires more labor? Such alternative possibilities, each with its economic justification, may be included in the activity narrative and must be shown in the budget as well.

Performance Evaluation Measures

A final section of the activity narrative may be the development of performance evaluation measures (PEMs). At times, this may be a simple matter, since it follows directly from the objective itself. In the case cited above, the measure is obvious; are 500 radios a week being produced by September 1st? Other PEMs may be more difficult to measure. An objective may specify the quality of the radio, perhaps in the number of malfunctions permitted per one hundred radios sampled. The PEM would be the number of malfunctions reported by the quality control engineers.

The PEMs are tied into the milestones. The explicit statement of PEMs, based on milestones, makes it possible to check progress routinely and rigorously.

The activity narrative, together with the budget and PEMs, is crucial for the next step in the planning process. The heart of the planning process is cybernetics. In planning there is a continual feedback of information and a continuing opportunity for revision.

Step 6: Implementation.

The implementation of the activities is closely related to the planning process, but is not in itself planning, except that the planners should see to it that implementation takes place. So, too, is the function of control. The implementation of activities, and control of these activities, is the concern of management in carrying out all the other central management functions discussed in this book.

The implementation of activities, of course, is also the start of the next planning step.

Step 7: Evaluation and reporting.

The place of evaluation and reporting is made evident by the PEMs and the milestones in the activity narrative. While planning is an activity of all levels of management personnel, the particular person assigned as planner, as well as the line personnel carrying out the activity, should monitor the activity on a continuing basis, as well as at the end of certain predetermined periods. Milestones should be reviewed by reference to a calendar, or some other memo. However, data should be provided on a regular and continual basis to permit the PEMs to be measured more often. In order to assure that PEMs and milestones are followed, a regular report may be written and filed. However, this step should be an ongoing activity, carried out throughout the implementation phase, and not merely as a conclusion shown in a written report after the fact. The ongoing evaluation need not be a formal, written report. It may consist of memos, notations on a calendar, any other kind of daily record, or even verbal reports of ongoing performance.

An example of ongoing evaluation is given in the chapter on *comparative management* [Chapter 15], where we take note of *Jidoka*. With Jidoka, a worker who spots an imperfection in the product can stop production until a correction is made.

There are two kinds of evaluation reports: those made during the activity and those made afterwards. We refer to them as prospective (ongoing, aimed ahead, prepared during the activity) and consummatory (final, after the activity is completed).

It is important to stress that in good management, the consummatory evaluation is not enough. In automobile factories in the United States, cars are inspected after they come off the production line. Those cars which have defects noted by the quality control engineers are sent back to a special room where the defects are corrected. In Japan, defects are corrected before the end of the line. This is one reason, many experts believe, that Japanese cars have a reputation for better quality than some American cars.

The purpose of evaluation of the products being manufactured is to avoid sending defective products to the users. The evaluation should include not only the actual physical product, but the productive process, the efficiency of the operation, and the answer to the question of whether the ultimate purpose of the firm is being served. A crucial part of planning is the ability it gives us to reconsider, reorganize, and correct. The cybernetic process works best when we can feed back information before it is too late to make the changes that are indicated.

Another option is to have the evaluation based not only on PEMs and milestones, but on an overall judgment of the activity as it relates to the mission and the goals. This is also well accomplished by a written report. Such a broad evaluation may be done at less frequent intervals than the activity milestones, but should not be done so seldom that major consequences may be ignored for long time periods. For example, some observers believe that the U.S. automobile manufacturers were too slow in moving into the production of compact cars. A more alert management, noting early indications of Japanese success in selling small cars, should have taken faster action to develop compacts.

There is another way of classifying evaluation reports — reports may be made by insiders or outsiders. Insider reports are more common, cheaper, easier to come by, based on direct working knowledge. However, some distance from the activity may be desirable. Thus, progress may be monitored not only by direct line supervisors responsible for the activity, but by other persons, such as planning officers, controllers, or other supposedly disinterested persons.

Outside evaluation is not common. However, there are many times when it is desirable to appoint an outside consultant, especially when there are severe problems, or indications that all is not well in the operations of the firm, or at least the particular division in question.

Evaluation is not an end in itself. It leads to the next step.

Step 8: Revise plan, if necessary.

No plan is forever. An important aspect of the planning process is the feedback which leads to change. If the radios are produced on time, but are of poor quality, the entire activity may have to be modified. If the trucks acquired by the railroad company are not being used fully, the company may have to consider alternatives, such as a better marketing effort, a price change, the acquisition of a different type of truck, or perhaps reducing the size of the fleet.

As has been noted previously, plans may be standing or single-use. A single-use plan may have to be modified if there are strong reasons for doing so. However, the main application of the cybernetic process is for standing plans. In such cases, we may think of the plan as a circular flow process.

HOW TO PLAN

Managers responsible for planning should take the following steps. (NOTE: Where possible, consult with other managers, especially when lower level decisions are involved.)

1. ***Ask yourself:* Are there formal plans on file?**

   a. Strategic plans?
   b. Tactical plans?
   c. Contingency plans?

   Are they up-to-date and satisfactory?

   Consider strategic plans first. Assuming that they are missing, old, or unsatisfactory in some way, continue as follows.

2. **Think about the outside factors which may affect the firm. Are there significant opportunities or threats ahead?**

   - Is there new legislation which may affect business?
   - Is recession or inflation predicted?
   - Is there new competition present or threatened?
   - Is there new technology in the field?
   - What are the industry trends (up or down)?
   - What are conditions in your local market?
   - Are there new markets where you might do business?
   - Are there new products your firm can handle?
   - Are there long-term opportunities on the horizon?

Though internal sources should be consulted in this kind of consideration of external forces, it might be helpful to bring in outside experts.

3. **Think about internal conditions in your firm. Are there any significant opportunities or threats ahead?**

   ■ Do you have extra funds available or is cash in short supply?

   ■ What are the trends in your profits, cash flow, sales, market penetration, costs, and other financial data?

   ■ What is the status of your employees, including such matters as employee relations, quality of management, depth of management, the availability of workers, relations with unions (if any, or the possibility of unionization), quality of your machinery and equipment (age, repair records)?

In these considerations, consulting internal sources is of particular importance.

Assuming you have satisfactory plans, consider the next guideline.

4. **Think about implementation, evaluation, and feedback.**

   ■ Are regular reports being filed?

   ■ Are you satisfied with the reports? Are you meeting milestones? Are you within budgets?

   ■ If there are deficiencies, are they being corrected?

   ■ Most important, even if the plans are being fulfilled, are you satisfied with the overall business results?

If any of the above questions yields results which do not satisfy you, it is time to make new plans. Refer back to the chapter for steps in the planning process and follow them.

You should then turn to tactical plans for consideration. Are such plans on file and being implemented?

5. **If you don't have proper tactical plans, follow the guidelines for strategic plans, with the exception that you should concentrate on internal factors rather than external environments.**

6. **If you do have tactical plans, follow guideline number four above.**

7. **Look ahead.**

   ■ Is there an opportunity for a new product, new market, or new technology ahead?

   ■ Is there a threat of strike, bankruptcy, or new competition ahead?

   If the answer to these questions is yes, prepare contingency plans.

8. **Follow steps, as outlined in this chapter, for planning.**

4

Strategic Planning

A key area of planning is *strategic planning*. Strategic planning analyzes the problems and opportunities of the organization from the point of view of top management and/or the board of directors of the enterprise. Strategic planning is concerned with the long-term future of the entire enterprise.

Major strategic planning decisions can affect the future of the organization for many years to come. After World War II, Montgomery Ward decided to keep much of its resources in cash, fearing a major depression. At the same time, Sears & Roebuck decided upon a major expansion of its stores into suburban shopping centers. The strategic plan of Sears led it to become, for a time, the number one retailer in the United States. Montgomery Ward's undue conservatism led to a smaller share of the retail market and, ultimately, to loss of independence through consolidation with a large oil company. As profits began to decline in retailing, Sears has made new strategic plans with expansion into financial services through growth of its insurance subsidiary and acquisition of real estate and stock brokerage firms. Later, this diversification was dropped as Sears decided to focus on retailing.

The top management of an enterprise should not make its decisions based on operating standards of the past. Top management must engage in strategic planning to ensure a positive future for the organization. Strategic planning of company-wide goals and objectives and strategy for long-term success is essential for a well run organization.

Top management of every organization, whether for-profit or not-for-profit, should ask three basic questions in its strategic planning:

1. Where is the organization now?
2. If no new strategic plans are adopted, where will the organization be in five years? In 10 years? Is this acceptable?
3. If not acceptable, what specific strategic plans and courses of action should be adopted by the organization? What are the pros (payoffs) and cons (risks) of such plans and actions?

Many organizations do not formally undertake strategic planning. They often succeed for a while by "seat of the pants" or intuitive strategies. Once an organization becomes large in size or there is a major change in the organization's environment, intuitive strategies are likely to become ineffective. Failure to engage in strategic planning at that point in time is likely to result in risks of expensive mistakes and, sometimes, bankruptcy.

An organization may gradually evolve into the use of strategic planning. Often, organizations may begin formal planning through financial planning and budgeting. As the corporation grows, it may begin to forecast its future and to begin to think strategically about marketing and the roles of competitors. Finally, the organization may move into a strategic planning mode wherein top management tries to plan to create a better future for the organization.

Strategic planning has several benefits for an organization that may help it perform better than competitors who do not similarly plan. First of all, the organization can take advantage in its strategic planning of the Boston Consulting Group's categories of business units. The organization can determine which units of the organization are *cash cows* (mature business units of little growth but highly profitable), *stars* (units that are growing rapidly), *question marks* (units that hopefully may turn into stars or cash cows in the future), and *dogs* (units that should be sold because of doubtful future profitability). Once this determination has been made, a strategic plan of investing profits from the cash cows into stars and question marks, and divestiture or dissolution of dogs can be developed and implemented.

Second, strategic planning can cause top management to focus its attention on critical issues for their organization instead of on the many other problems and prospects.

Strategic planning can thus help an organization improve its position in the marketplace and improve its overall profitability as measured by such means as increased value of common stock in the stock market or better earnings per share.

The process of strategic planning involves three major factors: (1) formulation of strategy, (2) implementation of the formulated strategy, and (3) evaluation of results (sometimes called control).

The formulation of strategy often begins with the use of the SWOT model of strategic factors. The initials SWOT stand for **S**trengths, **W**eaknesses, **O**pportunities, and **T**hreats. The internal environment of the corporation is scanned for **S**trengths and **W**eaknesses. The internal environment includes the structure of the organization, its culture, and resources. The structure of the organization deals with the chain of command as expressed by the organization chart. The culture of the organization deals with the values and expectations of the managers and employees of the organization. The resources of the organization consist of its human and financial assets, as well as other valuable assets, such as a popular trademark.

The external environment deals with strategic factors, **O**pportunities and **T**hreats, that are outside the enterprise. This external environment includes those groups that directly impact the operations of the enterprise — the stockholders, governments, communities in which facilities are located, competitors, suppliers, customers, and labor unions. General forces such as economic, cultural, political, legal, and technological forces also should be considered as part of a review of the external environment.

Basically, the formulation of strategy involves developing plans to efficiently and effectively deal with environmental **O**pportunities and **T**hreats after considering the organization's **S**trengths and **W**eaknesses.

Once strategic plans have been developed, they can be implemented through allocating resources to specific programs after careful budgeting.

Results can be evaluated or controlled by comparison of actual results with projections in the original plans. Use of reports on results in such terms as sales, return on investment, or net profits can be helpful in determining the success of plans.

Once the top management of an organization has scanned its internal and external environments through a SWOT analysis, it can move to looking at strategic alternatives. A number of questions can be asked, all leading toward a model of what the corporation should look like in the future.

Top management can begin these questions by asking whether the organization should stay in the same line of business. If the answer is yes, then top management will likely choose a stability strategy. A stability strategy involves no major change of course for the organization. An enterprise that adopts a stability strategy will maintain its present objectives and goals. It concentrates resources on its present business and tries to improve its performance. One variety of stability is called a *no change* strategy. Why change when things are going well? The *no change* strategy will be successful as long as internal and external environments remain the same.

A second variety of the stability strategy is a profit strategy in which present profits are emphasized, often with the loss of possible future growth in this part of the enterprise. Profits earned from cash cows can, of course, be invested in other units of the company under a growth strategy to be described later.

A third variety of the stability strategy is a pause strategy. This strategy may be allowed after a period of rapid growth to allow an enterprise to improve its management.

If the top management of an enterprise decides not to remain in the same business, it should ask whether it should leave this business completely or partially. In this case, the firm may decide on a retrenchment strategy. Personnel and "nonessential" expenditures are often cut back. Consultants may be brought in to reduce overhead and otherwise increase efficiency. Successful turnaround in operations may lead top management to change its view and expand again in the same line of work.

Alternatively, part or all of the business may be sold or merged with another enterprise in a strategy of divestment. A particular business unit may need more resources to succeed than the enterprise can make available, given other opportunities to use resources. Also, the corporate culture may render a particular unit a poor fit with the total enterprise. Divestment may bring an enterprise cash that can be used to fight off a takeover by corporate raiders or needed for other opportunities. Liquidation and/or bankruptcy may be followed if divestment is not possible and there is no hope for profitable operation in the future.

Top management may also ask whether the enterprise should try to grow larger in its present business by increasing its present size or buying competitors, or whether it should grow by buying or expanding into other businesses. If the answer to one of these questions is affirmative, top management should adopt a growth strategy.

Growth strategy is currently the most popular strategy found in major corporations. Growth means more sales and perhaps more profits through economies of scale. A growing firm will have more opportunities for managers to be promoted and receive more compensation. A growing firm may be able to attract more capital from the capital markets and thus be able to grow even faster than a firm that emphasizes stability.

A company may follow a growth strategy of horizontal integration. Horizontal integration involves acquiring by purchase or merger a company in the same industry. Stroh's purchase of Schlitz is an example of horizontal integration in the beer brewing industry. Horizontal integration may improve economies of scale or may help a firm enlarge its geographic market. One barrier to horizontal integration in the United States is the antitrust laws, which may prevent certain mergers or acquisitions.

Vertical integration is another growth strategy. In vertical integration a firm acquires a supplier of its raw materials or a distributor or retailer of its products. For example, Coca-Cola Company has acquired several of its franchised bottlers and distributors. Vertical integration may enable a firm to lower its costs and improve control. Vertical integration may have the disadvantage of tying up more assets in the same business — an unfortunate strategy if the business as a whole should decline.

Another growth strategy is growth through diversification. In this case, a firm acquires products or businesses that are different from those presently operated by the firm. Concentric diversification means that a company is adding products that are related to current products. When PepsiCo acquired Pizza Hut, it could sell its Pepsi Cola in the Pizza Hut restaurants. The addition of unrelated products or businesses is called conglomerate diversification. Conglomerate diversification may enable the firm to offset problems of seasonality. For example, a race track that operates in New Hampshire only in the summer may purchase a hotel that operates in the Bahamas in the winter so that cash flow occurs continually throughout the year. Employees may work in the Bahamas in the winter and in New Hampshire in the summer.

One argument in favor of diversification is synergy. Synergy means that two corporations can achieve more as part of a single company than they could as two independent entities. Philip Morris and Kraft both sell products through supermarkets. The consolidation of Kraft into Philip Morris might mean savings on distribution costs and better use of talented brand managers.

Firms can also follow a combination of strategies. One division may be following a strategy of stability, another may be in a growth mode, and a third might be sold off as part of a retrenchment strategy.

Some strategies should be avoided at all costs. The "home run" strategy may be adopted by the corporation that developed a very effective product. Xerox, for example, has been trying hard to find another product with the same impact as its xerographic copier, which it developed while a small company in the photo products business. It is seldom that a company can hit two home runs in a row.

There is a tendency for companies to continue to invest in the same area when it already has invested much in that field, even though the technology or the environment may have changed. A large office products company continued to invest in improving mimeograph equipment when its product was being supplanted by xerographic copiers.

After reviewing strategic alternatives, top management must choose a particular strategic plan. The plan must fit the goals and objectives of the organization. Each alternative can be evaluated after a forecast using pro forma profit and loss statements, pro forma cash flow forecasts, and pro forma balance sheets for expected sales. The sales can be further estimated over a range — most likely, outstanding, poor — for each alternative. Such quantification can help management make a decision among strategic alternatives, but other factors must also be considered.

Risk is an important factor in choosing a strategic alternative. Few top managers are willing to choose an alternative that requires betting the entire company on the success of the alternative, particularly if the company is successful in what it is presently doing. Thus, the amount of assets required for the strategic alternative is an important factor. An alternative that requires few assets will not endanger the entire company if it fails. Management of a publicly owned company with many stockholders dependent on its earnings and many employees dependent on the company for their livelihood may be more adverse to risk than an entrepreneurially directed new venture with stockholders deliberately investing in a risky situation in the hope of a large return on their investment.

Time is also a factor. If the alternative will result in quick profits, it may be more attractive to a company's top management than one that will bring a return only after years of development. Since analysts and institutional investors often place heavy emphasis on growth in earnings per share each quarter or each year, the top management of many publicly owned companies are under pressure for improved results each year or even each quarter. Alternatives with a quick return may appear more attractive to top management for this reason.

Other external factors should be considered as well. For example, customers in the United States may frown on a company that invests in a highly profitable alternative in a country which exploits "sweatshop" labor for manufacturing apparel. Employees who are unionized or may be considering joining a union may push for alternatives that will help them gain more job security or better wages. Public officials may favor plant locations that will help their reelection. The top management must consider which of these external factors are of importance in deciding on their strategy.

Internal corporate factors need to be considered as well. A company may have a long tradition of a certain style or culture. Walt Disney Corporation, for example, is known for family entertainment and for placing much emphasis on the personal ideas of Walt Disney; this emphasis continues many years after his death. Disney is unlikely to consider making X-rated movies in view of this tradition, no matter how profitable such a corporate strategy might be.

Individual personalities and wishes of the top management may also influence the selection of alternatives. A large corporation choosing a new site for headquarters of the corporation often picks a location near where the top management lives or would like to live or where it minimizes the personal taxes paid by key members of top management.

Once a particular strategic alternative has been chosen, the top management must move to implement the new strategy. Procedures, policies, and a plan of action must be developed. An organization must be developed or revised by top management to implement the strategy. This new organization structure must then be staffed by persons who will carry out the implementation of the strategic plan. Leadership or direction of this implementation must be provided by management. Finally, control must be installed to ensure that the plan is being correctly implemented as directed. Costs should be in line with plans and plans should be achieved as scheduled. Systems, such as *management by objective* and other systems, can be used to ensure that this implementation takes place as planned or that timely revisions in the plans are made in light of the actual experience and feedback.

5

Decision Making

Decisions! Decisions! Which tie shall I wear today? Should the United States bomb Beirut Airport? Which flavor ice cream do I want? Should income taxes be raised? These are all questions that require a decision.

Everyone makes decisions constantly, but some decisions are more important than others. Nearly everyone makes decisions eventually, but some people decide quickly; we call them decisive. Others agonize endlessly over decisions; they are indecisive. On the other hand, some fast decision makers make horrible decisions, while some who act slowly, and perhaps more carefully, may make better decisions. But not always!

Some people can't decide. They think that by putting off the awful moment of choosing they are buying time, or avoiding the inevitable. This may not be so. Not deciding is also deciding. To delay making a new investment may be to lose an opportunity forever. The general who does not strike in time may be giving up victory. To hesitate in making a purchase may be to miss a low price or lose out on a product in short supply.

Life is a process of continuous decision making. At every step we must decide — turn right or left, go on or stop, say yes or no. Most of these decisions are routine, intuitive, made unconsciously and instantaneously. There are other decisions which are difficult, take time and conscious effort; in these cases we are more aware that we are deciding.

For the businessperson, the decision making process is of special interest. The quality of decisions is a major factor in the success of a business. It is a major factor in the career growth of the manager; how superiors view the decision making ability of the manager is important to his or her advancement.

The businessperson makes decisions at every turn: should he or she raise or lower prices, buy new equipment or repair the old, hire or fire, borrow funds or not, increase or reduce output, seek new markets, advertise, change models? In the chapter on planning we pointed out that a crucial step in planning was choosing between alternatives. This, we said, was decision making.

DEFINITION

In everyday life we make decisions at every step, often without being aware of what we are doing; our decisions are automatic, unconscious. In teaching management, however, we refer to decision making as a conscious process.

In everyday life, choosing a blue striped tie in the morning rather than a blue paisley tie to go with a blue suit may be or may not be a conscious effort, but in a business, running a sale of neckties in a boutique is clearly a cognitive act. If sales are running ahead of schedule, the manager may have to increase the number of employees or authorize overtime. He must make a conscious decision.

Decision making, then, is the conscious selection of one alternative among two or more. Other definitions can be found, but they all include the idea of choice among alternatives.

Decision making is not a panacea for managers. Not all problems have solutions. Or we can say, at least, that not all problems have good solutions. Often, decision making is not absolutely right or wrong; there is seldom only one, best activity. Decisions are made by human beings, individuals who are less than perfect. Decisions are not always made by analysis of hard facts and by rational choice. They are based on value judgments, hopes, guesses, prejudices, habits.

Ordinarily, we conceive of choice as an individual activity, though in a business it is made in an organizational setting. We also discuss group decision making, but groups are made up of individuals. Each individual in the group, hopefully, has a mind of his own, and therefore makes an individual decision. A number of techniques of group decision making are discussed later in this chapter.

We often consider decision making in management a rational, normative activity of economic man, based on good information and dealing with a choice between unambiguous alternatives to reach desired goals. Modern management experts understand the complications that make the decision process a little less perfect than this description would suggest. People can be irrational, foolish, impatient, and do not always act in their own best interest. Consider, for example, the businessman who gambles away money he needs for inventory.

The focus of the theory of decision making has changed. Older approaches can be called *classical*. Classical decision theory assumes that the business manager is rational, acting in his own best interests as "economic man," that he has the information needed to make a rational decision, that he knows what he wants and how to get there.

Newer theory is called *behavioral*. Behavioral theory looks at the decision maker as a real human being, with limits to his rationality. Herbert Simon (*Administrative Behavior*, 3rd ed., New York: Free Press, 1976) introduced the idea that man has "bounded rationality," that is, that there are limits to rationality. Man is influenced by ideas he holds unconsciously, by the standards of the society of which he is a member, and by personal preferences which may or may not be best for the organization. Moreover, he acts without complete information; there is never perfect, absolutely complete information upon which to act. There are always factors ignored, unknown, unexpected.

Economists have long assumed that businessmen act to maximize profits. They insist that the businessman chooses an output and price which assures the highest possible profit. Simon points out that the businessman may not know precisely what level of output, or what specific price structure, would guarantee the absolute maximum profit. Economists love to demonstrate, by mathematics and diagram, exactly how price and output are determined in competition and monopoly. Today we know these are exercises in logic only. Simon replaced the idea of maximizing as the key to the behavior of businessmen with the concept of *satisficing*. According to this concept, the businessman probably chooses the first alternative he finds which meets his requirements, that is, the first alternative he finds which is satisfactory (which satisfices).

For example, economists teach that in monopolistic competition, the businessman raises prices until he gets a maximum profit. In fact, he may raise prices until he gets a satisfactory profit, perhaps in accordance with a rule of thumb or tradition in the particular industry. Thus, he does not make a rational choice between all alternatives available. He makes a choice of limited rationality by taking the first alternative which is good enough.

We are not suggesting that the businessman is completely irrational. We only point out that rational decision making is limited by the degree of certainty of the outcome.

CERTAINTY, RISK, AND UNCERTAINTY

Decisions can be made under conditions of certainty, risk, or uncertainty. These terms have very specific meaning and affect the decision process.

Certainty means we know what will happen under particular conditions. If you double the price of corn flakes, you will sell fewer boxes. If you invest surplus funds in a particular government bond, you will earn a fixed, known return by a particular date. If you sign a new labor contract, the cost of labor will rise.

Risk means that you cannot be absolutely sure, but you know the probabilities of the occurrence of a certain event. If you raise the price of a private label ice cream, people may think it's a better ice cream; the chances are 15 percent that sales will increase, 30 percent that they will drop, and five percent that they will remain the same according to a market survey. Insurance is based on the appraisal of risk. Actuaries can determine the probability of an event occurring if there are many similar cases. Thus, they know the likelihood of a building burning down, and they can set a fee structure for fire insurance so that the total fees collected from all building owners will be enough to pay claims and still yield a profit.

Uncertainty means that there are so many unknown factors that you cannot estimate the probabilities statistically. You cannot insure against uncertainty because the insurance company cannot determine actuarially what the chances may be of an event occurring. The actuaries don't know how likely it is that your new pizza business will succeed.

These three conditions are not completely separate possibilities. There are different degrees of possibility of each. Some outcomes are fairly certain. We can list others in an order which becomes less and less certain until we begin to face risk. The statistical assurance that we know the probability of an event, like the likelihood of a seven at the toss of dice, may be great in some cases. But at other times probabilities become very worrisome. Risks increase. We have all heard of the margin of error in a statistical statement: the survey shows John Jones will be reelected by 69 percent of the votes, with a possible error in the survey of two percent. But what if the survey shows Mr. Jones will be elected with a majority of 51 percent, with a possible error of five percent?

At some point in the continuum we can no longer talk of risk, for we are facing uncertainty. Somewhere on the list of outcomes we discover that probability cannot be assigned to the outcome. There are no sharp signs differentiating certainty, risk, and uncertainty. They are part of a continuum.

Of course, the process of decision making is different under each of the three conditions: certainty, risk, and uncertainty. Facing certainty, we can devise mathematical formulas to help us. We know the outcomes, but must decide which outcome we prefer. Facing risk, we can make good decisions by the use of actuarial tables, with the aid of computers, or by using reasonable models. Facing uncertainty, we use intuition, judgment, and prayers.

PROGRAMMED vs. NONPROGRAMMED DECISION MAKING

As we have pointed out, some decisions are made without conscious effort, while others take much time and trouble. Aside from nonbusiness decisions which are made automatically — like reaching for the blue striped tie — there are business decisions which are also made easily by following a clear procedure or an established rule. These decisions are called *programmed.*

Programmed decisions are those that are routine, made in accordance with an established rule or procedure, or based on habit, custom, and common practice. They need not be simple; some are complex but repetitive. For example, the rules may require that a typist hired for a typing pool must be able to type 40 words per minute with no errors, must be a citizen, must speak English, must have a high school education, must be in good health, and must be over 18 years of age. Those without these qualifications will not be hired. Period. The personnel officer need not lose sleep over the decision.

Some decisions are not made repeatedly. They are faced infrequently, irregularly. They are different, and cannot be solved by following a rule. Consider the plight of a man selling horse-drawn carriages in 1920 trying to decide if he should sell the new horseless carriages. He must make a decision that is not routine. This type of decision is called nonprogrammed.

Nonprogrammed decisions are not routine, not repetitive, and not based on clear rules and procedures. They deal with unusual or unique situations. They are often less structured, more ambiguous, less clear, more complex. For example, should the firm purchase a new machine for one million dollars which requires 10 employees to operate, or one for five million dollars which requires only five. The question is not merely one of mathematical costing. The manager must decide on factors that may include the reliability of the machine, the expected rate of breakdown, the life of the machine, trends in pay scales, the availability of skilled staff, problems with unions, the length of the work week, vacation scheduling, overtime rules, illness, lateness, and so on.

One example of nonprogrammed decision making is group decision making, in which nonroutine decisions are turned over to a number of persons for consideration.

GROUP DECISION MAKING

Autocratic business leaders and entrepreneurs often decide by themselves in the privacy of their subconscious minds. Modern consultants often urge that decisions be considered by more than one person. Group decision making is very trendy. Such decision making can be informal, as when a number of people are consulted irregularly and casually. Group decision making can also be formal, as when the process is assigned to a specific group designated for the purpose of deciding, or at least of recommending. In practice, there is a continuum of informal to formal decision making.

More will be discussed about group decision making in the section on participative management. However, we can note certain advantages and disadvantages to group or committee decisions. It is said that a camel is a horse designed by a committee. Certainly our tax laws, like camels, are a committee effort.

The major advantage of group action is that it avoids the limitations of a single person. It increases the variety of ideas and the number of alternatives which may be considered. In the section on *management by objectives (MBO)* we will show that one of the advantages of MBO is that it increases the chances of satisfactory implementation. People who participate in reaching a decision are more likely to make certain that the decision is carried out. A side issue is that participation in making decisions is good training for managers on their way up.

We are saying, of course, that group decision making increases the number and variety of alternatives that may be considered. We are not saying, however, that the quality of the final decision is necessarily improved.

There are problems in the implementation of group decision making in a business firm. One problem is that the process is costly and time consuming. When the plane hits an air pocket and starts to fall, there is no time for the pilot to consult his crew; he decides on his own to pull up the stick.

Moreover, lower level staff persons are often wedded to their own special interests and may ignore the higher level goals of the firm. While individual prejudices are washed out in the general consideration of the group, group prejudices may be substituted. The members of the group generally originate from one professional status, and are all subject to the same standards and beliefs.

Chief executive officers must also consider the possibility that once introduced to the decision process, the participants may want to be included in all decisions, even those which the CEO considers his private domain.

Lastly, we note that it is not always possible to reach a consensus. A group can become hopelessly tangled in dispute. In the final resolution of a problem, one person, the man in charge, will have to decide.

MANAGEMENT BY EXCEPTION

One use of nonprogrammed decision making is in the management style known as *management by exception (MBE)*. Under this management approach, decisions are made by lower level staff until a problem arises that cannot be decided by rules and regulations. Then the problem is referred to higher level management, where a more innovative approach is acceptable. In this case, higher managers are not involved in the petty details of day-by-day management, but are called in to resolve important questions.

We have pointed out that everyone constantly makes decisions, but some people make more nonprogrammed decisions than others. Nonprogrammed decisions are usually made by higher level managers.

NATURE OF DECISION MAKING

It is generally agreed today that the simplistic model of decision making under a purely rational formula is unacceptable. The behaviorists have made their point. We do not decide in a vacuum, at least under conditions of uncertainty. Even under certainty, decisions are colored by our feelings, our biases, our deeply held beliefs. We can maximize profits by making false claims, but we are honor bound not to do so. A paragon of virtue may know that he will go bankrupt selling bathing suits with long sleeves, but will continue because he thinks bikinis are immoral.

Even under conditions of risk, there is room for the human factor. How great a probability of success we demand before starting a new venture depends not on the mathematical percentages alone, but on whether we are risk averters or risk takers. The mathematical model gives us the probability, but we must decide to accept the risk, whatever it is. We have values, beliefs, habits, and customs which were ingrained in our minds during our growth to adulthood. We make decisions within the framework of these ideas. We do not act in a value-free environment.

Moreover, decisions are not made by choosing between a few unambiguous alternatives. Often there are multiple decisions to be made at one time, as well as many possible alternatives to the one decision. The effect of any decision may vary from the point of view of the observer. Some individuals may benefit from one decision, while others benefit from another. Self-interest may be involved in making a choice, rather than the interest of the organization. One decision may be in conflict with another if the first is aimed at a different goal than the second. There are times when no decision seems to be adequate to the problem at hand — there are no solutions to some problems.

Not all decisions are made calmly and coolly with adequate time. Too often, pressures of the real situation demand a fast decision, even though information may not be adequate and all alternatives are not explored. The stress of the business world not only makes careful thought a rare commodity, it makes slipshod decisions too common a phenomena. We cannot be assured of full rationality under these conditions.

Decision making is difficult because of risk and uncertainty. It is also difficult because of time pressure, conflict between goals, intangibles. In making decisions, certain parameters must be kept in mind: costs, existing policies, bias, and interrelationships. It is made difficult because of fear and timidity, resistance to change, problems in communication, conflicting criteria, and questions of feasibility.

CREATIVE DECISION MAKING

Programmed, routine decisions are usually not the subject of management texts. They are made by everyone, constantly and continuously. Some routine decisions are intuitive. The young lady buys the lavender blouse because she likes it. Some routine decisions are based on some rule or a prior decision. Arriving at the station later than usual, I take the more crowded express train instead of the local, because standing is less objectionable than coming to work late.

Nonprogrammed decision making can be mechanical or creative. Mechanical decisions can be made by computers, by groups, or by drudges. Creation is more often discussed in books on art. A creative decision is made by an innovative, sharp, bright, clever individual.

DECISION SKILLS

There is yet another side to decision making. Despite the irrational factors in the human mind, decision making can be learned and decision skills improved. While we will never eliminate judgment and bounded rationality, we can improve decision making skills. First of all, there are the decisions which can be reached by systematic, scientific, mathematical, computer-oriented methods, as in operations research. However, even in cases in which personal judgment is the main factor, the process of decision making can be improved by following guidelines.

A start in improved decision making can be made by becoming aware of barriers to good decision making. Some barriers include fear, lack of time, lack of information, illogical thinking, and failure to follow an orderly procedure.

Some managers are afraid to rock the boat. A major change may be called for, but the timid soul does not dare take action which may cause new problems. Of course, rash action must be avoided. However, a decision maker must be prepared to take strong, decisive action. Fear must be mastered.

We live in a fast-paced world. There is seldom time to do all the research we would like to do, to accumulate all the information we think we need, to consider all the alternatives which can be conjured up, and to decide at leisure like the Delphic Oracle. Lack of time is an important factor in the conceptions of bounded rationality and satisficing. Time is limited. We must do the best under the circumstances. At least, decisions should not be delayed consciously until the last minute.

Lack of information is closely associated with lack of time. Insufficient information, however, may be a result of other factors. There are cases in which the requisite information is simply not available. The plans of your major competitor may not be known until it is too late for an early response. Or information may be so complex that you cannot absorb and understand it in time. Sources of information may be unreliable. Good decisions are based on good information, but lack of information will not excuse failure. At least, the manager must accumulate as much information as possible.

Illogical thinking is a sign of poor management. Often, it is a result of emotional response to problems. A decision may be based on personal prejudices or on a point of view colored by values which are inconsistent with the purpose of the organization. One way to guard against blunder is to be aware of the values and personal prejudices guiding you. At best, the improper prejudices must be rejected in making a decision. At the very least, the decision maker must understand himself and know why he made a particular decision.

However, there is a different reason for some illogical thinking: basic stupidity. In such cases, there is little that can be done. In a competitive society, failure follows stupidity, the firm goes bankrupt, and the wound is cleansed.

The last barrier mentioned was failure to follow an orderly procedure. Systematic decision making, in the broader context of problem solving, requires full discussion.

SYSTEMATIC DECISION MAKING

We can look at decision making from a narrow or broad point of view. In the narrow view, decision making is choosing among alternatives. It is the act of choice itself. In the broad view, decision making is the entire process of problem solving in which we identify a problem, develop alternative solutions, choose the best alternative, and implement the decision. Systematic decision making is concerned with the broad view.

Management writers have little to say about the act of choice itself. Most discussions of decision theory reach a point in the systematic process in which they say: Choose! They specify factors to be considered in the decision, but cannot explain the internal process by which the mind selects.

One exception is Herbert A. Simon, who discusses the workings of the human mind. He suggests that the impressive outcomes of human problem solving are reached by the assembly, in the mind, of a small number of simple elements out of a large number of elements by a process of relatively simple interactions (Herbert A. Simon, *The New Science of Management Decision,* revised edition, Englewood Cliffs, New Jersey: Prentice-Hall, Inc., 1977). If this be true, someday we will be able to program computers to make complex decisions. Even now, scientists are working on the problem of artificial intelligence. At this time, however, we assign the job to live human beings.

We turn, then, to the broad view of decision making and find that it is very much like the process of planning. There are a number of steps involved, similar to those in planning. Following the general approach of Simon, we might say that the broad process of problem solving includes intelligence, design, choice, and review. Other authors propose a number of steps with minor differences, but all amount to the same process: identify a problem, develop a series of alternative solutions, analyze, choose the best, implement, and monitor.

Outlining the steps in problem solving is essentially a normative process. We are advising what should be done. Not all decisions follow this process; we argue that they should.

STEPS IN PROBLEM SOLVING

1. **Identify the problem.** We take it for granted that the problem is known, but sometimes we may stare at a problem without being aware that something is wrong. More difficult is knowing what the problem is. Sales are dropping but the solution may not be greater sales efforts. Maybe public tastes have changed. Maybe there is a new product on the market which has made our product obsolete. Perhaps the problem is that our quality is too poor. Maybe our prices are too high.

There is a danger that we will confuse the problem and the symptom, or the problem and the solution. The first step is to define the problem, to know what question must be answered.

2. **Affirm criteria and parameters.** We should be clear about the limits of action we may take, and the way we will judge our actions. This activity is often so well understood that many authors do not include this step in the list of measures to be taken in solving a problem.

Yet it *is* important! The limits may be financial. A small business firm cannot spend one hundred million dollars. A solution which destroys the natural environment must be rejected. This is the time to inspect the list of goals and objectives of the firm as a guide to future action.

3. **Develop alternative solutions.** There may be more than one way to catch a mouse. A cat may do . . . or a trap . . . or poisoned bait. There are often many ways to increase sales, or improve productivity, or raise profits. The trick is to imagine, invent, and inventory all the ways. Here creativity is important.

It is in this step that the benefits of group decisions are greatest. Presumably, more people can think of more solutions. But it is not always so. The creative solution may escape the group. There are a variety of situations in which alternatives may be explored.

First, there are cases in which there is only one possible solution. Others are simply not acceptable or are too weak, too poor to offer hope. In this case, the process of decision making is cut short. The sheriff, faced by a gunfighter with a gun in hand, doesn't consider multiple solutions. He shoots.

Second, there are cases in which there are many solutions. This is the case we have in mind when we discuss problem solving as choosing the best of a series of alternatives. The implication of multiple alternatives is that there are many possible solutions which are respectable on the surface.

Further analysis may disclose that one is better than the others, or that only one is truly acceptable.

Third, there are problems with no good solutions. An optimistic mind assumes that all problems can be solved. Sometimes this is not true. When the marshal is at the door, it is too late to decide to behave in accordance with the requirements of the lease.

The step involves listing all the possible alternatives that may be considered, fleshed out enough so that they can be examined with some degree of care. Elsewhere we discuss methods of group activity, including brainstorming, the Delphi method, and others. We note, here, that the various alternatives should be considered.

4.   **Evaluate and choose the best alternative.** Some authors list evaluation and choosing separately. There is much logic in this approach. We combine the two because (a) evaluation really predisposes us to choosing, and (b) because we have little to say about the mental process of choosing.

Evaluation is a crucial step. There are many factors to be considered in an evaluation, depending on the nature of the problem. Is the solution feasible for the firm? Some solutions may be better than others, but cannot be accomplished. It is important to ask whether there are other consequences of any action we might take. What is the purpose of our activity, to find a workable solution or the best possible solution? Do we want to maximize profits or satisfice?

If we have a priority system, we might rank the various alternatives. The alternatives may be subject to cost benefit analysis. They may be listed in a matrix or a decision tree. They may be analyzed by computer. These methods are discussed elsewhere.

The ultimate step is to make the choice. Usually choosing an alternative follows from the evaluation. In a sense, the analysis forces the choice, but this is not always so. Coca-Cola chose a new formula on the basis of market surveys. A more alert and sensitive chief executive might have rejected the statistics on the basis of consumer loyalty. But this is unusual. Most decisions are easy once the analysis is completed. In fact, a thorough analysis would have included consumer loyalty to Coca-Cola.

5. **Implement.** In pure logic, we might argue that decision making is just choosing. Implementing a decision is a separate topic. However, it is common in discussions of decision making to include the entire process of problem solving as a broader and more realistic model. We do not decide, in the business world, for the pure joy of the process. There is an ultimate purpose, a reason for deciding. And so we acknowledge that a decision, once reached, should be put into practice.

Earlier we discussed group decision making as a means of participation which made implementation easier. An example of participative management exists in Japan where decisions are made slowly, by many people. Naive Western observers are often critical of the long time involved in making a decision, and constantly surprised at the fast implementation afterwards. The speedy action, of course, is a direct result of the participative process of deciding.

6. **Measure, evaluate, and feedback.** The process does not end with implementation. Decisions may be good or bad, but we may not know until afterwards. It should be kept firmly in mind that decisions are not forever. The results of a decision, properly implemented, must be monitored. The results must be compared with expectations, existing conditions, changes in the overall situation. Once the decision or its results are evaluated, the good manager must feed back the information to a new

process of decision making. Perhaps the decision must stand. Perhaps the decision must be changed. The process is never ending, but continues as long as the process affected by the decision is in operation, or the firm is in operation.

6

Organization

Organization seems to be like divorce followed by reconciliation. First, we break organizations apart into separate departments, and then we try desperately to get the separate departments to live together in harmony.

Of course, the division is necessary. Division of labor into specialties is the essence of efficiency in our complex society. Imagine trying to design, build, and sell cars with thousands of welders, machinists, salespersons, engineers, and accountants all in one big happy family with no separate departments. Troubles would abound. The line manager doesn't have the skill to supervise welders, salespersons, and accountants with equal facility. Somewhere, somebody suggests the salespersons need a place to sell, away from the welders and machinists. We decide the accountants should act independently from the engineers. We form a sales department and a finance department. We organize.

We have solved one problem with this first step in organizing but new problems show up. Maybe the engineers designed an extremely expensive car and the welders and machinists turned out a vast number of them. Unfortunately, the sales department can't sell them fast enough and the accountants find that substantial losses result. Obviously, the various departments must cooperate or there will be chaos. Creating a structure with separate departments is not enough. Managers must devise ways to coordinate the parts of the structure. Organizing is more than creating departments. The departments must be made to work together.

DEFINITIONS

Organizing is a process of cooperative activities aimed at a goal. It is an orderly procedure for the rational allocation of resources in a goal-oriented management system. More specifically, it is an activity in which structures are created and relationships established in a distinct association to permit the members to work together effectively to reach objectives.

If organizing is a function or activity of management, an organization is the thing managers create in the process of organizing. It is a body, a structure, an association, a society, an entity, a systematic whole. Richard L. Daft says that "organizations are social entities that are goal-directed, deliberately structured activity systems with an identifiable boundary." (Richard L. Daft, *Organization Theory and Design*, 2nd Edition, St. Paul, Minn.: West Publishing Company, 1983, p. 9) He emphasizes four points: (1) An organization is a social entity, composed of people. (2) An organization has goals; it is purposive. (3) An organization is consciously divided into departments for efficiency. (4) An organization is a separate, bounded entity.

More formally, organizing is defined as a cooperative, systematic process in which a group of people create a structure and behavioral patterns in an association to achieve agreed upon objectives. The word "cooperative" means working together. The word "systematic" implies regularity, stability, duration. The word "process" implies an ongoing activity. The word "structure" means an articulated series of sections or departments. The words "behavioral patterns" refer to the way humans relate to one another in authority relationships. An "association" may be a firm, a business, a corporation, an institution, a club, a religious order, a union, a gang, an orchestra, a fraternity, a government agency, a political party, a community federation, or any distinct group of people. The words "agreed upon objectives" implies that the group has goals that are consciously accepted.

This definition (indeed, nearly all the definitions of organizing) gives the impression that organizing is always a rational process undertaken by informed and reasonable men and women. In part, this may be true; philosophers postulate that rationality among humans is a distinct possibility.

In the real world rationality is like virtue — desirable but not too common. Even to the extent that the organizers of a firm are personally rational, it is not clear that their personal goals are always the same as those of the firm. Too often the top leaders of an organization are more concerned with their own individual gain than with the life of the organization itself. This is particularly evident, for example, in the creation of golden parachutes, discussed in the section on hostile takeovers.

More often, however, managers do not have all the information needed for rational decisions. Even if they have good information initially, the future is clouded by uncertainty, so that current organizational decisions may not reflect later needs. Conditions may change, so that decisions made at an earlier time may not be valid at a later date. Or the problem may be that an organizational design is created with little thought; traditional design is easier to follow than new patterns made necessary by a changing environment. This is irrational management.

The organizing process takes place in a particular social and political environment. Good organizational design should be based on many complex factors, including the technology of the firm, morale and attitude of the employees, their education and skills, government regulations, social customs, and other external conditions. Organizational decisions reflect the social and political worlds in which they take place. Managers may not be aware that the decisions about how to organize take place in this dim atmosphere and not in an immaculate setting. Their decisions about organizing, nevertheless, are as much a product of social and political forces as a consequence of logic.

When we argue that decision making is rational, we view the decision maker as "economic man," that is, as a logical person who is concerned with his or her economic well being. The manager of the firm is viewed as seeking maximum profit for the firm. In truth, human motivation is far broader than profit seeking. It includes desire for fame, respect, security, and other goals. The narrow view of profit motivation results in a narrow view of what is rational. Many acts seem irrational from the point of view of "economic man" seeking profit maximization, but completely rational if we consider the complex desires of the whole human being.

However, for the purposes of this book, it will be assumed that the proper functioning of managers as organizers is intelligent, logical, reasonable, informed, and based on economic factors. Real life examples aside, we will assume that organizing is the rational process of "economic man."

DISTINCTIONS IN ORGANIZING

Organizing will be discussed as a standard process in a formal setting, but we should be aware of the informal organizational processes which take place behind the formal front. By informal organization, we mean the groups of friends and acquaintances, the networks of gossip, the amorphous collections of persons with common interests who communicate, consult, discuss, consider, influence, and sometimes decide outside the company hierarchy.

Another distinction in organizing is between mechanistic and organic structures. This distinction was made by Burns and Stalker (Tom Burns and G.M. Stalker, *Management of Innovation*, London: Tavistock Publications, 1961, p. 19.) in their study of an electronics firm. A mechanistic structure is the classical or traditional design, common in large, stable, authoritarian, hierarchical firms. It is ideal for well designed, programmable, efficient, predictable, and inflexible tasks. An organic structure is a flexible, adaptable design, useful in an open system, with participative management, subject to change and ambiguity, focusing on the mission rather than on narrow technical matters.

ASPECTS OF ORGANIZING

Organizing can be examined in two aspects — by structure and by human behavior. Many commentators on organizing use the terms structure and context, or structure and authority relationships to mean the same thing. The terms structure and human behavior will be used here for reasons that will become clear.

Structure is obvious. We have all seen the formal table of organization *(T of O)*, a diagram showing persons as little boxes connected by vertical and horizontal lines depicting relationships. The chart is merely a picture of the formal relationships of the various parts of an organization.

More difficult to understand is the role of human behavior in organizing, the strange antics of the mortals in the chart and their relationships depicted by the vertical and horizontal lines. We are dealing here with matters of authority, its acceptance, and the subsequent delegation which marks its use. We are concerned with power and its use and abuse. We are involved not only with delegation of authority, but with responsibility. We are interested in relationships between people on the organizational chart. These are matters of human behavior. Hence, "human behavior" is offered as the second aspect of organizing.

It should be emphasized that both structure and human behavior should be examined with several conditions in mind. First, they are seen in a systems concept. Structure and behavior are related to each other and to the rest of the environment. The relationship to the environment means it is an open system. Second, they are seen in flux. The environment, and the systems within it, are marked by constant change. Organizations which are immutable are probably dead.

Third, they are seen from a contingency or situational management viewpoint. In a world of uncertainty, change, and complexity, the specific situation determines the best solution. There is no absolute right and wrong in any distinctive organizational structure, nor in any individual process of organizing outside the specific case. It is necessary to fit the organization to the situation.

Last, we should remember that good organization permits efficiency and effectiveness, but by itself does not create efficiency and effectiveness. With these conditions in mind, we turn to structure and human behavior in organizing.

STRUCTURE

Structure is best understood by looking at an organizational chart or table of organization *(T of O)*.

The *T of O* follows certain conventions. Each little box refers to a department or position. Often it may be a single person, such as the president or the treasurer. At other times it refers to a group of people, such as the board of directors or an office, such as the office of the treasurer. Even if the box contains the name of a person (e.g., John Jones, vice president of manufacturing), the implication is that the *functions* of that person (manufacturing) flow from that box.

The position of the box on the chart is relevant. Higher up in the chart means higher up in the organization. The box at the bottom of the chart is low man on the totem pole. We hear talk of "lines of authority" or "chain of command." These are indicated by the lines which connect the boxes. The vertical lines can be read either up or down. Down indicates authority relationships; the person on top gives orders directly to the one below. Up indicates communication; the person below reports to the one above. Vertical lines signify unequal authority, with greater authority above and lesser below.

Horizontal lines indicate relationships among individuals of equal authority — boxes at the same level on the chart enjoy positions of similar authority in the organization. Sometimes the *T of O* shows dotted lines. These generally refer to informal lines of authority or communication, or more precisely, to staff relationships, which are discussed later in this chapter.

In all cases, the connecting lines show not only authority relationships, but lines of communication as well. The *T of O*, or organization chart, is a model.

Like a map, it shows major features of an organization. The individuals who are shown as boxes generally have specialized functions, different from the functions of others, while the lines depict relationships. The chart, therefore, shows the separation of the organization into departments based on the division of labor, as well as the integration of the departments based on authority relationships.

The organization chart shows the hierarchical structure of the firm and the formal lines of authority. The *T of O* is a pyramid, with one or a few people at the top, a larger number at the middle of the diagram, and the largest number at the bottom.

In one sense, the *T of O* is misleading. It shows the formal structure only and omits informal relationships between people. For example, a particular organization chart may show several vice presidents reporting to the president, all on the same level. Yet everyone in the firm knows that one of the vice presidents has more power than the others; he is the heir apparent and also the president's son. Or a person may appear to have great power since he or she is close to the top of the pyramid. In any particular case, however, the apparent position may hide the true relationship; maybe the "high level" little box is merely window dressing, a leftover from a previous administration, or an honorary title.

DEPARTMENTS

Important questions relate to why and how a large organization is broken up into separate parts or departments. Departments can be created according to a number of principles, as follows:

1. **Function:** A primary way of dividing up a large organization is according to what the employees do, that is, their function. All engineers, all salespersons, all accountants may be grouped. More precisely, in this type of organization departments are created according to the function of the department.

Functional departmental structure is highly efficient when specialization is of major importance. It permits the development of specialized skills, and makes the training of specialists easy. It creates a community of interests and easy communication among the members of the specialty, assuring effective operation. A functional department structure works best under conditions of stability and in a mass production industry where employees with specialized skills are logically grouped together.

The key question of functional departments is how to foster cooperation between them. Members of a department tend to think of the welfare of their department before the welfare of the entire organization. For example, a production department may want to maximize output. To do this, the department may sacrifice quality and ignore costs. The sales department may seek maximum sales and demand improved quality. The accounting department may believe that neither the production nor the sales departments are aware of the effect of their tactics on the bottom line.

Dividing a large organization into functional departments at the top will probably fail in conglomerates. It may also be weak in dynamic organizations in which new products and services are being developed constantly.

2. **Product:** Another common way of dividing up firms is by product(s). This is standard practice in a conglomerate or multiproduct firm, such as one which produces TV sets, microwave ovens, and office copiers. Such a firm would be divided into departments for each product.

Perhaps the most famous example of product division is General Motors, which at one time had separate divisions for Chevrolet, Pontiac, Oldsmobile, Buick, and Cadillac. Each division is treated like a duplicate of the mother firm. Each is a profit center.

Note that a functional division can be evaluated either as a cost center or as a revenue center, but not as a profit center. Unlike a product department, a functional department does not combine costs and revenues to reach a bottom line. The product department, however, must prove itself by producing a profit, since it combines both income and expense. The Chevrolet division of General Motors issues a separate financial report. The quality control department in Chevrolet does not. In our profit-oriented society we expect a "profit center" to be more efficient than any activity center which does not have profit motivation. In Chevrolet, the value of the quality control department depends on how well it raises the quality of the car. However, treating the Chevrolet division as a separate profit-motivated business permits efficient and effective total operation.

On the other hand, product departmentation makes coordination among functional units difficult. Each department is concerned with its own bottom line, even to the detriment of other departments in the firm. For example, let us assume that there are benefits from joint purchase of certain types of equipment or supplies. Normally, each product department would have its own purchasing division. Joint purchasing might be difficult to achieve with product departments acting independently.

3. **Territory:** In large organizations doing business over large geographic areas, departmentation by territory is common. A firm selling products worldwide may need one division for the United States and one for foreign sales. A large U.S. firm may want to divide sales areas into East, West, and Midwest.

Geographic divisions are of great importance when the characteristics of the region affect the business substantially. For example, production overseas deals with conditions vastly different than production in the United States or in Canada. Differences include laws and customs, pay scales, and attitudes towards unions and work. Sales may be affected by national income in various nations, and by local perceptions about the desirability of the product. Management must be sensitive to local conditions and pursue different policies in different areas. Thus, at times, territorial departmentation is necessary.

On the other hand, excessive regional divisions create a more complex management structure, may be costly, and may be difficult for top management to control.

4. **Customer:** Departments can be based on the needs of different customers. A primary example of a customer with special needs is the military. An airplane manufacturer may want to create one division to deal with private airlines and another to deal with the Air Force. Another example of departmental division is the retail and wholesale customer, each requiring a different sales approach and a different pricing structure. While such a structure reacts to the special needs of each class of customer, it may lead to unequal growth of segments of the firm.

5. **Other forms of departmentation:** Some firms, or divisions of firms, are broken up into separate departments according to the process or the equipment used by the department. For example, a firm providing landscaping may put manual workers in one department and those who use heavy tractors, cherry pickers, and other major pieces of equipment into a separate department.

A department can also be created based on time. For example, each of three shifts in a plant can be headed by a separate supervisor and managed as independent departments.

Divisions can be created merely by number or sequence. For example, large numbers of persons applying for public benefits (e.g., the hordes seeking unemployment insurance after a large plant is shut down) can be separated into groups for processing by serial (social security) number.

In the real world of business, all or most of these methods of departmentation are used at the same time.

Many of the problems of organization, so evident in the typical firm, can be dealt with by matrix management, discussed elsewhere in this book.

So far it has seemed that forming departments is easy. We have simply ignored the major questions about the shape of the *T of O*. Shall it be steep or flat is the first question. The answer requires a discussion of span of management (also called *span of control*) and the number of levels of management.

SPAN OF MANAGEMENT

The span of management refers to the number of subordinates a supervisor controls. The oldest example of a discussion about span of control is found in the Old Testament.

> Moreover, thou shalt provide out of all the people
> able men. . . . and such over them, to be rulers of
> thousands, and rulers of hundreds, rulers of fifties,
> and rulers of tens. . . .
> — *Exodus 18:21*

It is generally agreed that there are limits to the number of persons a supervisor can control. Old army practice held that six individuals could be supervised well by one person. In 1933, V.A. Graicunas argued that the limits to the span of control could be measured accurately. As the number of subordinates increases mathematically, the number of possible relationships between the manager and his subordinates increases geometrically. He expressed these relationships in a formula:

$$C = n \left(2n / 2 + n - 1\right)$$

where **C** is the number of possible relationships, and **n** is the number of subordinates. Graicunus concludes that a manager can supervise five or six subordinates. Of course, ideas change with the times, and today it is believed that the formula ignores the actual situation and loses much of its value because it refers to possible relationships, not to actual relationships. However, the idea of limits to the span of control is still important.

The modern view is that the span of control depends on the situation, i.e., we have a contingency view. What are the factors that permit a broad span or demand a narrow span?

The factors that matter include the similarity of functions, the complexity of the job, the proximity of the parts of the operation, and the level of management. If many workers are performing similar operations, a supervisor can control a large number, perhaps 30. If all workers are doing different things, the span must be narrower. A supervisor can control standard, repetitive, simple work with ease; his span is wide. In the case of complex, changing work, the span of control is smaller. What is important is the nature of the work and the skill of the manager. Research scientists in a laboratory may require little supervision; coal miners may need more. In general, top managers dealing with complex issues have a more limited span of control than lower level managers who deal with standard, repetitive work.

One factor in the span of control is geographic proximity. It has long been held that a manager needs a narrow span to adequately control subordinates who work at distant locations. On the other hand, some writers argue that employees in distant locations must be of relatively high caliber, requiring less supervision. This permits a broader span, as in the case of the control of outside commissioned salesmen. A new factor, evident today, is the computer. The ability of the computer to process large amounts of data permits supervision of distant operations centrally. The computer can provide information needed by the supervisor for control on a timely basis, and gives the distant subordinates information needed to carry out their duties, broadening the workable span of control.

MANAGEMENT LEVELS

The span of control has a direct effect on the number of levels of management in a firm. With a wide span of control, a given number of employees can be accommodated in a broad, short pyramid. With a narrow span of control, an organization with the same fixed number of employees must be narrow and tall since additional levels of control are needed.

There is no one shape that is good for all organizations — short or tall. The contingency view holds that the proper shape of the organization depends on the situation. However, certain factors must be considered. A tall organization is one with many layers of management. An order, transmitted from the top to the bottom, goes through many layers. A communication from the bottom to the top goes through many individuals. Thus, an extremely tall pyramid provides many opportunities for distortion of the orders or messages, takes excessive time, and is costly. A number of firms have found it desirable to reduce the number of management levels, creating substantial savings in the costs of management. However, if the reduction of management is accomplished by making the span of control too wide, there is another danger. Too wide a span may weaken supervision. There is no rule that governs every situation. In the end, intelligence and good judgment determine the best shape for an organization.

LINE AND STAFF

Another issue is raised when we inspect a *T of O*, especially one with dotted lines between some of the boxes, or with some boxes off to the side of the diagram, indicating people affecting the organization but not directly in it. We are concerned in these cases with differences between line and staff employees.

The differences between line and staff are explained in two ways. First, line positions are those with direct authority, while staff positions are advisory. Second, line positions carry out the central purpose of the organization, while staff positions provide support. Both explanations require comment.

Line and staff can be illustrated with an example from the army. The central purpose of an army corps may be to attack the enemy, advancing on a particular front. The infantry divisions assigned the job are line. The colonel gives an order to advance to the captain who passes it on to the lieutenant who gives the order to the sergeant who passes it on to the private. All the officers involved are line officers, giving direct orders to carry out the central purpose of the corps.

On the other hand, the colonel responsible for intelligence activities might inform the line colonel that an enemy tank corps is stationed in the woods on the left flank. He does not order the line colonel to avoid that area, or arrange for an artillery barrage, or make other changes in the plan of attack. His function is to inform; he provides a service. While the service is of tremendous importance, he does not give orders; providing intelligence service is not the central purpose of the corps. He is staff. This is not to imply that the line officer may ignore him; to do so would be folly.

Another example can be found in private industry. The foreman of the frimfram shop producing frimframs is a line manager. He gives direct orders to the workers and is involved in the main business of the firm — producing frimframs. An accident takes place in the shop and a worker sues the firm. The staff attorney gives advice to the foreman about posting safety rules. He gives advice, not orders, and his job is not the central purpose for which the firm was created. He is staff.

Unfortunately, the matter is not as clear as it seems in these examples. Complications cloud the issue. To begin with, there are two kinds of staff persons, personal and specialized.

Personal staff refers to positions which directly aid a line manager. Usually we refer to such jobs as "assistant to the manager," rather than "assistant manager." The difference is important. The "assistant to" has no authority of his or her own. The job is to relieve the boss of certain duties, to provide help, to ease the workload of the manager. On the other hand, the assistant manager (a line manager) does have authority, usually delegated from the full manager.

Specialized staff do not provide personal help to ease the workload of the boss, but provide needed services or information to carry out specific functions. The specialized staff person usually has specific skills and gives distinctive, expert services, often of a technical nature.

The distinction between line and staff is not as clear as first appears, especially in a firm with an organic structure rather than one with a mechanistic structure. In a firm with a less formal, organic structure, staff persons may be given functional authority.

Functional authority is line authority for a particular, limited task or function. It may not be permanent. For example, a planner may be given temporary authority to design a system. More commonly, it gives specialized staff authority in the narrow field of the staff person's expertise, e.g., a safety engineer may have the right to walk onto a construction project and order a bricklayer to put on his hard hat. He may not give any other types of orders.

The problem with functional authority is that it reduces the authority of the line manager. The central problem of staff is that of conflict with line. Consider the tough line manager who complains that he is given the responsibility of producing frimframs cheaply, only to have the safety engineer, the quality control engineer, and (worst of all) the human relations director insisting on changes.

In a more general sense, the existence of staff personnel interferes with the hierarchical chain of command which is so central to classical organization theory. One of the pillars of such theory is unity of command. We sometimes state the essence of unity of command with the old saying "one man, one boss."

According to this principle, one supervisor — and only one supervisor — has authority over a particular subordinate, and that subordinate reports to only one supervisor.

Henri Fayol warned against too strict adherence to this principle, at least with regard to communication. He took note of the need for persons in lower positions in different departments of an organization to communicate with one another. To follow the hierarchical structure, the communication would have to travel up the chain to the top of the pyramid and down to the bottom of the other chain. As a solution, Fayol suggested a bridge, or gangplank, between the two, i.e., informal, direct communication. Nevertheless, the gangplank is an informal device which merely ameliorates the conflict between the differing needs of separate departments; it does not fully resolve the conflict.

The problem of line staff conflict is real. It is all too common to find examples of staff infringement on line authority. The question that must be resolved to settle such conflict is who has the authority and responsibility. Problems of misunderstanding and resentment must be dealt with promptly. The line manager must accept staff functional authority as he or she would accept any parameters created in the environment. For example, an angry manager cannot shoot an inefficient employee! The line manager must also understand that the inefficient employee cannot be fired unless certain procedures are followed. Both the law of the land and the rules imposed by the human relations director must be adhered to.

On the other hand, the staff person must act with some discretion. He or she must be sensitive to the feelings of the line supervisor, must have empathy and an understanding of human nature. It cannot be assumed that line and staff will agree and understand one another automatically. Top management must take steps to assure such agreement and understanding.

There are cases in which the conflict between line and staff will not fade away under the gentle spell of cooperation and empathy. The obstacles to cooperation may be inherent in the mind of the line manager or the staffer. Obstacles may be a result of an inappropriate structure. If organizing is reconciliation after divorce, the problems of line/staff relationship are a mirror of the problems of organizing in general. They have existed since the beginning of organization, and are most evident in bureaucracy.

BUREAUCRACY

A bureaucracy is an example of mechanistic structure. In current use, the word bureaucracy is a malignancy. It wasn't always so. Today we associate bureaucracy with red tape, but formerly it was proposed as orderly, legitimate administration.

The concept of bureaucracy was introduced by Max Weber, a German sociologist (1864–1920). Of course, there were organizations we would call bureaucracies long before Weber, but he named and described them. In the ancient world, large scale organizations, especially military units and certain religious groups, were essentially of bureaucratic form. For years, hereditary rulers and their ministers had made use of intermediary groups of clerks to carry out the routine jobs of an increasingly complex government. Max Weber, however, gave the concept of bureaucracy precision and an explanation.

Weber wrote in Germany, about the turn of the century, when the German State was struggling to emerge into an industrial nation from a semi-feudal society. Weber reacted against the evils of the then-existing system of administration. The German barons made official appointments based on nepotism and favoritism, maintained a capricious attitude toward law, and a subjective attitude toward people. Tax collectors assessed lower taxes against favorites. The administration of the German States was characterized by inefficiency and lack of expertise. On the other hand, there was an example of efficiency in the Prussian army which attracted the German scholar and served as a model of an ideal administration.

Weber proposed standards for administration of the state, which we take for granted today, in a system he called bureaucracy. In essence, bureaucracy is a legal, rational system of administration based on the concepts of expertise and hierarchy. He proposed a number of requisites for public administration:

1. Division of labor based on specialized skills
2. Formal rules of law governing administration
3. A clear relationship between authority and responsibility; a distinct chain of command
4. An impersonal and formal relationship of superiors to subordinates
5. Employment and promotion based on expertise and merit

Today, we tend to think of bureaucracy as excessive formality and adherence to rules without regard for individuals. Originally it meant an orderly system based on rule of law and dedicated to efficiency. When examples of the errors of bureaucracy are pointed out, we usually mean excessive bureaucracy. Some order is needed. Employment and promotion should depend on merit. There must be rules to counter irregularity and discrimination. Specialization and the division of labor do promote efficiency. The excesses of bureaucracy are what causes concern, not the ideal case.

There is, however, a more general objection to the concept of bureaucracy. Weber, influenced by the Prussian ideal and writing before the behavioral aspects of management were understood, did not deal with human factors, the informal side of management structure and its political character. The strength of bureaucracy is as a legitimate system of authority, blessed with efficiency born of hierarchy and expertise. The weakness of bureaucracy is inflexibility, the omission of human relations, and its lack of realism. In modern organizations, we often create organic structures rather than mechanistic structures. The bureaucratic prescription is accepted without an overdose. For example, an exception may be made from a strict adherence to merit promotion in the case of minorities who have suffered from past discrimination. Today, managers more easily accept differences in human behavior and deviance from common standards. Managers are more accustomed to change, and do not shrink from new forms of organization.

ALTERNATIVE FORMS OF ORGANIZATION

Reports of the death of the bureaucratic, mechanistic organization are exaggerated, but a number of new species of organization have evolved. The major forces which account for the new types of organization are: (a) the increasing complexity of technology and information in modern institutions, (b) the need to reconcile the demands of functional and product departmentation, and (c) conflict between line and staff. The course of evolution of organizational structure is from pure line to line staff to matrix. All these new forms might be called organic. They depart from the hierarchical forms whose essence is unity of command. Included in these newer forms of organization are the committee, plural management, or the use of executive teams, project groups or task forces, and matrix management.

Committees. Committees are ubiquitous. They are found even in bureaucratic, hierarchical institutions. The committee is a group formed for a special purpose, often for better coordination or for decision making. Perhaps one reason for the popularity of committees is to shift responsibility or to kill an idea. Suppose that a proposal is made to a manager; he or she doesn't like the idea but is reluctant to say "no" for political reasons. The manager refers the proposal to a committee, confident that the idea will die a natural death in the prolonged deliberations, especially if the committee is loaded with friends and chatterboxes. But this is a cynical view. Committees have other, better uses.

The committee is useful in solving complex or sensitive problems and for difficult decision making. Two kinds of committee may be noted — the *ad hoc* committee and the *standing* committee. The ad hoc committee is a temporary committee created for a special purpose. Perhaps a new product is being considered for development, or the purchase of expensive equipment is suggested, or a major change in government regulations is expected, or there is a new trend in the competitive environment. The firm may appoint a special committee, an ad hoc committee, to examine the problem and make recommendations. The job done, the committee expires.

A *standing committee*, sometimes called a *structural committee*, is a permanent part of the corporate structure of a firm, and has a place in the *T of O*. A standing committee is often used for decision making and coordination. For example, an endowed institution may have a finance committee to make regular decisions on investing endowment funds. A management committee may help coordinate diverse departments. Perhaps the most common standing committee is the board of directors (or board of trustees in a nonprofit institution).

The board of directors is a *decision making* committee. It has full authority to manage the affairs of a corporation. Its powers are derived from the bylaws and corporation law. It elects the officers and acts on major business decisions. For example, board approval is ordinarily needed to appoint the independent certified public accountants and the law firm representing the corporation. Board approval is needed to acquire or dispose of major assets, approve major contracts, or to change the main business of the firm. The salaries and other benefits of the chief executives are often set by the board.

Typically, members of the board have formal power only during meetings of the board and on matters which are properly on the agenda of the meeting. In between meetings, their formal powers are limited to those specifically assigned by the board at a legal meeting. Normally, the official powers of management are carried out by the duly elected officers. Of course, the board members may have substantial informal power because of their position; an employee is not likely to thwart an important director on the technical grounds of lack of formal authority.

The real power of the board depends on the situation. Where the chairman or president is the major stockholder, or where he or she holds great power for reasons of history or practice or common consent, the board may be a rubber stamp. However, absolute power in business firms has a way of disappearing over time as in political institutions.

The committee is much used and much criticized. The advantages of the use of a committee are many. It is said that several heads are better than one; of course, this trite saying has been proven false by many brilliant individuals. However, many minds may be needed when a problem requires a variety of expertise and special knowledge. The use of committees helps focus attention on a problem. It helps secure support for new ventures or ideas and permits participation in planning and decision making, resulting in better communication, understanding, and improved motivation of participants.

On the other hand, committees can be costly and are time-consuming. With committee decision making, it is difficult to assign ultimate responsibility. Too often, committee decisions are compromises. The result may be mediocrity when innovation is required. Lastly, note that all this discussion assumes that the committee functions as a joint process. In some cases, the committee may be dominated by one person, or by a small group within the committee. In such cases, the committee really functions as a mere public forum for the real power operation.

A special type of committee is the *executive team* or *corporate office*. It is sometimes called the office of the president or the office of the chairman. The plural executive consists of a small group of top officers who make joint decisions on major operational questions. The executive team has been developed in large corporations as tasks have become more complex and the need for specialized knowledge has increased. The typical executive team includes persons with different skills — perhaps a financial expert, a marketing specialist, and an attorney. Problems with the plural executive are similar to those of the committee.

Task Force. We often think of a task force as an array of great ships steaming to the defense of the nation. Indeed, the naval task force is a perfect example of this breed of organization. A naval task force may be made up of units drawn from various groups, such as an aircraft carrier from a carrier group, numbers of destroyers and cruisers, supply ships from a support unit, and perhaps a battalion of marines. Each of the ships or battalion normally belongs to a permanent fighting unit, but is assigned, temporarily, to the special force. Thus, the task force, or project group, is a temporary organization made up of members drawn from permanent positions for a particular purpose.

The task force or project group is common in industries where a temporary objective is important. For example, a large construction firm may be building several, separate construction projects at one time. If special groups of engineers, architects, and accountants are created to deal with each of the separate projects, the management may be improved. Similarly, the development of a new product might be more successful if a separate team shepherds it through the early stages. An advertising agency has a number of separate clients, each with different needs. The agency might organize a series of separate groups, each serving the client with all the important functions: a creative group, a cost control accountant, a production team, a media specialist, and an overall director. Chrysler recently developed a series of new cars in half the normal time by creating interdepartmental teams to handle the differing objectives of the design, production, and marketing departments.

The task force shares some advantages and disadvantages with the committee, though it typically has more operational status. In a naval task force, the commander is the unquestioned leader. In some private groups, the authority of the director may not be clear. A major problem of a temporary structure is that the need may not be temporary. The advantages of cutting across the normal structure, combining the benefits of functional and product departmentation, have become urgent in a world characterized by complexity, special knowledge, and the need for vast amounts of information. We are led, then, to the matrix organization.

Matrix. The matrix organization was developed in the space age industries in the 1950s and 1960s. An early examination of the matrix organization was made by Davis and Lawrence (Stanley M. Davis and Paul R. Lawrence, *Matrix*, Reading, Mass.: Addison-Wesley Publishing Company, 1977). They argued that the distinguishing feature of the matrix organization was that it gave up the unity of command principle. Matrix does not insist that there be a "one man, one boss" relationship. They defined matrix (*op. cit.*, p. 3) as:

> . . . any organization that employs a multiple command system that includes not only a multiple command structure but also related support mechanisms and an associated organizational culture and behavior pattern.

In one way, matrix is a permanent task force. There is not much sense in pretending that a construction project which may last 10 years is transient. The development of a new missile system for the army may take years and is hardly temporary.

The underlying need is to combine the advantages of functional and product departmentation. The functional structure permits technical excellence by merging persons of a particular skill; for example, a group of engineers, working together under single leadership, should be able to produce a good engineering design. On the other hand, the project structure can be helpful in developing a new product effectively; it focuses on coordination of all the functions required for completion. A successful matrix combines the technical excellence of functional structure with the effective coordination of project structure. Of course, an unsuccessful matrix may blunder into poor design.

Specifically, a matrix organization is one in which each of the members of the group has more than one boss, usually a supervisor in the functional area and another in the product area.

Let us consider a matrix to develop and build a new missile. A giant midwestern corporation sets up a new plant in the west. A project manager is appointed. The manager runs the western operation, and is responsible for completing the project on time and within budget. He or she is a generalist, and has broad supervision over all the employees in the plant. However, many of these employees are specialists, perhaps engineers, or scientists, or cost accountants, or lawyers. In their specialty they look to the functional manager stationed in the midwest for guidance. For example, assume a new technology is developed in the use of computers. The central data processing manager might call the western computer expert to discuss the new technology for the special project. In the traditional, hierarchical organization, the formal relationship to a central computer manager would be advisory; the central computer manager in the midwest would act as a staff advisor to the western computer engineer who is line. Yet in a more realistic view, the central data processing manager would probably have functional authority based on position, knowledge, influence, or tradition. Calling the relationship advisory is really disingenuous. In a matrix organization, the superior position of the midwest manager on technical matters would be formally acknowledged. However, on personnel matters, such as pay, promotion, vacation, and working conditions, the western computer engineer would turn to the western project manager. The western computer expert would know that he or she must deal with a distant, functional authority on narrow technical matters and with the local project director on all other matters.

Matrix management is not easy. Since it violates the principle of unity of command, special training of participants is urgent. Each person involved must learn a new role. Each supervisor must learn how to supervise with an eye to the needs and demands of the other supervisor. Untrained managers cannot cope with this unaccustomed role; some trained managers never learn to accept such a role.

The exercise is difficult for the subordinates as well. They must learn when to turn to one boss and when to turn to the other. They must also learn how to tell one boss that the order just received is in conflict with orders from the other, without playing one against the other for personal benefit.

In general, it is necessary to minimize conflict and power struggles in matrix organization. It is important to avoid the anarchy that sometimes results from the lack of clarity as to who is in charge. Also critical, a sense of responsibility must be fostered as some members of a matrix team may try to shed responsibility on the grounds that lines of authority are unclear. Matrix management is desirable not only where it is helpful to combine the advantages of functional and project structure, but also in environments of complexity, uncertainty, and when there is an unusual need for coordination. These conditions are especially true in space age technology, such as the development of missiles, and in large building projects, as with the construction of a hydroelectric plant or a great tunnel.

7

Management of Change

We live in a world of rapid change. New technology quickly replaces old and is itself replaced by newer technology. Use of carbon paper is replaced by mimeographic, which in turn is replaced by xerographic copying. The economy changes from recession to recovery to rapid growth, and from stable prices to inflationary prices and back again. Interest rates fall and then rise. Government adds new regulations in some fields and deregulates other fields. Leadership changes in organizations gradually over time or suddenly. Control of corporations changes rapidly due to takeover fights and leveraged buyouts. Change is constant for every organization.

Change may bring new opportunities. Change may also bring threatening developments to an organization. An organization must plan for changes to take advantage of opportunities and to avoid threats. Change must be managed constructively.

Any change is disconcerting to some individuals. The manager must adapt the organization to change in such a way as to avoid some of the negative effects of change on both individuals and the organization as a whole. Thus, the speed of change, the kind of change, and the total amount of change must all be carefully implemented.

Often, individuals in an organization will resist change. Change brings uncertainty about the future. One reason that individuals resist change is they may believe that the change will hurt them individually — they may lose income or prestige or power within the organization or status outside the organization as a result of the change. If there is poor communication within the organization, individuals may fear that they are not receiving the entire reason for the change. They may believe that the change has other purposes that will affect them adversely.

Different individuals can validly have different judgments about the value of a particular change to an organization. Different individuals have varying experience and varying points of view about any policy adopted by the organization. A change in a company's credit policy will affect the sales manager differently than the financial manager. A new policy of tighter credit, for example, may help the financial manager reduce bad debt loss but will make it more difficult for the sales manager to increase sales.

The facts possessed by individuals may differ. The financial manager is very conscious, for example, of bad debt losses. The sales manager is very knowledgeable about what other companies' credit policies are. Accordingly, the sales manager may oppose a tightening of credit terms because he or she believes sales will be lost to competitors. The sales manager's opposition to the changed policy might be based on better information. In such a case, the sales manager's opposition to the change might be healthy for the organization. The supervisor of both the financial manager and the sales manager may meet with them to resolve the differences and come up with a changed credit policy that may reduce bad debts somewhat less than the financial manager would desire, but may help the sales manager better meet sales goals.

Managers must work to reduce the resistance to change by individuals. If a change is to be effective, it must be accepted by the individuals in the specific situation. If these individuals do not accept the change, they may completely reject it or sabotage it, may delay it or only partially implement it, or may behave in some way that will harm the organization (such as a strike or slowdown in production). They may also leave the organization if they are strongly opposed to the change.

There are a number of steps that managers can take to make change more acceptable. First of all, managers can let employees know why a change is necessary. Good communication can do much to facilitate change even when the change may involve some less than desirable features. For example, an airline faced with the problem of competing with new carriers paying lower wages in the new environment of deregulation may have to cut its labor costs to keep its prices competitive. Giving employees the data on wages paid by other carriers and its significance to the airline's competitive position may help employees better understand the need for cuts in personnel, wages, or both.

Once the information has been communicated, the manager can next seek the involvement of the employees involved in the situation. Those employees can help in coming up with a change that will help the organization. For example, the employees of the airline facing lower cost competition may come up with a number of feasible changes to help the airline compete better. Some of the changes suggested by the employees of the airline might be better than some of those envisioned by the manager, who may not have had direct experience as a mechanic or as a flight attendant. Working with the employees, the manager may be able to find solutions that solve the cost problem and are also acceptable to the employees.

When the change is being resisted by employees out of fear, it is important for the manager to be as supportive as possible. For example, if layoffs are necessary as a result of the change, the manager can help employees by providing outplacement services.

Sometimes, formal negotiation can be helpful in implementing change. A labor union may accept changes in work rules if some of the savings from a more efficient production process are passed along to the workers in the form of a raise.

Some managers may use threats (e.g., job transfers, demotions, loss of some privileges, etc.) to force change down the throats of unwilling individuals. Others may lie to employees and try to mislead them about the consequences of change. Such tactics may be effective in the short run, but may be counterproductive over the long-term.

Professor Larry E. Griener has studied change to identify why change is sometimes successful and why it sometimes fails. Based on his studies, Professor Griener has come up with a model for successful change in organizations. He found that there are two key factors involved in successful change:

1. Organizations that have redistributed power so that decision making practices make more use of shared power.

2. Organizations that undergo a development change process to lead to such a redistribution of decision making power. Successful changes require a series of phases — they do not occur in a single step.

Professor Griener has identified six phases which appear to be common when successful change takes place. Each of these phases involves a stimulus on top management and a reaction or response to the stimulus.

PHASE 1: PRESSURE FOR CHANGE AND RECOGNITION OF THE NEED FOR CHANGE

The pressure on top management for change may occur because of an external factor, such as introduction of a new product by a competitor, or new advertising, or changes in taste or style, or through better services. New technology or a change in resources (a gasoline shortage after war in the Middle East) may also be an important stimulus. The pressure of top management may occur because of internal forces such as poor communication, a labor problem, internal staff conflicts, or lack of profitability. The pressure for change, whether internal or external, then leads management to a recognition that action must be taken — a change is needed. This often occurs through the control function of the organization — data indicates that revenues have declined, market share has shrunk, profit per unit has decreased, etc.

PHASE 2: INTERVENTION AND REORIENTATION

Although management feels pressure to change, it may make no useful response. The situation may be viewed as temporary or caused by forces over which management has no control (change in interest rates, increased government regulation). Often, intervention by someone outside the management of the organization is necessary for a useful response. A new member of senior management or a consultant often plays this role. He or she can reorient management to proper responses to change.

PHASE 3: DIAGNOSIS AND RECOGNITION

In this phase, Griener's shared approach to power concept is important. The consultant or new member of the top management team, along with the involvement and strong support of the entire top management, begins to study facts and discuss solutions to problems at various levels in the organization's hierarchy. Problems are identified, some solutions begin to emerge, and roadblocks or opposition within the organization are identified. The shared approach to power concept benefits the organization since people at all levels in the organization learn that top management values their ideas, suggestions, and participation; that problems are being identified and acknowledged; and, finally, that change is possible which will benefit lower level employees as well as top management.

PHASE 4: INVENTION OF SOLUTIONS AND COMMITMENT TO NEW COURSES OF ACTION

The consultant or new member of top management can now lead the organization to identify possible solutions to the problems that have been acknowledged. Again, Griener's concept of a shared approach to power is useful in this phase as all levels of the organization participate in developing solutions. Solutions that have been developed under the shared approach to power concept are more likely to receive a positive commitment from the organization for the requisite new courses of action than those that have been imposed from above.

PHASE 5: EXPERIMENTATION AND TESTING

The proposed new solutions are now tested on an experimental basis on a small scale, if possible. For example, a loss in market share by a soft drink manufacturer might lead to their experimental introduction of a new product, such as a diet drink, in a small test market. Proposed changes in a production process might be tested on one production line in one plant or in several under different conditions. Small changes that work will reinforce positive behavior and help make possible the introduction of larger changes.

PHASE 6: REINFORCEMENT OF POSITIVE CHANGE AND ACCEPTANCE OF CHANGE

In this final phase, as acceptance of the smaller changes grows, the changes are now introduced on a large scale or throughout the entire organization. The reinforcement of positive results permits a more widespread change and the acceptance of the widespread change throughout the entire organization. Professor Griener believes that the success of the process will have the side benefit of increasing acceptance of use of the shared power approach.

The Griener model has all the characteristics of any model. Remember, all models are simplifications of reality. In large, very complex organizations, it may not be easy to fully utilize the shared power concept, especially when different parts of the organization must compete for resources. Moreover, it is not always feasible to use a consultant or bring in new members of top management when change is needed. The model is useful, however, to help us understand what occurs in successful change efforts. Management needs to identify areas of resistance to change and work with employees to encourage a positive response to change. This activity can benefit the organization by increasing productivity, reducing costs, or in other ways.

One systematic way of institutionalizing positive change is to adopt a program of organizational development (OD). An OD program is one that hopes to positively change the attitudes of the individuals within an organization to improve the effective performance of the organization. There may be examples of less than adequate performance, such as high rates of absenteeism, poor quality of output, or extreme factionalism among employees. The OD program is based on the concept that these symptoms and problems have human causes that can be overcome.

OD programs must be tailored for each organization individually. Nevertheless, they have a number of common goals and objectives. OD programs are designed to increase trust and cooperation among employees. They encourage discovery and review of problems rather than avoidance of them. They are designed to increase communication and employee job satisfaction. OD programs try to encourage authority based on knowledge and skills to support formal authority. They try to gain "win–win" solutions in which everyone wins through cooperation — both the employees and the organization. Finally, OD programs try to increase responsibility by individuals and work groups for planning and implementing activities that benefit the organization.

Organizational development programs are designed to help an organization plan for long-term change. OD is a continuous process over a long period of time. It is not designed as a "quick fix" for an organization. Sometimes it may take years to achieve the changes planned. As the organizational development process continues, feedback and experience is used to modify the process.

OD programs are built on such behavioral sciences as psychology, anthropology, sociology, economics, and political science. A variety of fields of psychology are involved. Industrial psychologists bring contributions in relations between managers and employees. Personality theory is adapted from clinical psychology. Group behavior is taken from social psychology. Political science and sociology contribute knowledge about how power works in a system. Cultural traits and characteristics are brought to the OD programs from anthropology. Economics adds the motive of financial incentive.

OD programs assume that employees desire a work environment that is satisfying and challenging. Employees are capable of growing on the job if they are encouraged, supported, and challenged by their work environment. Employees also desire acceptance by their colleagues or work groups. When group members trust each other and share in leadership, the group will be more effective in their work. Work groups are interrelated and sometimes overlap. The OD program should be designed to get groups to work together so that all groups and individuals will benefit. Behavior in work groups can be changed to increase the satisfaction of individuals and success of the group.

Successful OD programs stress the setting of goals or objectives. Personal goals, group goals, and enterprise goals must be harmonious. Use of MBO can help the OD program in increasing the effectiveness of the firm.

An OD program can be implemented in an enterprise with the help of a number of change techniques. The particular technique used will, of course, depend upon the particular situation and the particular problems facing the organization. The manager must try to fit a particular technique to the situation so as to achieve a desired outcome.

One way that managers try to improve results is by changing the structure of the organization. The nature of each worker's task and the authority relationship can be altered within an organization.

The nature of a worker's job can be changed in a number of ways. New methods can be used, such as job enrichment, job enlargement, and work simplification. Use of time and motion studies (scientific management or Taylorism) can also be used to change a worker's job.

Job enrichment is based on Frederick Herzberg's two-factor theory of motivation. In Herzberg's words, job enrichment:

> . . . seeks to improve both task efficiency and human satisfaction by means of building into people's jobs . . . greater scope for personal achievement and recognition, more challenging and responsible work, and more opportunity for individual advancement and growth.
>
> (SOURCE: Frederick Herzberg, "One More Time: How Do You Motivate Employees?" *Howard Business Review,* January–February 1968, p. 53.)

According to Herzberg, job enrichment provides a worker with the opportunity to grow psychologically and mature in a job. The worker's control over the job, his or her autonomy, and responsibility are increased. The number of activities on the job may also be increased as part of this job enrichment.

Job enlargement is less encompassing than job enrichment. Job enlargement increases the number of activities or tools on the job as in job enrichment, but does not necessarily increase worker control, autonomy, and responsibility. Job enlargement may make work more interesting and less boring — an assembly worker may build an entire fuel injection system for an automobile instead of just assembling one component.

Work simplification, on the other hand, may reduce the number of activities on the job.

In addition to changing specific jobs, management can change authority relationships. Line–staff relationships can be changed. For example, authority over marketing could be shifted from a functional basis where local marketing people act as staff to the branch manager of a bank and report to a vice president for marketing in the central office of the bank to a regional structure where each branch is responsible for its own marketing and has a director of marketing who reports to the branch manager. When such line–staff relationships are changed, it will change many things in the organization. The bank which has changed its marketing structure as outlined here may now find that the marketing person at each branch is less responsive to the marketing needs of the bank as a whole as he or she now reports directly to the branch manager and is more concerned with the local marketing needs of the branch.

Change techniques need not focus on job structure. Some techniques try to change people themselves in order to improve worker attitudes, skills, and job knowledge. Change techniques focused on changing people's behaviors usually function on a training approach.

One such training approach is sensitivity training. Sensitivity training is based on the idea that poor performance may be caused by poor interrelationships among workers who must work as a group to accomplish their work goals. A training group (often called *T group*) is set up to meet as a group, often outside the regular workplace. A trainer leads the group in discussion that is not focused on any particular topic and has no formal agenda. The purpose of the T group is to encourage members to learn about themselves with regard to how they deal with others and to build sensitivity toward others. The trainer's job is to help people learn more about themselves and to increase one's sensitivity to oneself and others. Training sessions are open, permissive, and supportive. The job may not represent the same environment as the T group, which may be a weakness. In addition, some individuals find T groups to be stressful — what they learn about themselves and their relationships with others may even be harmful to their self-image and counterproductive to the goals of the sensitivity training. On the other hand, some individuals have found sensitivity training to be helpful in improving communication skills, participative leadership skills, and perceptions. Increased perception may help lead to positive changes in some people. Others may make no real change.

Another technique of people change is to use team building. This technique involves a work group trying to solve a problem facing the group. After a problem has been identified, the team (work group) is asked to review the problem — i.e., why it occurred, what alternatives are available to solve the problem — and the team is asked to come up with a solution to the problem and to put this solution into effect over time. It is believed that team building through problem solving will help team members become more knowledgeable about each other and about the problem. Team "ownership" of a solution will lead to more employee commitment to implementing the solution. Team building may be effective if the group members have similar status, are open and trusting of each other, if they need to exist as a group to complete a task or solve a problem, and they must have appropriate experience and ability to complete the task or solve the problem. More evidence is needed.

In addition to changing structure or people, the task can be changed by new technology. For example, use of a robot to paint a car on the assembly line in an automobile factory may reduce the costs of painting a car, may result in more even application of paint to the surface thus increasing quality, and/or may avoid worker illness due to inhalation of paint fumes. Any or all of these reasons may lead to increased use of robots or other machinery and less use of people on an automobile assembly line.

Displacement of humans by machines (automation) may have dysfunctional effects as well. Workers may resist such a change via strike, slowdown, sabotage, etc., out of fear of loss of income/employment. On the other hand, automation may lead to more job security or economic benefits for those workers who remain after the technological change has been implemented.

Some specific OD techniques may be used to minimize the potential of dysfunctional change, whether the change is one of structure, changing people, or technology.

One specific technique often used is survey feedback. Worker attitudes on a specific topic, such as how decisions are made or what process is used, are surveyed. The results are fed back to the workers so that the workers can evaluate them and design changes for improvements themselves.

This may lead to a change in structure, a change in people, or a change in technology. Survey feedback can be combined with team building or even with sensitivity training in specific situations.

New technology, such as use of automation, may be successfully introduced provided that human factors are not ignored. Workers may respond favorably to new technology if an OD program is in effect and they believe they will benefit through improved working conditions, better safety, and/or increased financial/ status/group rewards.

Employees must want to be involved if change is to be effective. They must be able to contribute their suggestions and ideas. Managers must be receptive to ideas from workers and not see such suggestions as threatening to their position.

Such employee involvement and use of shared authority may help lead to successful implementation of change. However, there are limits to such an approach. A problem may require an immediate solution. When there is a fire, the fire chief cannot take the time to discuss with his or her crew how the fire should be fought — quick action is necessary. Even in such situations, by use of scenarios in advance, the fire chief can get the participation of all firefighters in drawing up contingency plans for fighting certain kinds of fires in the future. Then when a fire does occur, the appropriate plan can be implemented.

Implementing any change requires both time and a decision as to exactly how much change should occur. Timing will depend on how critical the change is and what the attitudes of the people in the organization are towards change. The amount of change is also dependent upon the critical nature of the change and the attitude of the work force.

After change has been implemented it is useful to evaluate the change. Did the change accomplish the goal? Could it have been done more effectively? How? Should the change be modified? Can we learn from this experience to make future changes with fewer dysfunctions? Evaluation of change should be done in both the short-term and the long-term as part of the normal control of any organization. Change, like any other process, can be managed to benefit both the organization and the individuals.

8

Staffing

Staffing is an important managerial function. It is often called by other names, such as human resource management. Staffing involves filling the positions in an organization and keeping them filled. The function of staffing involves the recruitment of people to fill existing positions; the selection of the best candidates to fill the positions from the available persons who have been recruited; the actual placement of people in positions; the evaluation or review of persons; the retention, promotion, or separation of persons after evaluation; the training of all personnel; and the compensation of personnel.

Staffing should only take place after the organization has been structured into positions with appropriate job descriptions. Some writers combine staffing with organizing as one function of management. The authors of this book believe staffing should be listed as a separate function of management because of its importance to successful management. Filling positions properly and keeping them filled are just as vital to the success of an enterprise as proper structuring of the organization.

People are often the most important factor in an enterprise although they do not normally appear on the balance sheet, as does equipment or cash. A capable employee may mean more to an enterprise than any other asset of the company. For example, the pitcher who can win 20 games in a season and draw fans to the ball park because of his style may mean a great deal to the success of the professional baseball team.

Although a star may be very important to a baseball team or to a movie company, most organizations depend upon many people working together for success. Indeed, it is often said that management *is* getting things done through people. For this reason, managers are crucial to the success of a company. The manager of a baseball team may deserve a great deal of credit as a result of his skill in getting the players to work together as a team to achieve their goal of winning the pennant.

Managers have many roles: they are decision makers, leaders, entrepreneurs, influential role models. Their many activities guide the company.

Successful managers have many different goals and needs. They come from all races, creeds, colors, sexes, sizes, ages, and varying backgrounds of education, experience, and economic resources. Some managers are challenged mainly by their work. They like to solve problems, make decisions, and get things done by working with people. Some managers like the power that comes with their positions. Other managers are challenged more by their rewards. Success in management may lead to excellent salaries and perquisites of office. Recognition in the form of status, awards, and election to prestigious charitable boards also is meaningful to some managers. This psychic compensation may be more important to some managers than their salaries or their satisfaction in successfully accomplishing their duties.

Management as a career also has its disadvantages. Most successful managers have to work longer hours than other employees. Managers have the burden and stress of their responsibilities. The heart attack, ulcer, or nervous breakdown may come to the manager who tries to do too much or who is frustrated by lack of success in achieving all of his or her goals. Proper staffing along with good planning, organizing, and excellent leadership and control will help the enterprise through proper selection, placement, and evaluation of managers. This will help the managers avoid excess stress and job dissatisfaction.

Organizations require different members and kinds of managers depending upon their plans, organization structure, and factors such as turnover and business prospects (growth, stability, or decline). External factors such as the availability of managers in the needed specialties and the demand for managers will affect staffing as well. A "high tech" industry may need managers with extensive educational backgrounds and long experience in the industry. A firm that is sales-oriented may need managers with more human relations skills than a firm whose orientation is in financial services, which needs people whose main expertise is "number crunching." The government agencies may complicate staffing with regulations to promote equal opportunity for minorities, women, the aged, and handicapped citizens. Such complications may benefit enterprises in the long run through emphasis in selection by merit unless the government regulations give absolute preferences for hiring veterans for some government positions.

Some companies favor policies whereby managers are promoted from within. Such policies are said to benefit employee morale. However, sometimes employees would prefer someone from the outside be hired when there are strong internal rivalries among candidates for a managerial position. Promotion from within policies have the disadvantage of making the pool of potential applicants for a position smaller and may exclude better people who have better qualifications for a particular position than internal candidates.

A policy of opening the selection of managers to both internal candidates and candidates from outside the firm may have several advantages. A policy of hiring by merit gives the firm the opportunity to select the best available candidate from a larger pool of candidates. Even if an outside candidate is not chosen, the interviewing of a broad range of candidates may bring fresh ideas which are useful to the enterprise to the attention of top management. Obviously, if a system of wide open competition is chosen, the company should make its selection as fairly as possible. Any other method of selection may lead to lower internal morale if an outsider is always chosen or to a bad reputation for the company if it ordinarily conducts a wide search and always selects someone internally after the search, no matter how poorly qualified that candidate might be.

A company needs to adopt a human resources plan based on its objectives and goals, its organizational structure, and its business forecasts. This plan will provide for specific position requirements for every managerial position in the firm. Each position should be designed to best meet the needs of the organization. The needs of the individual must also be considered as very important if skilled individuals are to be recruited successfully and retained for long periods of time.

Job requirements can be explored in terms of factors such as the scope of the job, skills required, and specific design of the job. A job should not be so broad that a manager cannot handle it nor so narrow that it will not be challenging for long to the person assigned to the job. The skills required for a position should be defined. In a company where rapid change is occurring, broader skills may be needed to allow persons of ability to better cope with executed change. The needs of the firm for specific tasks to be accomplished must be met in the design of the job. Individual needs can also be met by looking at such devices as use of work teams or group-set quality control, provided that the organization structure permits such flexibility.

Positions need to be evaluated vis-à-vis similar positions in other organizations and vis-à-vis other positions in the organization. Similar positions, such as credit manager, job manager, or vice president for operations can be compared with other companies in the industry or other companies in general. Trade associations usually compile salary data for similar positions in a variety of companies in the industry, often ranked by size of assets, number of employees, sales, or some other indicator. Such companies need to be adjusted for a number of factors such as risk. A company with high risk of bankruptcy may have to pay much more to attract a capable treasurer, for example, than a larger, more stable company in which the treasurer has a broader responsibility. The style of the management is also a factor — a company that provides more autonomy to a manager may have to pay less than one in which there is more centralized control.

Comparisons within the company may be very important as well. If other managers perceive a certain position to be of lower status and less responsibility, morale of the managers will suffer when that position is filled at a higher level of compensation than they perceive it worth — regardless of the external level of compensation at other companies.

Some companies, particularly large ones, develop elaborate point rating systems wherein each skill or area of expertise is rated, often with the use of an outside consultant, and assigned points. The jobs are then graded according to the number of points and placed on a salary scale by grade.

All systems to rate jobs, whether based on comparisons or on points or some other factor, are imperfect. Regardless of what is stated in the position description, no two persons will perform exactly the same in a managerial position. Also, even though titles may be the same in different companies, the duties may be different.

Managers need a variety of skills to accomplish their tasks successfully. First of all, they need interpersonal skills — the ability to communicate well and the ability to get people to work together to accomplish the firm's objectives. Sometimes they need the ability to inspire others. Managers often need specific knowledge of their industry or of business in general. A credit manager, for example, must be familiar with balance sheets and know how to interpret credit information and other financial information before deciding on the amount of credit to be given to an account. As managers move up the hierarchy, they may need to know fewer technical details than at lower levels of the hierarchy, where there is less concern with problems of general management and more need for hands-on knowledge. Managers need problem solving and conceptual skills. They must be able to find solutions to whatever problems face their enterprise.

In addition to skills and knowledge, managers need to possess other characteristics. They must have a bias toward action. It is not enough to find a solution to a problem — the solution must be implemented. Managers must act. Good managers also generally want to work as managers. They derive satisfaction from getting people to work together to achieve goals and objectives. Honesty, candor, and good character are characteristics that are also highly important for long range success as managers.

Matching a manager with a specific position begins with the position description. Once the position has been specified, a recruitment process can begin. Companies often use executive search firms (popularly known as "headhunters") to select senior managers. The executive search firm typically has a network of contacts to facilitate recruitment of senior managers. Managers with a good current position may not respond to open advertisement as readily as they might to a confidential telephone call from an executive search firm. Public agencies, which may have to recruit under "sunshine" laws requiring the whole process to take place with public and press scrutiny, may have difficulty in getting first-rate candidates to apply due to the public nature of their recruiting process. Some potential candidates do not want their present employer to read in the newspaper that they are being considered for another position. Public sector recruiting may also suffer from political interference, from requirements that applicants be citizens or residents, and from rigid civil service testing requirements. These problems may be somewhat offset by public agencies through better perquisites in the public sector, such as more generous pension plans, longer vacations, and, in some government agencies, more job security than in similar private agencies.

Employment agencies are also used by companies to help recruit suitable candidates — usually for lower level management jobs and for clerical and factory jobs. The government also maintains employment agencies to help people find work.

An enterprise may choose to recruit managers directly using advertisements in newspapers and magazines and, increasingly, using broadcast media. Firms also may contact placement offices at colleges and universities as well as in trade and professional associations. Customers and suppliers can often help identify candidates. Internal applicants and employee suggestions of candidates can be sought by making known all openings by posting them on bulletin boards or placing them in company newspapers or other house organs. Applications received from persons who would like to work in the firm may also be screened whenever a particular opening occurs.

Once one or more candidates for a position have been identified, a selection process takes place. First, candidates usually are required to fill out a written application which includes information on education, experience, skills, previous and current employment, and names of references. This written application enables the company to screen out candidates who do not possess the skills needed for a position. For example, an exporter of goods to Germany might require a salesperson to speak German. The candidates who cannot speak German are screened out at this point in the process. The written application also is useful to the potential employer at later stages in the screening process — such as in checking references and in verifying previous employment.

A screening interview may then take place to further screen candidates. This interview may enable a preliminary judgment to be made as to the better candidates. These can then receive further attention. Others can be kept in reserve in case more candidates are needed at a later date or can be identified by future openings. The screening interview may be accompanied by tests of personality or tests of specific skills, such as the ability to operate a computer.

Next, the candidates who have survived this screening may be interviewed again at several levels. Employees who may work with the candidates at the same level of the organization may interview the candidate in free interviews. The candidate may be interviewed by the person who would be his or her superior, sometimes by that person's superior, and sometimes by superiors at higher levels of the organization.

Interviewing is a skill that is important both to the interviewer and to the candidate. Interviewers must know what they wish to learn from the interview. Carefully prepared questions are helpful and should include: What has the candidate accomplished on their present job? How is this experience relevant to the job currently being filled? Why is the candidate willing to consider another job? Sometimes, an interviewer will begin an interview by trying to be less structured. He or she might ask a general question to get the candidate to begin talking. If the candidate does not answer the questions that the interviewer hopes to get answered by this indirect approach, direct questions can be asked by the interviewer.

The candidate also has questions that need to be answered. He or she will be interested in the response of the interviewer to their questions — both as to substance as well as what it tells the candidate about the point of view and attitude of the interviewer. The interviewer is also interested in these attitudes in addition to the substance of the answers.

After the interviews are completed, the candidates must be rated. The immediate supervisor can then list the applicants in order of priority. The ultimate decision as to who should receive a job offer is ordinarily made by the person to whom the applicant will report, typically with a veto authority from higher management. If someone is responsible for managing an area, he or she ultimately should pick the persons who are hired to work in that area, barring unusual circumstances.

Before a formal job offer is made to the preferred candidate, references and employment background information should be checked. Many companies insist on checking references by telephone. Employers today are often reluctant in this age of lawsuits to put anything negative in a written reference. There may be more candor expressed over the telephone.

Once a person has been hired, a key step takes place. This step involves orienting the new employee to the company and its other employees. Some orientation should be given as to the history of the organization, its mission, goals, and objectives; the mission, goals, and objectives of the particular department; company products, organization, and regulations. Salary and benefit programs need to be explained. Co-workers should be introduced. It is often helpful to the new employee for some other employee to be selected who will help the new employee learn such mundane facts as how to obtain a parking permit, where the company cafeteria is located, how to pick up paychecks on pay day, etc. Such a facilitator can do much to lower the normal anxiety of the new employee and to help smooth the transition to new employment.

Every employee needs to be appraised or evaluated on a regular basis by his or her supervisor. Regular evaluation of each employee is a major method in making certain that each person is managing or performing his or her duties as effectively as possible.

A systematic plan of management evaluation will help accomplish several goals for the organization. First of all, regular evaluations will help management development. If a manager learns as a result of an evaluation what areas of management he or she is weak in, the manager can then take steps (sometimes with the aid of the supervisor or of company or external management development programs) to correct deficiencies. Such management development may lead to better performance as a manager — another key goal of a management evaluation plan. The measurement of performance on a regular basis is a useful goal in itself. The management evaluation plan will also help supervisors award fair compensation to the managers who help identify persons who may be ready for a promotion or additional responsibility. Implementation of a management evaluation plan can provide useful feedback to the supervisor and may improve communication between levels of management.

People are hesitant to evaluate others, especially when the evaluation is in writing. Despite this normal reluctance, people do need to be evaluated by their supervisors. Former New York City mayor Edward Koch, when walking about the city, frequently asked people, "How am I doing?" If someone is not doing part of a job well, it is helpful to that person to know where improvement can be made. A good system of evaluation will help improve performance.

Management by objectives is a tool that has helped improve evaluation. If a person's tasks are stated as objectives, with milestones of expected accomplishments, then performance of tasks can be evaluated with fair standards and objectivity, provided the individual being evaluated has had input into setting the objectives and milestones. Evaluating a person as a manager may be more difficult to fully implement in terms of objective standards. One way to attempt to do so is to list the functions of each manager (planning, organizing, staffing, directing, and controlling) and try to set objectives to be evaluated for each management function. Then, each manager can be evaluated in terms of his or her objectives under each function of management.

Although this may seem simple to accomplish, there are complexities to be considered. The specific objectives set for the person being evaluated may be too modest. Some organizations try to overcome this problem by setting "stretch" goals — such as a change in the business cycle, a strike, inclement weather, etc. — that may affect performance without regard to the objectives that have been set. The evaluation should be made in light of these unexpected circumstances although it is difficult to do so. For example, a real estate salesman may find it much easier to reach an objective of selling one house per month if interest rates on home mortgages are eight percent versus 14 percent. How much of the success is due to the level of interest rates? How much is due to the agent's skill and hard work? How much is attributable to the listings of homes available for sale at any one time?

Some organizations evaluate managers in terms of traits. Trait rating systems list personal characteristics, such as initiative, intelligence, leadership, industry, and ability to get along with others. Managers are then rated for each trait on a scale of excellent, good, average, fair, or poor. A manager may be assigned an overall rating as some kind of an average of the traits rated. A major difficulty with trait rating is that such ratings may lack objectivity. In addition, managers should be rated on their actual results (adjusted for the internal and external environment) rather than on traits of character or ability. Results are what count in the long-run. This is why many organizations have moved away from trait evaluations and moved toward evaluating success in accomplishing objectives.

Regardless of what system of evaluation is used, supervisors must work hard to see that their evaluation is fair and objective. Much time and effort is needed for the superior to adequately evaluate each subordinate.

Effective staffing requires much attention to the selection, training and development, and evaluation of each manager and all subordinates. Effective staffing will do a great deal to enumerate success for the enterprise, provided it is based upon careful planning and careful structuring of the organization, as well as good leadership and control.

9

Leading

Many people confuse the terms "leadership" and "management." Not all leaders are managers and not all managers are leaders. Keith Davis, in his book *Human Relations at Work* (New York, McGraw-Hill, 1967, pp. 96–97) defined leadership as follows:

> Leadership is a part of management but not all of it . . . Leadership is the ability to persuade others to seek defined objectives enthusiastically. It is the human factor which binds a group together and motivates it toward goals. Management activities such as planning, organizing, and decision making are dormant cocoons until the leader triggers the power of motivation in people and guides them toward goals.

There can be leaders of unorganized groups. Managers may not be the leaders in their groups. Thus, leadership and management are not synonymous.

Basically, leadership is a process by which one person influences others to accomplish some goal or goals. Leaders guide others and motivate them to achieve these goals. Hopefully, the leader will help the group to achieve the goals of the organization with as much efficiency and as little dissonance as possible. The manager of a baseball team endeavors to lead his players to the goal of winning the pennant and the World Series. The manager of the baseball team's function is to have the players work together to win each game. If the players have talent, the manager can lead them to success by getting them to coordinate their efforts as a team. Similarly, the conductor of an orchestra gets the members to work together to produce music. In business, the successful leader of an enterprise uses the multiple talents of all the employees working together as a team to achieve the objectives of the firm.

Leadership will not work without "followership." The baseball player who ignores the signals of the team manager is indicating that he does not wish to follow his team leader. Only when persons are willing to follow a leader can leadership be effective. People will only follow a leader (unless coached) if they believe the leaders will help them achieve their own goals and needs. Thus, leaders must motivate their followers by demonstrating that the goals of the organization are congruent with the goals of the followers. Hence, motivation (discussed in Chapter 10) is a key aspect of leadership.

We need also to distinguish between formal leaders and informal leaders. Someone may be designated as the manager of a particular unit of an organization. This person may lack the attributes and skills of leadership. Someone else in the unit may be the informal leader of the group — he or she may have the respect and confidence of the other workers. Sometimes this system will work, especially if the designated leader is smart enough to let the informal leader lead. Ideally, the formally designated leader will also be the real leader of the group.

Leadership is based on power. Power is the influence a person has on others. Such power can be based on a variety of bases. *Coercive power* is power based on fear. If one does not do what the leader wishes, he will be punished (e.g., fired, transferred to a poor working assignment, have pay cut, or receive a reprimand). Therefore, compliance with the leader's wishes will prevent this punishment. *Reward power* is the direct opposite of coercive power. If one follows the leader, she will be rewarded with better pay, a better job, or with praise. *Legitimate power* comes from the position of the leader–president of the company, foreman of the work group, etc. The general of the army has more legitimate power than the lieutenant who has more legitimate power than the sergeant. *Expert power* is the power of a person who has special knowledge or skills. One follows the advice of an accountant in filling out tax returns because she possesses expert knowledge of the tax regulations. *Referent power* comes when a follower identifies with a leader. This identification may come about from admiration of personal traits to a desire to carry out the wishes of the leader.

Formal leaders in organizations usually have coercive, reward, and legitimate powers depending on their levels in the hierarchy of the organization. The foreman may be able to reprimand a sloppy worker but may not be able to fire that worker without the approval of his supervisor. The manager of the baseball team can overrule the pitching coach on a change in pitchers. Referent and expert powers tend to be based on the individual traits and characteristics of the manager. The individual leader has more control of referent and expert powers than the organization, which has more control of coercive, reward, and legitimate powers.

There is not consensus about exactly what leadership is. Leadership is more than power. It is more than authority. Some people claim that leadership is holding some position of authority. Others claim that leadership is the possession of certain traits or personal characteristics. Still others believe that leadership is a category of behavior — the process whereby a person acts in a way that influences other people to follow him or her. For the purposes of this text, we will define leadership as a process by which one person influences others to accomplish some goal or goals of the organization.

Every organization that is effectively achieving its goals and objectives must have one or more persons skilled in leadership. The skills of leadership include several elements — the authority and power of the leader, the ability to understand motivation and to use it to achieve the goals of the organization, and personal characteristics or style.

Power has been discussed here and motivation has been discussed in the previous chapter. Style and personal characteristics of the leader are important. The British people turned to Winston Churchill in the dark days at the beginning of World War II because of Churchill's ability to inspire confidence in resisting the Axis powers. When the war was almost over, the British people voted Churchill out of office: they desired a different type of leadership for peacetime needs. People tend to follow those whom they believe will help them achieve their personal objectives. Effective leaders understand this principle and try to use motivators and style to ensure the effective operation of the organization.

The impact of a leader can be great on a nation. Winston Churchill successfully motivated the British people to resist the Axis powers and win the battle of Britain. President Franklin D. Roosevelt restored confidence in the United States during the Great Depression. Martin Luther King, Jr., achieved many of the goals of the Civil Rights movement because of his effective moral leadership. Golda Meir provided effective leadership to Israel during a time of crisis. Not all political leaders have been positive. Hitler was able to inspire the German people to follow him with the long-term result being the destruction of Germany in the war begun by him and the eventual dismemberment of Germany. Stalin ruled the Soviet Union by coercion resulting in the death of millions of people.

Similarly, the impact of a leader can be great on a business enterprise or on a nonprofit organization. Lee Iacocca turned Chrysler Corporation around with his dedicated and inspiring leadership. The Watson family built IBM from a small office products company to the largest manufacturer of computers in the world. In earlier days, business leaders like John D. Rockefeller (Standard Oil Company), Theodore Vail (AT&T), Andrew Carnegie (U.S. Steel), J.P. Morgan (stocks and banking), and Alfred P. Sloan (General Motors) provided leadership in industry. In nonprofit enterprises, Robert Moses became known as a great developer of roads and bridges in the New York metropolitan area; Charles W. Eliot, president of Harvard, and others provided leadership in our universities; and Basil O'Connor built the National Foundation (March of Dimes) into a great charitable organization.

Despite these individual names and others that we may recall as well-known leaders, no leader does his or her job in isolation. The leader must be influenced and supported by followers. Lee Iacocca did not come up with all the ideas to turn Chrysler around by himself. Thomas Watson, Jr., did not develop the prototypes of the successful IBM computers by himself. The sharing of influence between a leader and one or more followers can benefit everyone concerned. A well-run organization has give-and-take between the leader and followers. A good leader will listen to followers and adopt their advice when it is sound.

There are a variety of theories about leadership. Historically, the approach to leadership theory was to look at traits that were important to leadership. A trait is some characteristic that explains a person's behavior. The "great man" theory, dating back to the Greeks and Romans, held that leaders were born, not made. Leadership occurred because the leader had certain traits necessary for leadership. Some of those traits were physical — energy, looks or appearance, height, age, and weight. Unfortunately, there have been no conclusive results about a relationship between physical traits and leadership. Some effective leaders have been short (Napoleon), some tall (Abraham Lincoln); some have been energetic while others lazy; some have been handsome, some ugly; some have been old and some young; some have been fat, others skinny.

Behavioral psychologists began to look at other traits beginning in the 1940s. Ralph M. Stogdill identified intelligence traits, personality traits (e.g., self-confidence, aggressiveness, ability to adapt) to related traits (e.g., initiative and persistence) and social traits (e.g., administrative ability and cooperativeness). Edwin E. Ghiselli studied personality traits (e.g., intelligence, initiative, supervisory ability, decisiveness, maturity, and self-assurance) and motivational traits (e.g., the need for job security, financial reward, power, self-actualization, and achievement).

Despite these studies, it is very difficult to come to useful conclusions about leadership based on traits. Trait studies do not generally tell us how much of each trait someone should have — how much intelligence, for example, is important? Trait studies also completely ignore the role of followers or subordinates. Leadership is a dynamic process. The relationship between the leader and the followers is important to successful leadership. Furthermore, many psychologists disagree about which traits are important or even about how many traits should be considered. Some believe that some traits are really just patterns of behavior. Perhaps some list of traits can be used to predict effectiveness of leaders. If so, we have not yet reached a point in time when we can effectively make such predictions.

Some studies of leadership have concentrated on the personal behavior of leaders in trying to develop useful theories of leadership. Perhaps leadership is based on the style of the leader. Unfortunately, no specific style has received universal acceptance. At first it was posited that there were three basic styles of leadership: autocratic leaders, participative (sometimes called democratic) leaders, and free-rein leaders. The autocratic leader makes the decisions and expects followers to carry them out — he or she leads by reward and punishment. The participative leader consults with followers on proposed decisions and encourages their participation in resolving the decision. Free-rein leaders let their followers select their own goals and perceive their role as facilitators as helping their followers carry out their goal.

These three styles of leadership are perhaps overdrawn. Actually, leadership behavior is more of a continuum, as explained in the work of Tannenbaum and Schmidt. Leaders sometimes have difficulty in deciding whether they should make a decision on their own, seek participation from others, or leave it completely to others. A leader could make a decision and announce it to subordinates. A leader could make a decision and try to sell it to subordinates. A leader could present his or her ideas and ask for suggestions from others before he or she makes a decision. A leader could define the parameters of the problem and ask a group (including the leader) to make a decision. A leader could let subordinates make the decision. Depending upon the circumstances, the leader might be autocratic or participatory with his workers on discussing the order of process on the production line, but might be autocratic in imposing rules to ensure plant safety (such as no smoking in areas with flammable materials).

Rensis Likert and other researchers at the University of Michigan have conducted a series of studies of leadership since the late 1940s. Leadership was studied in business, government, and hospitals, and data was obtained from thousands of employees. Based on this research, Likert and his colleagues concluded that leaders were either job-centered or employee-centered. In job-centered leadership, the leader closely structures the job of subordinates, supervises them closely to ensure that specified tasks are completed, and uses time study and incentives to increase production. In employee-centered leadership, the leader devotes his or her attention to building effective work groups with high objectives for performance and devotes much time to the human factors of his or her followers. Likert concluded that employee-centered leadership tended to result in higher production. Thus, employee-centered leadership is more effective.

Robert R. Blake and Jane S. Mouton developed the managerial grid in the early 1950s. This grid looked at two variables: concern for production and concern for people. Many researchers have used this grid to identify a number of combinations of leadership styles.

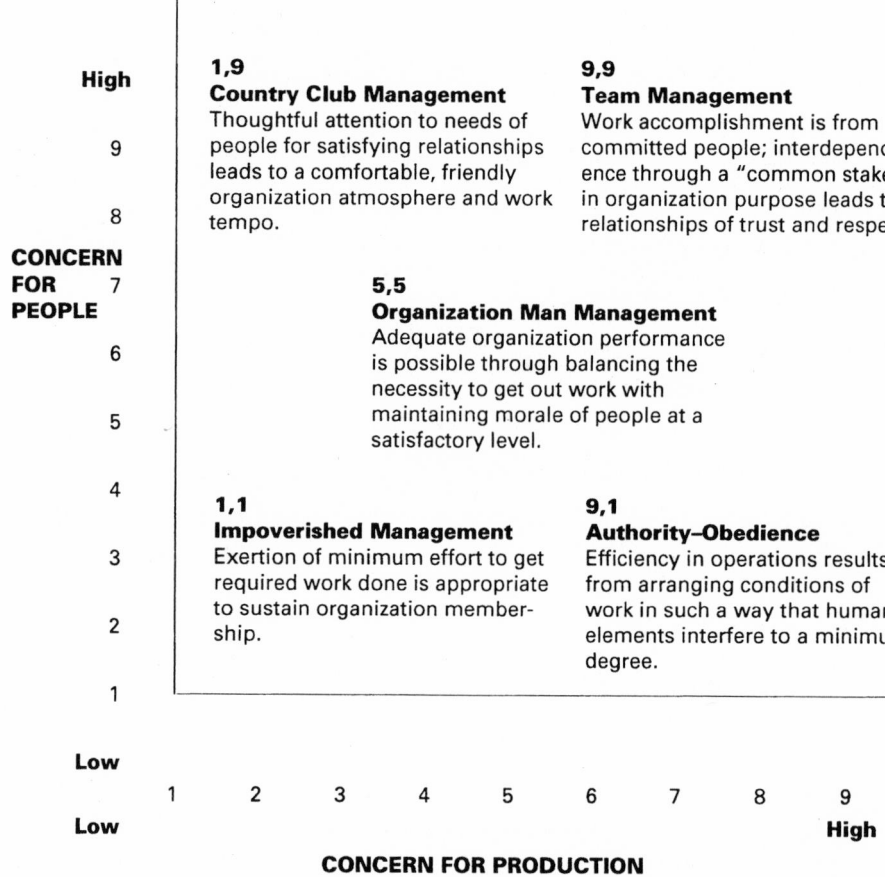

High

9

8

**CONCERN
FOR** 7
PEOPLE

6

5

4

3

2

1

**1,9
Country Club Management**
Thoughtful attention to needs of
people for satisfying relationships
leads to a comfortable, friendly
organization atmosphere and work
tempo.

**9,9
Team Management**
Work accomplishment is from
committed people; interdependence through a "common stake"
in organization purpose leads to
relationships of trust and respect

**5,5
Organization Man Management**
Adequate organization performance
is possible through balancing the
necessity to get out work with
maintaining morale of people at a
satisfactory level.

**1,1
Impoverished Management**
Exertion of minimum effort to get
required work done is appropriate
to sustain organization membership.

**9,1
Authority–Obedience**
Efficiency in operations results
from arranging conditions of
work in such a way that human
elements interfere to a minimun
degree.

Low

| 1 | 2 | 3 | 4 | 5 | 6 | 7 | 8 | 9 |

Low   **High**

CONCERN FOR PRODUCTION

(SOURCE: Blake, Robert R. and Jane Srugley Mouton. *The Managerial Grid III
The Key to Leadership Excellence.* Houston: Gulf Publishing Company, Copy-
right © 1985, p. 12.)

Blake and Mouton use this grid by asking an individual leader questions
about his or her leadership style and positioning them in the appropriate place on
the grid. While many styles can be shown on the grid, five styles are highlighted
as examples of styles of leadership. Four of these styles — 1,1; 1,9; 9,1; and 9,9
— are at the extremes.

In 1,1 style leadership, called *impoverished management*, the leader concerns him or herself minimally with either people or production — the leader makes a minimum effort. He or she virtually does nothing.

In 1,9 style leadership, called *country club management*, the leader is concerned mainly about the people. There is little or no concern about completing tasks such as production.

In 9,1 style leadership, called *task management*, the leader is concerned mainly with efficiency in completing the task. In this style there is little or no concern about the employees.

In 9,9 style leadership, called *team management*, the leader is equally interested at the highest level in both employees and tasks. This is the ideal style. Such leaders are team leaders who do an excellent job in meeting the needs for accomplishing tasks with the needs of the employees.

Other steps of leadership can be placed anywhere on the grid. In 5,5 style leadership, called *middle of the road management*, the objectives are adequate employee morale and satisfactory task efficiency.

The managerial grid is frequently used in management development programs to train leaders to come closer to 9,9 style leadership (team leadership). The Blake and Mouton recommended management development program begins with one week of laboratory seminar groups discussing the managerial grid and leading the participants to analyze and assess their management styles. In the second part of the program, teamwork is introduced. Managers from the same department get together and work to their description of a 9,9 style leadership for their organization. In the next phase, intergroup discussion is held to analyze tensions and conflicts and further analyze 9,9 style leadership. Next, goals are set by the leaders in the program for such areas as profit, safety, and cost control. In the next phase, participants meet to try to attain the goals set by the group. Finally, a stabilization phase attempts to stabilize the improvements and modifications made by the group process. This management development program is different in that the line managers or leaders run the program using the managerial grid concept and all hierarchies of leadership participate in the program.

The managerial grid concept is provocative but only limited research has been done to test the grid. Will a 9,9 style leader always be more successful than one from another style? Much more research must be done on this grid and on 9,9 style leadership before this question can be adequately answered.

Another approach to leadership questions both traits and particular leadership styles as being effective in all situations. This approach to leadership believes that the specific situation or contingency is important in the emergence and effectiveness of a leader. Churchill emerged as an effective leader for the United Kingdom during World War II. He was not perceived by the voters as being a desirable leader in a different situation — peacetime. Situational or contingency leadership supports both the interrelationship between leader and followers and the theory that followers support leaders whom they believe will help them accomplish their own needs and wishes. A number of behavioral scientists have focused their research on identifying by situational factors in leadership and identifying their specific performance.

Fred E. Fiedler and his associates at the University of Illinois developed the first contingency theory of leadership. It is probably still the most popular situational leadership theory. Fiedler believes that there are three critical or situational dimensions that influence the effectiveness of a leader:

1. **Leader–Member Relations.** Fiedler regards this situational dimension as the most important from the view of the leaders. This has to do with the amount of confidence that followers have in their leader. It also includes loyalty to the leader and their trust in him or her.

2. **Task Structure.** In this situational dimension, Fiedler considers the extent to which followers' tasks are clearly spelled out and people held respon-

sible for them (routine tasks) or, on the other hand, tasks that are unstructured or vague (nonroutine tasks).

3. **Leader Position Power.** In this situational dimension, Fiedler considers the power that is inherent in a specific position. It includes the authority of position. The leader with a clear position and direct organizational authority can more easily obtain "followership" than one with unclear position power. The rewards and punishment power of the position and support from superiors are important to position power.

Fielder measures the leadership style by a unique method of research. He evaluated leader ratings to questionnaires called least preferred co-worker (LPC) questionnaires in which the leader responded to questions regarding the person in his group who he would least like to work with. If a leader rated his least preferred co-worker in more positive terms (high LPC), then Fiedler assumed that the leader was people-oriented and supportive. If a leader rated his least preferred co-worker in low or unfavorable terms, then Fiedler assumed that the leader got his major satisfaction from task performance, or was primarily task-oriented.

While he understood that personal views of workers might be unclear and/or inaccurate Fiedler concluded:

> Leadership performance depends . . . as much on the organization as it depends on the leader's own attributes. Except perhaps for the unusual case, it is simply not meaningful to speak of an effective leader or an ineffective leader; we can only speak of a leader who tends to be effective in one situation and ineffective in another. If we wish to increase organizational and group effectiveness, we must learn not only how to train leaders more effectively but also how to build an organization's environment in which the leader can perform well!
>
> (Fiedler, Fred E., *A Theory of Leadership Effectiveness*, New York: McGraw-Hill Book Company, p. 41.)

Situational favorableness is defined by Fiedler as the degree to which a situation makes it possible for a leader to exercise influence over his group. Leader–member relations can be either good or poor, task structure can be either high or low, and leader position power can be either strong or weak. Each of these three critical situational dimensions can be combined so as to be feasible, moderate, or unfavorable.

This research shows that task-oriented leaders seem to generally perform best in both favorable and unfavorable situations. Relationship-oriented leaders seem to perform better in moderate situations. The basic conclusion of Fiedler's research is that leaders who are task-oriented and leaders who are people-oriented can each function best in different types of situations. There is nothing necessarily good or bad in either style leader (task-oriented or people-oriented). Effective leadership depends upon the situation.

Fiedler has a number of suggestions for improving leadership. He believes leader–member relations can be improved by restructuring the leader's group of subordinates in such a way that the group is more similar in terms of levels of education, technical expertise, ethnic origin, and general background. While this might be good theory, it is difficult to carry out in practice due to laws requiring equal opportunity, affirmative action, and union work rules.

Fiedler believes that the task structure can be modified either in a more structured or a less structured direction. Some followers prefer more structure, others less. Jobs can be described in more detail to satisfy those who want more structure. Tasks can be made less structured by providing more generalized instructions.

There are several ways, according to Fiedler, to modify leader position power. The leader can be given more power over subordinates (e.g., performance evaluations) and better job title or reporting relationships. Fiedler does not believe that leadership training can be effective based on his research, which shows that people with much training perform about as well on average as people having little training.

Critics of Fiedler's *Contingency Theory* question his methodology in measuring LPC, his particular group of subjects for his research, and the limitation of using only high and low LPC scores. Some of Fiedler's findings are not statistically significant according to these critics. Despite disagreements with Fiedler's specific theories and research methods, it seems clear that the effectiveness of the style depends in part on the situation or contingency.

More research may be helpful in clarifying this relationship in the future. Fiedler is owed a great deal for stimulating thought about the relationship between effective styles of leadership and particular situations.

Fiedler's research is important to managers for several reasons. First of all, managers can deduce from Fiedler's findings that some managers will perform better in some situations than in others. Managers need to be matched to jobs that suit their particular style of leadership. Second, the job can be tailored to the particular manager to make the manager more effective. By changing a manager's position power, for example, the job can be done more effectively in some situations. Of course, such job structuring is not always possible — others may object to a changed reporting relationship.

Robert J. House has developed another situational theory of leadership, which is called the *path–goal* theory or approach to leadership effectiveness. This approach combines Vroom's expectancy theory of motivation with situational factors. In the path–goal theory, the main function of the leader–manager is to spell out and set goals and objectives with followers (subordinates), and to help them attain the goals through finding the best path and removing obstacles.

In the view of House, a leader's function has two basic elements:

1. **Goal elements.** The leader must increase the kinds and number of rewards followers attain for achievement of work goals.

2. **Path element.** The leader must remove obstacles that retard achievement of goals by making the paths to the rewards easier.

House suggests that there are four styles of leadership:

1. **The directive leader.** In this style, the leader directs and followers (subordinates) have no participation in decision making.
2. **The supportive leader.** In this style, the leader is friendly to followers (subordinates) and is interested and concerned for the needs of his or her followers.
3. **The participative leader.** In this style, the leader asks for suggestions and consults with followers before making decisions.
4. **The achievement-oriented leader.** In this style, the leader sets challenging goals for followers and has confidence in their high levels of goal achievement.

In path–goal theory, the *same* leader can utilize any of the four steps of leadership. This is different from Fiedler's contingency theory, which suggests that different leaders must be used in different situations.

The leader should be a directive leader in situations in which there is great ambiguity about the task. The leader should be a supportive leader in situations which are dangerous, monotonous, or have high amounts of stress. Support from the leaders makes it easier for the subordinate to complete such tasks. The leader should be a participative leader in situations that are very complex. In such situations, participative leadership will build commitment from subordinates to complete the task. The leader should be an achievement-oriented leader in situations in which subordinates are confident about their abilities to achieve high goals of performance. Setting high goals and expressing confidence that subordinates can achieve them are important in achievement-oriented leadership.

Thus, the way the leader affects the paths is the big factor in a path–goal theory. The leader does this by helping followers (subordinates) find the best path to achieve their goals, by setting goals that are challenging, and by removing obstacles.

Path–goal theory has only been tested in a limited number of research studies. These studies have had mixed results to date. Path–goal theory is very complex. This has caused difficulties in applying path–goal theory to real world situations and has made it difficult to isolate the variables for research purposes.

The path–goal approach is important to the manager by stressing that effective managers (leaders) need to use different styles of leadership in different situations or contingencies. Managers can improve the effectiveness and satisfaction of their subordinates by increasing rewards for goal achievement and by eliminating obstacles that retard achievement of the goals. Effective managers must be prepared to adapt their leadership style to the situation, the task, and the particular subordinates involved.

Victor Vroom and Philip Yetton, in their book *Leadership and Decision Making* (Pittsburgh: University of Pittsburgh Press, 1973) and in other published work, have developed another situational theory of leadership. They call their theory a normative theory of leadership service. It offers normative guidelines for how decisions should be made in specific situations.

The Vroom–Yetton Theory suggests five styles of leadership:

A–I: **Autocratic I.** The leader solves the problem alone, using whatever information is available.

A–II: **Autocratic II.** The leader obtains the necessary information from followers (subordinates), then makes the decision alone. The leader may or may not tell the followers why he or she wants the information.

C–I: **Consultive I.** The leader shares the problem with followers individually. The leader obtains their input without bringing followers together as a group. The leader then makes the decision alone.

C–II: **Consultive II.** The leader shares the problem with followers as a group. The leader then makes the decision alone.

G–II: **Group Participation.** The leader shares the problem with followers as a group. The group works together in looking at the problem and alternatives, and the leader and other members of the entire group reach a solution together.

The appropriate leadership style to be used from among the five styles can best be determined by the answers to seven questions. The first three questions relate to the quality of the decision, the latter four are designed to test the acceptability of the decision by followers (subordinates). These questions can be shown on a decision tree.

The Vroom–Yetton theory is being tested in a variety of research studies and settings. One advantage of the Vroom–Yetton theory is that its application results in specific answers for how much subordinate participation should be involved in a specific decision. Critics have pointed out that there are more decision making methods than the five suggested in the Vroom–Yetton theory (A–I, A–II, C–I, C–II, G–II). Critics also suggest that there should be more than seven questions in some situations. For example, the size of the work group may be an important variable.

Despite criticism of certain aspects of the Vroom–Yetton normative theory, this theory has some practical value to the manager. The Vroom–Yetton theory suggests that the leadership style of the manager should vary from situation to situation. This is different from Fiedler's contingency theory which suggests that a manager's style of leadership doesn't change. In this aspect, the Vroom–Yetton theory is consistent with path–goal theory. Vroom–Yetton theory means that the manager must assess the situation before choosing his or her leadership style. The decision tree will help the manager in this assessment.

This chapter has discussed a number of approaches and theories of leadership. Both the older trait approach and the behavioral approaches (such as Likert and the managerial grid) seem to conclude that a number of factors, including intelligence and leadership styles, are important for effective leadership. Apparently, no one trait or style is best for every situation. The various situational theories of leadership have built on this conclusion by stating that leadership style should vary depending upon the situation.

Much more research and experimentation is needed on leadership. Knowledge and review of the major theories of leadership and motivation can help any manager reflect on what style of leadership and motivation is appropriate for any given situation. Good leadership is important in organization if goals are to be accomplished effectively.

10

Motivation

A motive is a thought or feeling that makes one act. Motivation is the will to achieve or complete a task or goal. Motivation applies to the entire list of needs, desires, thoughts, feelings, and drives. Motivation of employees and of oneself is a major task of a manager. Motivation in business is more than just the task of motivating a worker to produce 50 units per hour or motivating a salesperson to sell 30 units per day, although motivation of both production and sales at an acceptable rate are important. Motivation in business also includes the task of attracting people to join the organization, to stay in the organization, and to develop their full potential as employees.

The problem of how to best motivate employees is one that faces all organizations. The purpose of looking at motivation is not to manipulate people but to help them and the organization achieve goals through designing a work environment that emphasizes performance.

There are many theories of what motivates behavior. People sometimes behave in unexpected ways. Sometimes they know why they behave as they do; other times they cannot explain their behavior — the reason may be explained by their subconscious. Some social scientists explain motivation through a content approach. The content approach to motivation deals with what within people causes them to behave as they do. Content theories of motivation deal with the needs of people as motivators. Other social scientists approach motivation through a process approach. The process approach deals with how people are motivated. It concentrates on the choice or direction of behavioral patterns.

This chapter will look first at the content approach to motivation. There are a number of content theories of motivation. Perhaps the best known is Abraham Maslow's needs hierarchy theory. Maslow theorized that people have a hierarchy of needs that must be satisfied in an order from the lowest to the highest level of needs. Once one level of need in Maslow's hierarchy has been satisfied, this need would no longer motivate behavior. Maslow's hierarchy of needs is as follows:

1. **Physiological needs.** These needs are the most basic ones — air, water, food, clothing, shelter, sleep, and sexual satisfaction.

2. **Safety or security needs.** The need for safety and security or freedom from fear of physical danger and the fear of loss of job, property, shelter, etc.

3. **Affiliation or social needs.** The need to be accepted by others, for interaction with others, the need for friendship and acceptance.

4. **Esteem needs.** Once people satisfy their need to belong, they need to be held in esteem or respect by their peers, themselves, and others.

5. **Self-actualization needs.** The highest level of needs — to maximize one's self-potential and self-fulfillment.

There has been much social science research on the validity of Maslow's concepts that people are motivated by a hierarchy of needs. Some social scientists believe that there are only two or three levels of need rather than the five outlined by Maslow. For example, Alderfer claims there are three basic needs: existence needs, relatedness needs, and growth needs.

Regardless of the exact number of levels of need, social scientists also hold variant theories as to whether needs are in a hierarchy, as Maslow states. Some research seems to indicate that once existence needs and physiological and safety needs are satisfied, different individuals may differ in their pattern of which of the higher levels of need they wish to satisfy next.

The value of Maslow's theory to managers is in several areas. First of all, an identification of needs is useful to the manager. Basic needs must be satisfied — food, clothing, shelter, safety — somehow if people are to be motivated. One of the difficulties for managers is that individuals may differ in how much of each of the basic needs they desire. Most people have multiple needs that vary from each other. Different people have different needs. One person may be more interested in gourmet food. Another may desire a large house or a prestigious automobile and be content to eat simpler food. Managers must, therefore, apply Maslow's theory according to the situation that faces the manager. The needs of the people supervised by the manager should be identified so as to try to provide satisfaction linked with performance. Needs may also vary over time. If managers do not satisfy needs of employees, there may be dissonant effects, including frustration, reduction in output/sales, or higher employee turnover.

Managers can look at each level of need on Maslow's hierarchy of needs and develop methods to improve motivation of employees.

Psychological needs can be addressed by such measures as salary improvement, adequate lighting, heating/air conditioning, subsidized meals in the company cafeteria, and help with housing (a company guaranteed mortgage, for example). Safety or security needs can be addressed by giving better job security (tenure for a faculty member, for example), providing hospitalization and other insurance including a pension plan, and safe conditions in the workplace. Affiliation needs can be addressed by encouraging social and athletic activities at work and by office parties and lunches with associates. Esteem needs can be addressed by praise and awards for a job well done, by promotions, titles, publicity, and by a better office. Self-actualization needs can be addressed by providing challenging jobs or tasks, by giving more self-direction and autonomy, and by encouraging creativity and other achievement.

A major variant on Maslow's hierarchy of needs has been developed with research conducted by Frederick Herzberg and other social scientists. In the 1950s Herzberg developed a two-factor explanation of motivation. This explanation is generally called the two-factor theory or the motivator–hygiene approach to motivation. Herzberg and his associates interviewed accountants and engineers and asked them to give the interviewers examples of times they felt exceptionally good or exceptionally bad about their jobs. Herzberg discovered that the factors producing satisfaction on the job were completely separate from factors producing job dissatisfaction. For example, an unsafe work site might not be given as a reason for satisfaction on the job. Herzberg concluded that job satisfaction and job dissatisfaction are not simple opposites; he concluded that two factors are needed to explain motivation.

The factors that produce satisfaction on the job are known as motivators in two-factor theory. Motivators include such things as achievement, recognition, advancement and personal growth, challenging work, and responsibility. The factors that lead to dissatisfaction on the job are called hygienes by Herzberg. Hygiene factors (also called maintenance factors) include such factors as pay and working conditions, relationships with peers and supervisors, supervision itself, and personal life. Motivators produce job satisfaction. Hygienes or maintenance factors prevent job satisfaction. When hygienes are absent from a job there will be dissatisfaction. When hygienes are present, dissatisfaction will be prevented but hygienes will not bring about satisfaction. When motivators are absent from a job, dissatisfaction will not be caused. When motivators are present, motivation will take place on the job.

Some social scientists have disagreed with Herzberg's conclusions about motivators and hygienes. There is some evidence that some hygiene factors, such as pay and achievement, may be important for satisfaction as well as dissatisfaction. In addition, Herzberg's research was performed on professional employees (accountants and engineers). Other kinds of employees may have different motivators than professional employees, as is indicated by several studies. Some individuals may be more responsive to hygiene factors. Others may be more responsive to motivators.

Even though two-factor theory may be questioned, it can be helpful to managers in certain areas. An employee can be happy and dissatisfied at the same time. He or she may be happy with the pay and dissatisfied with the work or vice-versa. Employees may be happy, they may be dissatisfied, or they may be both happy and dissatisfied at the same time.

An improvement of hygienic factors such as working conditions may ease dissatisfaction but may not provide any positive motivation. Motivation may be increased by providing more opportunities for recognition, advancement, autonomy, and growth through job redesign. Two-factor theory may thus help some employees gain increased motivation through job redesign provided that hygienic factors are maintained.

Both Maslow's hierarchy of needs theory and Herzberg's two-factor theory deal with *what* motivates people. They are content approaches to motivation. There are a number of theories that deal with *how* people are motivated. This process approach has focused on the choice or direction of behavioral patterns.

Victor H. Vroom has developed expectancy theory, which is based on the belief that people will act to maximize their rewards or benefits and minimize their losses. Expectancy theory suggests that a person's motivation at any time towards an action would be determined by that person's values of all outcomes (positive and negative) of the action multiplied by the strength of that person's expectancy that the outcome would result in the derived goal. Thus, motivation = valence × expectancy. Valence is the value attached to specific rewards or losses, such as receiving a raise, being promoted, or being fired. Expectancy is the belief that effort or action will be rewarded. In an expanded model of Vroom's expectancy theory, expectancies are divided into two types. *Expectancy 1* is the belief that effort or action will lead to performance and *Expectancy 2* is the belief that performance will lead to rewards. Thus, Expectancy 1 is a belief in personal effectiveness and Expectancy 2 is the belief that good performance will receive a reward. An employee may be high in Expectancy 1 (that is, believe he or she is very effective) and low in Expectancy 2 (the employee may believe that a good performance will receive no reward). If a person is high in both Expectancy 1 and Expectancy 2 and has a high valence (personal value in a specific reward), then that person will be very highly motivated to perform the task or goal desired.

Expectancy theory is currently considered to be a good framework for understanding motivation. It is criticized because of its complexity, which makes its application in the real world difficult. How would managers consider Expectancy 1, Expectancy 2, and valence in making decisions? Despite its complexity, expectancy theory has the benefit of recognizing the importance of needs and motivations of various individuals. Expectancy theory will help the manager recognize the necessity to design the environment based on desired performance. The manager must pay attention to Expectancy 1 by setting performance goals that employees believe they can attain. If personal goals are set too high, motivation will decline. The manager must also consider Expectancy 2 by linking desired performance to positive rewards. If performance is not linked to rewards, motivation will suffer. Finally, managers must focus on valence by seeing that the rewards to be given are meaningful to the employee.

Vroom's expectancy theory has been further developed by a number of social scientists. Motivation is not a simple cause and effect. Managers must consider individual differences in successfully motivating people.

David C. McClelland has suggested that there are three types of basic motivating needs: a need for power, a need for affiliation, and a need for achievement. People with a high need for power want to exercise control. They tend to be forceful and seek positions of leadership. People with a high need for affiliation enjoy friendly interaction with others. People with a high need for achievement work hard, take responsibility, and look for success.

Some research indicates that people with a high need for achievement and some need for power tend to advance faster in management than do those with a high need for affiliation. Companies in which human relations factors are important will need some managers with a high need for affiliation. In small companies, achievement motivation is especially important for top management. In larger companies, power needs and affiliation needs tend to be more prevalent.

Another process approach to motivation is reinforcement theory. Reinforcement theory (also called behavior modification) is primarily based on the ideas of Harvard's noted psychologist, B.F. Skinner. Skinner's concept is fundamentally that human behavior is a function of its consequences. In the workplace, work behaviors that lead to undesirable consequences will generally be less likely to occur again.

There are three components involved in reinforcement theory:

1. **Stimulus.** An event or occasion that results in a response.
2. **Response.** A unit of behavior that occurs as a result of a stimulus.
3. **Reinforcement.** A consequence of a response.

A person's past history of reinforcement is the only determination of current behavior, according to reinforcement theory. Therefore, if a particular stimulus–response leads to a desirable occurrence for the worker (such as praise or a raise), it will be more likely that the same stimulus will lead to the same response in the future. If the particular stimulus–response leads to an undesirable consequence for the worker (such as reprimand or a pay cut), the response in the future to the same stimulus will likely be different than it was the first time.

Under reinforcement theory, there are a number of types of reinforcement that may be used to modify behavior, either by strengthening it or weakening it.

Positive reinforcement is used to strengthen behavior that is seen to be beneficial to the organization. Thus, if an employee produces more units of output than set as the standard for production for a given period, such as a day, the employee will receive a bonus. If the bonus is sufficiently attractive to the worker, the employee's behavior is reinforced and the employee is likely to try to exceed the production standard in the next period. Other types of positive reinforcements in the workplace might be additional time off or a more flexible work schedule, an award, or a better title.

Avoidance learning is also used to strengthen behavior in the organization. Avoidance learning takes place when employees respond to a stimulus in such a way as to avoid undesirable consequences. If the worker who is late in coming to work is reprimanded by the supervisor, the worker may learn to come to work on time to avoid the unpleasantness of being reprimanded.

Punishment is used to weaken undesirable behavior in the organization. Such punishment as pay cuts, demotions, reprimands, and fines are used to weaken behavior that is seen as undesirable.

Extinction is also used to weaken undesirable behavior. It is less drastic than punishment, as extinction merely withholds desirable consequences (such as pay raise or praise) when behavior is not what is desired by the manager. If no positive reinforcement is presented to a specific behavior, the undesirable behavior may become "extinct" in the future.

The timing of reinforcement of behavior (either strengthening or weakening of behavior) is important in reinforcement theory. Continuous reinforcement is used when a desired behavior is always followed by a specific result such as a bonus every time the production standard is exceeded or praise every time a task is completed. Intermittent reinforcement, on the other hand, takes place when rewards (punishment) are given on a periodic basis — such as a pay raise every year after review of performance or when praise is given sometimes after completion of a task but not each time.

From the viewpoint of the manager, reinforcement theory is important. Rewarded behavior tends to be repeated. Unrewarded or punished behavior tends to be avoided. This is important to the manager in setting up pay and other reward systems. Rewards, under reinforcement theory, should be performance based. Obviously, employees must be given performance guidelines in advance, detailing what performance will be rewarded and what will not be rewarded (punished).

There is much criticism of reinforcement theory. First of all, reinforcement theory seems to ignore individual employee differences. Extra pay may be more important to one individual. Praise may be more important to another. Second, reinforcement theory seems to ignore group dynamics. The reward from the manager may mean less to an employee than the attitudes of co-workers. Thus, a worker may be motivated to produce more units than the standard by the prospect of a bonus, but will not do so because of pressure from co-workers to slow down production to a level desired by the group. Reinforcement theory also tends to stress the importance of such external factors as pay increases and promotions at the expense of internal factors such as a feeling of accomplishment for completion of a task. Some social scientists also question the ethics of reinforcement theory. The use of behavior modification through positive reinforcement or punishment may be manipulative or even exploitive in some situations.

Managers need to use elements from whichever theories of motivation lead them to get the job done. Often there is no single "right" answer as to how to best motivate people to accomplish the goals of the organization.

Money remains an important motivator to many. Behavioral psychologists tend to rate money as less important as a motivator than do economists and many in the world of work. Money is important to many people but not to all. Sometimes money is not used as a motivator but merely as a means of filling jobs — if each company in an industry pays at about the same rate, money may not be the key motivator to attract and keep people. Nevertheless, money may be important. Lack of adequate (as perceived by the employee) monetary rewards may lead to reduced performance, strikes, or employees looking for greener pastures elsewhere.

Some managers believe that money is the best incentive for good performance — that it is the best motivator. Managers with this belief often favor incentive compensation plans. One type of incentive compensation plan is a production incentive plan — the more units one produces, the more one is paid. Alternatively, an incentive compensation plan may be based on the profitability of a division or of the company as a whole. For example, a Wall Street investment banking firm will give large bonuses to each partner in a year when the firm has earned a good profit. In such a case, the firm may set salaries lower than for competing firms but grant good bonuses based on the firm's profitability. Stock options may also be given as bonuses in lieu of cash payments.

An alternative that has been growing in popularity for workers in industries with many production workers is an all salary plan for employees. All salary plans are often more popular with workers than piece rate pay plans, especially if more employment stability can be built in.

Fringe benefits are often considered to be maintenance factors. Hospitalization plans and other health benefits, pension plans, life insurance, extra vacation time for seniority, maternity/paternity leaves, etc., are all of varying importance to workers but are less apt to be viewed as positive motivators than an increase in salaries and wages.

Job enrichment is another possible motivator in the workplace. The "quality of life" in the workplace may be of importance to many employees. Some workers are frustrated by repetitive jobs, such as jobs on an assembly line. Job enlargement may be used to limit this repetitiveness. Job enrichment goes beyond job enlargement by trying to build more achievement and recognition, and more challenges into jobs. Job enrichment builds upon the two-factor theory of Herzberg. Herzberg maintains that job enrichment will help employees grow psychologically in a job.

In job enrichment, workers may be given more scope and responsibility in such methods as sequence, pace, and acceptance or rejection of materials or finished product. Job enrichment tries to encourage employee interaction and participation in decisions, in feedback or performance, and in such factors as layout of the plant or office. The significance of the task (is the job worthwhile?) is also a factor in job enrichment.

Some large firms have endorsed job enrichment with the belief that it will increase productivity and morale and help reduce dominant factors such as absenteeism and employee turnover. The results of job enrichment have been mixed. Some employers have found job enrichment to be very successful. Others have found that some workers, especially blue collar workers, seem to be motivated more by pay and job security than by job enrichment.

Despite its advantages in some work places, job enrichment has limitations. Some jobs are repetitive in nature — they cannot be changed to be more stimulating whether due to cost, lack of appropriate technology, or the low level of skill required. Few labor unions have negotiated for job enrichment — organized labor seems to prefer economic incentives such as higher pay, fewer hours of work, better fringe benefits, and increased job security to job enrichment. At professional and managerial levels, job enrichment may be more important.

Simple human factors may be more important than job enrichment. As can be seen from the Hawthorne experiments of Elton Mayo and Fritz Roethlisburger, workers like involvement. Whether the amount of light was increased or decreased at Hawthorne didn't matter — performance continued to improve because of the mere fact that management was paying attention to the workers. Feedback — even negative feedback — on performance may be more important than pay or job enrichment to many workers in terms of motivation. Workers also like the opportunity to be consulted and to make suggestions for improvement.

A combination of approaches may be helpful. Job enrichment may become more useful when workers receive extra compensation from some of the savings seen from higher productivity and when human factors such as feedback, involvement of workers, appreciation, and recognition of results are present.

Behavior and motivation of individuals and groups depend upon many factors. Every situation is different. The manager must be aware of what motivates individuals and what motivates group behavior. The style of a leader may also be important to individuals and groups. This will be discussed further in the chapter on leadership.

The process of management is equally important to motivation. If goals and objectives are clearly set with proper participation, if there is a good organizational structure, proper staffing, adequate leadership and controls, it will be easier to motivate than if the functions of management are not being properly considered.

At best, motivation is a difficult and complex factor in management. Understanding why people behave as they do and how to motivate them to best accomplish the goals of the organization is a challenge to every manager.

11

Communication

Sophisticated communication distinguishes humans from other animals. When a beaver slaps the water with his broad tail and dives, other beavers get the message. Danger lurks! But what kind of danger? A wolf? A hunter? The other beavers don't know.

Human society depends on intricate and rational communication. Management, no less than other human activities, also depends on good communication. Indeed, Roger D'Aprix says that management *is* communication (*Communicating for Production*, New York: Harper & Row, Publishers, 1982). Plans mean nothing unless they are made known. It is impossible to direct, command, or inform without communicating. Control depends directly on receiving communications and communicating orders for changes, if needed. Modern writers often do not include communication as one of the functions of management because communication is implicit in each of the management functions, especially in leading.

Managers, like other human beings, spend most of their daylight hours talking, writing, and sending messages, i.e., communicating. Communications are so urgent and so pervasive that we sometimes forget to learn another skill — when not to communicate. Is it not said at times that "silence is golden?" But in any joint activity, such as management, effective communication is golden. We must communicate effectively to give direction, transfer information, or plan, organize, staff, lead, and control.

Early writers on management did not consider communications to be a separate function. Instead, they considered it a subfunction, usually part of the function of directing since you cannot give directions without communicating.

Communication was discussed by Henri Fayol, one of the first writers to analyze administration. Fayol pointed out that the formal structure of large organizations, if slavishly followed in all communications, could restrain communication between persons in separate divisions. Thus, there was no necessity for communications to follow formal lines up and down a long table of organization to get from a person in one low level branch to another in a distant branch. Fayol argued that direct talk between two such persons was not only common sense, but was also not a violation of principles of management organization.

Chester Barnard discussed communication as part of organization. He argued that communications must be understood, consistent with organizational purposes, compatible with personal interests, and feasible (C. Barnard, *The Functions of the Executive*, Harvard University Press, Cambridge, Mass., 1938, p.165). Modern management theory continues the tradition that communication is part of all management functions, but puts greater emphasis on good communications. Elaboration of the problems of communication between persons in distant branches of a table of organization has led discussion of ways to improve line–staff relations and new concepts, such as matrix management, discussed elsewhere in this book.

DEFINITION

There are many definitions of communication. *Webster* defines communication as intercourse by words, letters, or messages; interchange of thoughts or opinions; the act of imparting or transmitting; a process by which meanings are exchanged between individuals through a common system of symbols (as language, signs, or gestures).

Many management writers stress the transmittal or transfer or exchange of information from one person to others as the essence of communication. It seems to the authors that the use of the word "information" is unduly restrictive. A broader definition would stress the transfer of meaning, understanding, or ideas. The authors prefer to define communication as the process of transmitting meanings between people by use of symbols.

The word "process" in the definition is important. Communication is an activity which takes place over time. It is a series of actions or operations leading to an end, hence, a process. Of course, communications must be considered in a systems context.

Communication takes place in varied forms. Communication will be discussed in these various contexts. There are many types of communication, from writing letters to frowning disapproval, from direct commands to public speeches, from publishing in-house newsletters to advertising. Communication can be interpersonal (between individuals) or organizational. It can be verbal (oral or written) or nonverbal, using signs, facial expressions, gestures, and body posture. In an organization, communication can be internal or external, and formal or informal.

Internal communication may include rules, procedures, memos, and newsletters, but most commonly, orders and directives. External communications may include advertising, public relations, and government relations. It may deal with the public, customers, or shareholders. However, communicating with shareholders may also be considered internal. Internal communication can take place upward, downward, or laterally.

However, all communication follows a pattern, best described in a model:

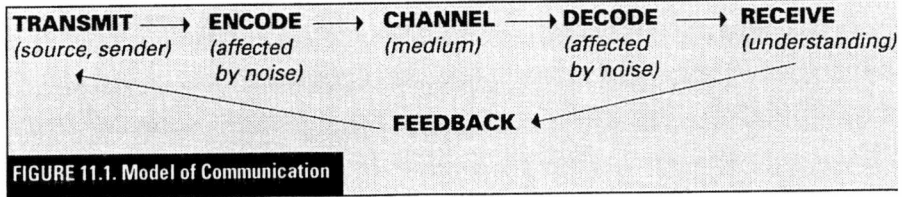

TRANSMIT ⟶ **ENCODE** ⟶ **CHANNEL** ⟶ **DECODE** ⟶ **RECEIVE**
(source, sender)   *(affected*   *(medium)*   *(affected*   *(understanding)*
                      by noise)   *by noise)*

⟵ **FEEDBACK** ⟵

FIGURE 11.1. Model of Communication

MODEL OF COMMUNICATION

A model, like a map, clarifies but may oversimplify. A model of communication which presents only the main elements in all communication may imply more effective communication than is often the case. The simple picture of communication is usually altered to include "noise," or some interference with the transmittal of meaning. The problem is whether the student fully appreciates the difference between ideal communication in the model and actual communication in the real world. Some of these problems will be discussed in a later section on barriers to communication.

The model of communication can be illustrated in a diagram *(see Figure 11.1)*. The elements of the model are: (1) The source *(sender)*, (2) encoding, (3) the channel *(medium)*, (4) decoding, and (5) understanding *(receiving)*. Additions to the model include (6) feedback from the receiver to the sender, and (7) noise or interference with understanding.

Source

The idea for the matter to be communicated begins with the sender. It may be an order, a request, a casual observation, an opinion, a response, a question, a bit of information. In discussion of management communication it is assumed that the sender has a reason for communicating a message, but not all communications have a purpose. Some communication is nonsense but it will be assumed, for purposes of discussion, that communication is meaningful. The essential element is that there is a sensible idea to be transmitted to another person or persons.

Encoding

The second step is to put the idea in such a form that the other person will be able to understand it. Usually we think of encoding as putting the idea into words, but messages can be expressed in other ways. Sending messages without words has been raised to an art form by skilled mimes; a raised eyebrow, a shrug, or a smile can convey as much meaning as a multitude of words.

Nor is clear prose the only alternative for managers who have not mastered the art of the mime. Messages can be sent in numbers, as in a financial report, or with diagrams and pictures.

Channel

A decision must be made as to the medium to be used in transmitting the message. An idea can be sent in writing, orally, by gesture, or by a symbol. A flag is used to convey a message in car racing. A written message can be sent in the form of a memo, a letter, a telegram, a printed report, or by computer. Often, the sender may not consider carefully the full possibilities offered by various channels. Good managers do. An oral order is easy to give, fast, direct, and permits prompt feedback. A written order may be necessary if it is complex, difficult to understand, if the long range impact is important, or if a permanent record is necessary.

The medium to be chosen depends on the message. A lengthy and detailed financial report could hardly be presented orally. In some cases, to indicate approval or disapproval a frown or smile is message enough; a written statement in such cases would be overkill. A photograph or diagram may convey more meaning than words.

However, as Marshall McLuhan has noted, "The medium is the message," i.e., the medium chosen influences the meaning of the message. A written letter of censure carries far more weight than a verbal reproach. A telegram may carry a message of urgency missing in a letter. A look of supplication may convey more desperation than the words of a prayer.

Decoding

The receiver of the communication must perceive the message and decipher it. It is not enough to receive a letter; one must read it. It is not enough to scan a letter; one must concentrate on the contents. Have you ever heard a statement and nodded agreement while your mind was elsewhere? For a communication to be completed, the receiver must be aware of the message and must then interpret it.

It is common knowledge that a secret message in a code must be deciphered, but so must a statement in jargon (the technical language of a profession). The use of jargon by experts in a particular field saves time and makes communication easier among the insiders, but it may cause confusion among outsiders who are not initiated into the mysteries of the special language. Yet the most common decoding deals not with secret codes or jargon, but with the ordinary message. It is not always easy to determine the true meaning of a message. Is the request you just received a suggestion or an order? Does "at once" mean right now or in five minutes? Is the "no" an absolute denial?

Understanding

The object of communication is to convey a meaning. The sender wants to know if the message is understood. It is all too rare that the original message conveyed and the message received are the same. If they are, there is effective communication. Too often, orders are misunderstood, information misinterpreted, requests misconstrued. The process of communication is seldom perfect.

Feedback

It is argued by most management experts that feedback is an essential element of good communication. *Good communication!* But feedback is not an element of all communication. A person can conceive of an idea, encode it in the English language, broadcast it by shouting. The receiver may perceive the message, decipher it, and understand it. Finis! There may be no feedback.

Feedback is necessary in effective management communication. One reason is to let the sender know that the message received is the same as the message sent. If the sender has a motive for the message, the feedback completes the process, and satisfies or rejects. The feedback may take many forms. The soldier says, "Yes, sir," the worker proceeds with the activity required by the boss. The response may be a nod, rejection of an order, a letter of reply, applause, or the continuation of a conversation.

Noise

By noise we mean anything that interferes with the process of communication. It may be physical noise, making it difficult to hear. It may be the fault of the sender or the receiver. It may be caused by interference in the environment. Some writers speak of filters. By this they mean that the message goes through a series of individuals in the line of communication, with each person making subtle changes in the message, i.e., each person filters the message. What emerges may be very different from what was intended.

FORMAL COMMUNICATION

Communication can be formal (official, carried out as part of work) or informal (outside the work procedures of the firm, usually known as the "grapevine"). When a manager carries out his or her functions — planning, organizing, staffing, leading, and controlling — the manager is engaging in formal communication.

A major problem in formal communication is just how much is needed. We are accustomed to the image of the taciturn mountain man in the movies; he would not make a good manager of many men. Nor could the chatterbox be tolerated in a busy factory. Somewhere in between is the golden mean, the manager who imparts just enough information. Elsewhere we discuss information "overload," the curse of unbridled computer information. Just how much communication is needed is a matter of judgment. Good communication must be complete and accurate, but it must be concise as well.

Formal communication can occur downward, upward, laterally, or diagonally.

Downward

Downward communication refers to orders, directives, information, and requests passed down the chain of command. It may include rules, policies and procedures, and assignments. It can consist of verbal or written orders, memos posted on bulletin boards, letters, reports, or computer printouts. Downward communication may take place in meetings, conferences, speeches, on the telephone, or person to person. We usually discuss the importance of two-way communication, and managers are exhorted to encourage feedback. However, there are situations in which communication is essentially one way. In time of war, when the officer gives the order to advance, he expects no formal response. The only feedback is visible by the back of the advancing soldier.

Upward

Upward communication includes all meanings transmitted from subordinates to superiors, usually consisting of ideas, requests, and responses. The subordinate may reply to a request for information by submitting a report. He or she may request further information or clarification of an order. He or she may be filing a grievance, responding to a question or a questionnaire.

Upward communication is many times distorted. Information is often suppressed. The subordinate may not want to transmit information which hurts his or her position. Bad news is commonly disguised or delayed. In ancient Rome the bearer of ill tidings was slain. Modern managers seldom go so far.

Lateral

Lateral communication takes place between persons of equal rank, either in the same department or in separate departments. Our main interest is in communication between members of distinct departments where the purpose, or benefit, of communication is coordination. The unit making fan motors may inform the main assembly line that production of fan motors is falling behind schedule so that the assembly line foreman is able to take corrective action in production plans.

In extremely bureaucratic organizations, direct lateral communication may be inhibited. In most organizations, it takes place in accordance with the principles enunciated by Henri Fayol. More complex is lateral communication between departments that are widely separated geographically. Today, such distant communication is made easier by computer-assisted communication systems. When communication between dispersed units becomes more and more complex and urgent, new forms of organization become important, such as matrix management.

Diagonal

Diagonal communication, like lateral communication, does not follow up and down the formal table of organization, but cuts across the hierarchy. It is different from lateral communication in that it links persons at different levels.

A major use of diagonal communication is between line and staff. Such communication can be advisory in nature. Where line really has authority (perhaps due to expertise), such communication may be similar in essence to downward and upward communication.

INFORMAL COMMUNICATION

Informal communication in an organization is usually referred to as the "grapevine." *Webster's Third New International Dictionary* says the grapevine was probably so called as a humble substitute for a telegraph line. Outside management circles, it is also thought of as rumor, often without foundation. Management experts acknowledge an important role for grapevine communication in large organizations.

The grapevine does not follow the hierarchical table of organization. It is multidirectional. Various patterns have been identified.

One pattern is referred to as the probability pattern. In this case, information is spread randomly. In the single-strand pattern, the flow of information is along a line, from one person to another, and another, and another. In the cluster pattern, the flow of information is more select than in the probability pattern. Only certain, select individuals are included in the chain. Finally, there is gossip, which is most widespread and may follow no set pattern.

The common opinion in the past was that the grapevine was highly inaccurate. But a number of studies have indicated that the grapevine can, in fact, be very accurate. There is still dispute over this issue. However, everyone acknowledges the importance of the grapevine. It is a fact of organizational life and cannot be eliminated. The suggestion for managers is that the grapevine should be monitored and used. If a false rumor is started, it may be necessary to issue formal statements correcting the rumor. Another approach is to use the grapevine directly. One advantage is that it permits communication without commitment. For example, management may want to know how employees will react to a certain plan. Some details of the plan could be dropped into informal channels. Management would then wait to see the reaction. Or suppose management wished to discuss an embarrassing or sensitive matter without making a formal acknowledgment, as in giving the real reason an employee was discharged. The grapevine may have its uses in such a case.

NONVERBAL COMMUNICATION

It is often assumed communication must be written or spoken. This need not be the case. Facial expressions, symbols of position, dress, gestures, body language, and images are also used in communication.

Nonverbal communication can be classified as signs, setting, and actions. Signs include physical signs, such as flags and images. A corporate logo is an image which tells us something about the firm. Flags may be used as a substitute for language in yachting.

By setting, we usually mean the physical location in which communication takes place. A plush, oversized office gives one message, while a spare, small office gives another. Within an office, the arrangement or use of furniture is important. If the person who occupies the office wants to increase feedback and elicit franker responses, he or she may move from behind a big desk to a chair alongside the guest.

Setting can also mean attire. You may dress informally if it is not important to impress the person with whom you are communicating. At other times, as during an interview for a job, it is common to wear more businesslike clothing, perhaps a dark suit. Grooming affects communication as well; it gives a message about the speaker.

Action is often called body language. Body language encompasses many things, including facial expressions, gestures, and posture. Among the barriers to good communication are inconsistent communication, such as friendly words accompanied by a scowl, criticism, and a smile. The receiver judges a communication by the way the sender acts, as well as by the actual verbiage.

Words can be emphasized by gestures, movements of the arms and hands, and posture. Have you ever spoken to someone who fidgeted while you spoke, looked at the ceiling or his watch, and doodled? You would have known that you were not getting your message across. The end of an interview can be signaled by walking to the door. Lack of interest can be highlighted by accepting a series of phone interruptions.

Effective communication, in which the message received is the message intended, is made difficult by barriers of understanding caused by language, perceptions, conditions, or noise.

BARRIERS TO COMMUNICATION

It seems, at times, that misunderstanding is more common than comprehension, especially in world affairs. While such pessimism may not always be justified, good communication is all too rare. Despite efforts to get a message across, there seem to be a host of barriers deliberately designed to block the way. Some of these barriers are part of human nature and show up in interpersonal communication. Others are more evident in organizational communication.

The major barriers to interpersonal communication are semantics and the unique perceptions of individuals. One major culprit is semantics, the use of language which hinders understanding. This may be a matter of poor coding. Another culprit has to do with the perceptions, or the mindset and prejudices, of the sender and receiver.

The use of words is personal. Usage varies with the user. Words have varied meanings, and may therefore convey different things to different people. Increased efficiency to the manager may mean a speed-up to the worker. Some people take "never" to mean "hardly ever."

A complication is the use of jargon, the technical language of a profession. Used by insiders, jargon saves time and makes for greater clarity and precision of meanings. For outsiders, those who are not initiated into the secrets of technical language, jargon is unintelligible. Worse, meanings may be assigned which were not intended by the user.

Unfortunately, we often suffer from poor communication not because of the complexities of language, but from the common lack of language skills. Poor writing skills and ungrammatical speech is a major cause of poor communication. Good writing requires clarity, brevity, an active voice. One is tempted, in the training of managers, to give lessons in writing clearly. In fact, management schools do offer courses in writing business letters and memos, as well as in public speaking.

A problem related to poor writing is poor thinking. It is typical that the misuse of language is associated with lack of logic. Often, forcing a person to correct the grammar of a written statement also forces the person to think more clearly and more rationally.

Another barrier to good communication is inconsistency between verbal and nonverbal communication. We can say one thing, but the receiver knows we mean something else by our looks. The worker explains why he is late, and the foreman says it is okay, but his frown betrays his true meaning: it is not okay.

Considering the ambiguities of verbal communication and the greater uncertainties of the nonverbal, it is no surprise that the receiver of apparently conflicting verbal and nonverbal messages does not always get the message.

Other barriers to interpersonal communication deal with perceptions. Often the receiver has preconceived notions and prejudices, and makes premature evaluations. Moreover, all people have selective perceptions. We hear what we want to hear. We are motivated by self-interest, emotionally involved in the subject matter of the communication, and do not always make a rational analysis of the message. This may be a matter of poor decoding.

Of course, communication in organizations usually is carried out by individuals; communication between computers is newer. Thus, specific communications are interpersonal. However, certain facets of organization in themselves have a great effect on communications.

The hierarchical structure of an organization may tend to dampen communication from lower to higher echelons. In an autocratic organization, upward communication is likely to be inhibited. The process of communication is affected by status, power, and authority. In a firm with excessive central authority, communication is often in one direction, downward, and feedback is generally limited. Without feedback, the sender cannot be certain the receiver understood the message as sent.

The shape of the organizational structure is important. If there are many layers of management, messages get distorted by many carriers as the message moves up and down the hierarchy. Each carrier acts as a filter, and the result may not be what was intended.

On the other hand, an extremely wide structure presents problems of communication. Classical organizational theory established strict limits to the number of persons an individual could supervise. Managers have come to realize not only that the limits depend on the situation, but that a crucial factor in the structure of organizations is communication. This observation leads to some newer conclusions. A broader span of control is now considered feasible. Modern communication permits more centralization.

Organizations are more complex today than formerly, with an explosion of information, especially in industries at the edge of new technology. As a result, in many organizations, positions are created as centers of communication. These positions are not commonly thought of as communication centers, despite the fact that their main advantage is in communications. Formal communication goes through the table of organization, and individuals' positions in the *T of O* for directing and controlling must communicate in order to direct and control.

With modern technology, often based on computer systems, information can be dispensed more quickly, more easily, and more widely. With improved communications, a supervisor can deal with a larger number of employees, even at distant sites. Thus, the span of management is increased. With better information available, fewer positions are needed as communication centers. Therefore, the number of layers of management can be reduced, and the table of organization can be shortened.

The conclusion is that without modern communication systems, too broad a structure can affect communications adversely. Moreover, too many layers of management inhibit communication, though this problem can be overcome with modern technology. Put positively, good communication permits a broader, shorter management structure.

Less amenable to technology is the problem of overload, and the related problem of time pressures. An early result of computer technology was the production of vast amounts of information. A corporate officer on his way to a meeting was likely to be handed the latest information packet in the form of a 500-page document, providing enough information for a doctoral dissertation. Add to this barrier to understanding the many demands on the time of a busy executive, and you can see that increased information is not necessarily better information.

It is common knowledge today that computer experts must limit the amount of information communicated to relevant facts. The lesson of good writing applies to computer printouts. The communication must be succinct, clear, brief, and to the point.

Problems related to overload and time pressures include not only the many competing demands on the receiver of a communication, but also environmental interference. These barriers are sometimes referred to as noise. The environment in which managers operate is not quiet and calm. There are other messages clamoring for attention. There is real, physical noise, making it difficult to hear on the telephone or engage in quiet talk.

Other barriers can be cited. The closed door to the office of a top executive inhibits upward communication. Lack of communications planning may be the root of the problem in a large institution. Bureaucracy can reduce effective communication, especially if the members of the bureaucracy ignore the wisdom of Henri Fayol and demand strict adherence to hierarchy.

Overcoming Barriers

If semantics can be a barrier to communication, it can also be a solution. The secret is to use words well. Good writing and speaking are requirements of good communication. Writing should be clear, concise, complete, specific, correct, simple, and grammatical. The prior sentence can be expanded into a course or text on good writing. Effective managers must possess good language skills.

However, certain hints can increase success with writing for managers. Professors of English warn against redundancy. Yet, if the objective is important, it may be necessary to repeat particular ideas, using alternative words and phrases. It is also helpful to use multiple channels in communicating; a verbal order can be followed by a written order. A written statement can be augmented by a picture or diagram. A report full of numbers, as in a financial report, can be clarified by written comments. A short summary may highlight a lengthy report. Managers have been known to be upset by employees who do not follow a particular procedure. One solution is for the manager to emphasize the importance of the procedure by constant repetition. For example, the order "no smoking" or "wear hard hats" might be emphasized by many signs around the workplace, by taking action against violators and publicizing the action, and by repeated oral statements. Controlled redundancy has its uses.

Another hint is to take small bites when giving information. Don't try to overwhelm with a torrent of information. Give out instructions a few at a time. Most important is to clarify your ideas before you communicate. But we will have more to say about clear thinking in due time.

PERCEPTIONS

An important element in communication is perception. The sender has an image of what he means when he sends a message based on his background, education, experience, mental set. The message may have a different meaning to the receiver. The government official thinks a new regulation means protecting the public interest, while the manager in private business thinks it is an example of bureaucratic interference. The manager gives an order to improve productivity, while the union takes it as an unjustified speed-up.

The first step in overcoming barriers of perception is awareness. The sender must be aware of the point of view of the intended receiver. The sender must have empathy with the receiver. When a memorandum is issued, the audience must be kept in mind. It is essential to mind the overtones of a message. It is important to be aware of personal attitudes as well. Too often the sender of the message is defensive instead of positive.

Personal attitudes color our communications. Successful communication depends on our attitudes. It may be better to be conditional, rather than absolute. Criticism of an employee may be more successful if stated as description rather than as an evaluation. While control of a situation may be important, at times spontaneity is preferable. A manager is disturbed by the actions of an employee and he responds by becoming abusive. Rational analysis of the situation will show that the purpose of the manager should have been to correct the activity of the worker, not to satisfy his ego by shouting. A better corrective action might be to discuss the problem calmly. It takes a sense of public relations to understand what kind of message will have the intended effect.

The importance of awareness has been noted. Not only is self-awareness important, but so is awareness of the perceptions of others. Know your audience. Understand the self-interests of the receiver of your message. Have empathy. A common problem is sexist attitudes. A patronizing attitude by a male to a female employee may turn her off and make your message ineffective.

If a manager wants to welcome a new employee, he should ask the person to sit down. If he is interested in what the employee is saying he won't doodle, look at the ceiling, or accept interruptions. To have effective communication, it is important to cultivate trust and to ensure your credibility. Make certain that your messages are correct. Keep your word.

Perhaps the most important element in good communications is listening. Successful communications are usually two-way. A manager must listen as well as speak. Orders may be necessary, but feedback tells the manager whether the order was understood. Good managers often encourage an open door policy. They make it possible for upward communication to flourish.

A related method of overcoming barriers is to use a survey to elicit opinions. A good manager will also walk around a plant or office, visiting sections, observing activity, talking to employees at all levels. Indeed, "management by walking around" is useful in every organization. Meetings with various groups of employees can augment communication and bring urgent problems to the attention of the top administrators.

The open door policy and attention to feedback can be greatly improved if the communicator will take steps to eliminate noise. This may mean closing an office door during an interview to block out environmental disturbances, or having meetings away from the hubbub of the production line.

Another route to good communications, especially in an organization with modern computing capabilities, is to avoid overload. A number of firms have introduced the internal newsletter to pass on information to members of the staff. Larger firms use videotapes to circulate important messages. The grapevine, discussed previously, is an important source of information.

ORGANIZATIONAL COMMUNICATION

Organizational communication can be improved by specific changes in the structure of the firm. On one hand, a shorter table of organization means fewer filters in transmitting an order downward and receiving information from below. On the other hand, improved communication may permit a broader table of organization. Computer information can assist centralized control, as executives have faster and more complete access to information about widespread activities. But modern communications also may mean the possibility of greater decentralization. This apparent contradiction is nevertheless a fact. Distant, decentralized units are able to make better decisions if they are armed with information provided by a computer-based information system. The conclusion is that improved, modern communication gives management the option of creating an organization that is more or less centralized, depending on factors other than communication needs.

COMPUTER-BASED INFORMATION SYSTEMS

The proliferation and improvement of the computer-based management information systems (MIS) is an important factor in modern management. Most noticeable is the effect on the modern office, including a reduced role for secretaries and typists.

Consider a typical office scenario: A researcher signs onto his computer in the morning. He scans the menu for his electronic mail. One item is memos. He calls for memos and finds one from his boss reading: "Don't forget your report is due Tuesday." It is Tuesday. He calls up his unfinished report on the screen, makes a few corrections, adds a paragraph, and enters it into the data bank. Then he sends a memo to his boss; "Report ready!" His boss is too busy at that moment, but later calls up the report on her screen, reads it, takes appropriate action if needed, and files the report. Nothing has gone into the four-drawer steel file cabinet. No secretary was involved.

The elements of modern communication include the electronic typewriter and word processing program on the computer, e-mail, storage of messages, voice synthesizers and voice mail, as well as video teleconferencing. Modern systems may permit a widespread conference in which the participants speak into microphones and hear from loudspeakers without the necessity of holding the instrument in hand, all while watching each other on a private viewing screen. It is said that computer communication, as opposed to face-to-face communication, is impersonal. The video screen makes it less so.

12
Control

The purpose of the managerial function of control is to assure that the objectives and plans of the organization are being efficiently and effectively accomplished. Because there is constant change in the world, control is necessary to measure performance, revise plans, and make corrections to assure that goals will be accomplished. Every manager has a role in controlling functions of his or her department to ensure that the goals are being efficiently and effectively accomplished.

The word *control* has a negative meaning to some people, yet many controls protect individuals in a variety of ways. For example, the purpose of an airbag in an automobile is to provide a sudden restraint to prevent a person from going through the windshield in case of an accident. It controls the motion of a person, but only under certain circumstances. Similarly, a modern control device on an automobile brake (an ABS system) releases the brake on the appropriate wheel in the event that the car skids. A temperature control (thermostat) protects a computer from heat damage by starting up the air conditioner when the temperature of the computer room rises to a certain point. Controls may be positive as well as negative.

Before an organization can implement a control system it first must establish goals and plans to carry out the goals. Without a plan, it is impossible to exercise control. Controls themselves may be a part of a plan. A budget, for example, is a financial plan with built-in controls or limits on behavior. The main purpose of the budget is to allocate funds to accomplish the goals of the organization. The control purpose of limiting how much may be spent in any one area of the organization's operation is subsidiary to the major purpose of the budget or financial plan.

Secondly, the enterprise must establish an organization structure before it can implement controls. If plans are not followed, someone should have the responsibility to review events and the authority to make changes to ensure that the plans are accomplished or to revise the plans in light of changing circumstances. Lack of attention to who is responsible for overseeing a system of controls will make such a system ineffective.

The control process has three major steps. They are to: (1) establish standards, (2) measure actual performance against the established standards, and (3) correct shortcomings and follow up on successes.

Standards can be established to define what actual performance is expected in every major area of operation. Standards are measures taken at key points on actual performance. For example, market share is important to a manufacturer of disposable diapers. Changes in market share should be monitored closely on a periodic basis by the manufacturer. The disposable diaper manufacturer will also be interested in monitoring how many diapers are produced by each worker, how profitable the production and sale of the diapers is, what resources in money, facilities, and equipment are needed to purchase, produce, warehouse, and transport the materials necessary for making diapers and the finished product, and the performance of management in getting the workers to produce the number of diapers needed at an appropriate level of quality. The disposable diaper manufacturer will also be interested in innovation — how to make the diaper more effective, if only to prevent a competitive edge for other manufacturers. Most manufacturers will be interested as well in social responsibility — running a factory that is a safe environment for the employees, in not polluting the physical environment by dumping waste, and similar factors.

Standards may be set in quantitative terms such as 500 diapers per hour or four reject diapers per 100 produced. Alternatively, standards can be set in terms of dollars — profit per diaper, sales of diapers, etc. Standards are best expressed in terms of the goals and objectives of the firm — through using a system of management objectives such as producing 500 diapers per hour with certain tolerances of thickness, shape, etc. Standards can be expressed qualitatively , such as producing better diapers. Quantitative standards are easier to verify than qualitative standards and should be used whenever possible.

Once standards have been established, it is possible to measure actual performance against the standards. If standards are drawn carefully on a quantitative basis it may be possible to measure actual performance easily, at least for routine operations. For example, if the standard for a worker is to produce 500 diapers per hour, it is easy to measure how many diapers are actually produced per hour. For less routine operations, it may be much more difficult to draw appropriate standards and to then measure them. Should the credit manager's performance be measured on how much bad debt is incurred per $100,000 of sales on credit? Such a simplistic measure would clearly be inadequate as the credit manager under such controls would doubtless give credit only to very creditworthy accounts. The firm may be better off to give much more credit and take larger bad debt losses than to screen out most potential credit problems. A general appraisal may be more useful for a senior executive than a strictly quantitative appraisal, particularly if the department appears to be meeting its goals at a reasonable level of costs.

Once performance has been measured in terms of the standards that have been set, it is next in order to correct shortcomings and reinforce success. Management often gives first attention to negative deviations from the standards. The negative deviation may be due to factors beyond the control of management, such as a strike at a sole source supplier. (Even here management could consider going to several sources in the future to prevent this from happening again.) If performance has been unsatisfactory, steps can be taken to improve performance through better leadership and/or a change in duties or procedures or by changing the personnel involved. Alternatively, plans may be altered or goals changed to meet different circumstances. Quick action might be necessary to influence results for the longer term. Managers need good feedback from control systems to enable them to make corrections or changes in time to be of use to the organization for the future.

If the deviation from the plans is positive, management can give praise and other recognition to those who have performed better than expected. It is possible that the good results are due to poor standards rather than to better than expected performance. In this case, it is necessary to try to redefine the standards for the future, although such changes in standards has become customary.

Control, as mentioned earlier, gives management useful input that can result in revision of plans, rethinking of organization, new staffing, and better methods for leadership and direction. All functions of management are interrelated. We consider them separately in this text for purposes of learning the functions but the manager must consider these functions almost simultaneously.

In his book, *Cybernetics: Control and Communication in the Animal and Machine*, Norbert Wiener stated that information transfer or control takes place in many different types of systems and that such controls are self-regulation or "cybernetic." Such cybernetic controls take place through feedback of information which causes the system to automatically correct errors. For example, in the body of a human, cybernetic systems would control body temperature, pulse rate, blood pressure, etc. In formal organizations, feedback also takes place in a similar manner if proper control methods are instituted.

Management uses a number of different control mechanisms. Some are used on a regular or constant basis such as self-control by employees, control by groups, and company processes and rules. Self-control by employees avoids many other controls. The employee who comes to work each day on time, is a self-starter, works hard for the work period, and does not leave work early will need fewer controls than the worker who is chronically late and needs someone to stand over him. Individual initiative is important for self controls to work.

Control by groups may also be important in many companies. The work group may set its own standards and methods of behavior that are followed by employees who wish to be part of the group. Such controls may be positive and lead to favorable results in, for example, number of units produced per worker with high quality, or may be negative, leading to work slowdowns and low levels of production and/or low levels of quality.

Company rules and procedures may also be important in a system of regularly used controls. The rules and procedures may provide a control system for handling certain routine tasks, such as how purchases of a certain dollar amount are made, a requirement that recruitment of employees follow certain procedures, etc. Rules and procedures can control behavior with proper implementation. Rules and procedures do need to be reviewed periodically to see if they are still necessary or need revision to achieve the goals of the enterprise.

Some controls are used on a periodic basis. The development of a management information system (sometimes called a real-time information system) is one form of periodic controls. The period may be short, such as every day, or longer — monthly, quarterly, or annually. For example, supermarkets often have devices at the checkout counter that transmit to headquarters which items are sold at the time of sale. Such information may lead to a system where inventory is reordered automatically when a certain number of sales are made. This data can also be analyzed store by store to see whether regional differences, competition, or special promotions have an effect on sales. A university may develop a system of on-line computerized registration to help it gain information more quickly on which classes need to be closed off and additional sections set up to best accommodate the needs of students without having to conduct registration in one week in the gymnasium. The feedback from the students as to which classes are desired can also be used in planning for the future by the university. A management information system helps management by collecting, comparing, analyzing, and distributing data or information.

Management information systems may cover more than sales data. Such a system may be used in a factory to help control quality. Prompt reporting of the number of rejects due to poor quality may help management determine whether there are serious problems in quality control. If rejects reach a certain level, this information can be reported to management through the management information system, thus alerting management that a problem exists. Then management can study why there are problems and can take steps to correct the problems. Promptness may or may not be important in every case. Where promptness is important, as in ordering food for a supermarket or determining the number of available seats in a classroom at the beginning of the college term, the use of a management information system may be essential to the organization's success in meeting its goals and objectives.

The need for promptness points out the need for controls to be directed at helping alter future behavior. It is, of course, important to study historical data such as accounting reports, reports of previous sales, etc. Such data, if it is to be most useful, should be reviewed in time to help management change what is happening to bring about a more favorable future performance. There are a number of control systems such as PERT, which will be discussed later in this text, to help management use data to affect future behavior so as to achieve desired results.

Other periodic controls are helpful to management in addition to management information systems. Annual audits by independent outside certified public accountants are used to help provide management and other stockholders (such as government stockholders, the public) with financial statements for the enterprise that have been prepared in accordance with generally accepted accounting principles. The auditors will sample a variety of items that go to make up the financial statement. For example, they may check with suppliers to see whether the invoices paid by the company represents actual transactions or whether they are really in stock. The external financial audit may result in controls being strengthened on the use of the firm's physical and financial resources if procedures are sloppy or fraud is found.

A firm may also use an audit of its management on a periodic basis as a control device. A management audit involves an inventory of the firm's key human resources — its managers. When compared on a periodic basis, the management audit can be useful to top management in reviewing the quality of its managers.

The budget is another periodic control that is helpful to management. The budget is a plan for the future use of physical and financial resources. Budgeting as a control device will be discussed later in this text in more detail.

In addition to regular and periodic control devices and systems, there are other control devices that are useful to management on a special or occasional basis. One of these devices is the use of special reports. For example, if a firm finds that it has a quality control problem in one part of its production process a special study may be made of the problem. A report may then be issued with recommendations to management dealing with the specific problem. Special reports may also be available from trade associations, government agencies, and management consultants to help a firm deal with special problems.

One special control device that is very valuable to management is management by walking around. Personal observation by the manager provides firsthand knowledge of what is going on. This requires top managers to walk around the plant or visit branch locations often — but not always with advance announcement. By walking through the plant, the manager can see what is going on: Is the workplace neat? Are workers reading newspapers or having "bull sessions" when they should be working? Does morale seem good? The manager can often find out much by such experience. Some organizations carry this one step further — they require their key executives to actually work in the field, such as sitting at the car rental desk and renting cars once a month in a car rental agency. This direct hands-on experience can help the manager learn firsthand what problems exist in the field and can lead to changes in company policies and procedures.

Many of the controls we have discussed so far are designed to help performance conform to plans in a specific area. It is necessary to look also at control of total performance of the enterprise. Often an organization is divided into many units — a Fortune 500 corporation may have hundreds of business units. At some point, management must look at the big picture — how the organization as a whole is doing.

Most such big picture controls are financial in nature. For profit enterprises, all have the objective of at least making some profits if they do not have the objective of maximizing profits. Not-for-profit enterprises must offset their expenditures with revenues and donations if they are to be viable in the long run. Financial measures, such as profitability, are the chief ways of keeping score of success in achieving our goals and objectives.

The profit and loss statement (also called income statement or statement of operations) is a big financial control in for-profit enterprises. It shows how much profit or loss was earned in a particular period of time. It can also be used on a *pro forma* basis as a forecast of future results. Profit and loss control can be used for the enterprise as a whole and for major divisions or departments. It is a summary of the results of the enterprise's operation for a particular period of time — a month, a quarter, a year, etc.

On a departmental or a divisional basis, profit or loss control is used for the same purpose — measuring how the department or division has done (or is expected to do) for a period of time. At the departmental or divisional level, profit and loss control must include some factor for general company overhead. This overhead may be allocated to the department or division on the basis of sales or square feet or space used or some other factor. Such allocation of overhead is often not very precise, especially if it requires considerable accounting effort which may not be worth its cost to the enterprise. As a result, managers are sometimes unhappy with the amount of overhead allocated to their department or division. In addition, the manager of the department may not have wide enough authority to run this part of the enterprise in such a way as to influence the level of profit. Despite these weaknesses, departmental or divisional managers do their part in achieving the overall level of profit targeted by the company.

Departmental or divisional profit and loss controls are easiest to apply when divisions are organized as strategic business units or on a regional basis. When a firm is organized on a functional basis, a more elaborate system is needed to use profit and loss control. In this case, the manufacturing division will sell the complete product to the sales division which, in turn, will sell the product to the customer. Difficulties often arise in such a system as to what price the manufacturing division will sell the product to the sales division. The problem of control of staff and service departments, such as the computer center, can further complicate such a system. Generally, these costs are allocated as overhead in such a system of profit and loss control.

While profit and loss controls highlight the importance of the bottom line and may, therefore, increase responsibility of each division's manager, such controls have some weaknesses. The difficulty of accounting fairly for intercompany transfers and the cost of accounting for such a system are often major difficulties. Instead of keeping one set of books for the company, each department or division may need its own set of books and accounting records at higher total cost to the company. Profit and loss controls also may not adequately measure all that is desired. The development of a new product may be more important to the future of the company than present products. Allocation of costs of this development to existing production divisions, for example, may make divisional managers feel they are being improperly assigned costs. Managers of divisions may become unduly competitive with each other to make their own profit goals, at the expense of the best results for the company as a whole.

On the other hand, profit and loss controls have some advantages. They force managers to concentrate on the goals of the company, making their targeted level of profit. If internal pricing policies are based on what would be charged on the outside market, managers must keep their costs controlled. Therefore, profit and loss control may be a useful tool for the manager of the division or department as well as the company as a whole.

An alternative approach to traditional profit and loss control is to look at return on investment (often abbreviated to ROI) of capital. This can be done for the company as a whole by comparing earnings with the amount of capital invested (often equity plus debt is used as the amount of capital). Similarly, a division's or department's return on investment can be measured by comparing its earnings with the investment in capital in the division or department. In this approach, the goal is to emphasize return on capital employed in the operation of the company, department, or division.

A variety of systems are used to compute the return on investment in various enterprises. Some companies use fixed assets after depreciation as the base instead of equity plus debt capital. Within an organization, it is important that one system be used consistently throughout the organization. In looking at more than one company, investors or competitors must be careful to adjust various systems of computing ROI to a common basis if the comparison is to be meaningful.

Some companies find return on investment a useful concept of control on a product basis. Each product is evaluated by comparing profits with investment needed to produce and sell the product. As a refinement, comparisons can also be made between profits and total sales of each product or other measures as well. Allocations of cost for use of such costs as accounts receivable and sales expenses can be made in some relationship to sales. Return on investment thus can be used to determine how effectively capital is being used for each product. Products can be categorized into those which are growing in profitability (stars), those that are stable (cash cows), and those that are declining in sales and profitability (dogs).

There are some weaknesses in using the control measure of return on investment. It may be difficult for a company to allocate costs to each product properly. For example, a large branded goods company selling through supermarkets may find it difficult to allocate the cost of the salesperson's call on a supermarket to each product sold to the supermarket by that salesperson. Even if the costs can be properly allocated to each product and the return on investment on a particular product is small, this does not mean that a decision should be made to discontinue the product with a small ROI. The salesperson may save only a minute of his or her time on a supermarket call if one product is discontinued, but he or she will still have to call on the supermarket. Furthermore, that product may be manufactured in space that is otherwise unusable in the factory or by workers who need to make this product to fill out a full working day. ROI in itself may not provide enough information to determine whether or not a product should be discontinued.

ROI also presents the difficulty of deciding what is a minimum return on a product. Often a company will rely on what is customary elsewhere in the industry as a standard rate of ROI.

Some companies have found that selling at a standard maximum rate of ROI may cause it to pass up good opportunities. A number of large companies turned down investments in the process of xerographic copying because they believed it would result in a smaller ROI than their minimum rate of return on investment. Often, it is difficult to estimate in advance the likely rate of return on investment. Some companies have adopted flexible rates of return based on probability of achieving success or probable risk of failure. A company may be willing to accept a smaller rate of ROI for a small project than for one which will use a substantial amount of capital.

Return on investment has several advantages as a method of controlling performance of a company or its divisions. It causes management to look closely at what profit is being earned on each product or investment of capital and on the overall return for the company as a whole. If each product manager or each department head is forced to look at performance in terms of return on investment, each manager must look at their performance using one common measure. This helps unify all managers behind the goals set by top management.

ROI as a system of control also enables top management to spot weaknesses. If one division has rising accounts receivable because it has become very lax on credit terms, this will affect the return on investment negatively as the total investment in that division will rise due to the increased accounts receivable, while the return in the form of collections may rise at a smaller rate. Top management can then review the situation and make a decision as to the wisdom of the looser credit terms in this division.

Return on investment may be improved in a variety of ways. One way to improve ROI is to increase profits on each sale by raising prices if sales volume will not decline (demand is inelastic). A second way is to decrease profits on each sale by cutting prices if sales volume will increase more in total units than the decreased price per unit — increased turnover or mass merchandising often increases the return on investment when demand is elastic. In addition, return on investment in assets can be increased by using assets more intensively. If a factory layout can be revised, for example, to permit greater production with no increase in investment, the ROI of the factory will be increased. ROI as a control concept may give managers an incentive to try to improve performance.

Another control concept that is increasingly becoming important in North American business is the concept of measuring total performance of the company by earnings per share of common stock. Many institutional investors and analysts of common stocks concentrate heavily on this measure. This often forces top management of the corporation to use this as a system of control even if they would prefer to concentrate more on ROI.

If earnings per share of the common stock of the corporation decline, the market price of the common stock will tend to decline. If the price of the common stock declines, the corporation may become more vulnerable to a hostile takeover bid. Thus, management may have to adopt goals and strategies that will give highest priority to increasing earnings per share of common stock.

This pressure from stock market investors has caused many corporations to place their highest attention on short-range financial factors — what can we do to improve the earnings per share next quarter or for the year? This may cause top management to make decisions which will look good in the short-term but may be less beneficial to the long-range success of the corporation. For example, corporate funding for basic research and development may be given a lower priority because of this concentration on short-range growth in earnings per share. The corporation may look better in the short-term but may fall behind competitors who spend more on research and development now to gain technological advantage in the future.

In addition to overall financial controls like profit and loss control, return on investment, and earnings per share, a number of detailed financial controls are available to every organization. Courses in business finance and accounting focus on these controls and are of use to every manager. Financial control can be aided by use of various financial ratios which show relationships among different items on the balance sheet and profit and loss statement.

Harold Geneen, former chairman of ITT, believes that "any significant variation [from plans] is a signal for action." In an article in *Fortune*, "The Case for Managing by the Numbers" (October 1984), Geneen said: "If one of your products is selling above expectations, you may want to increase production immediately. If . . . one . . . is not selling as well as expected, then you may have to find some way to get those sales up or begin to reduce the costs and expenses involved, and the sooner the better." Geneen used his financial controls to point out exceptions, which then would be carefully reviewed at monthly meetings with all his managers.

Profit and loss control, return on investment, and earnings per share are all useful concepts for overall corporate control. Nevertheless, financial measures by themselves are not adequate for total corporate control. Corporations must also be concerned with human factors — employee morale, ability to attract and retain good personnel, relations with customers, the government, and with the public at large.

Financial controls are easier to apply than controls dealing with human factors. Companies tend to measure human factors indirectly through measuring results against plans primarily in financial terms. More can be done in this field by consciously attempting to measure human factors in terms of plans and results in nonfinancial areas.

For example, turnover of executives can be quantitatively measured. If turnover of executives increases at a company, it may be due to a number of factors. Perhaps salaries are not competitive with other firms. This may be determined via industry surveys through trade associations or in other ways. If salaries are not the factor, high turnover may be due to better future prospects in other companies that are growing faster where executives may realize more responsibility in a shorter time. If this is a not a factor, the high turnover may be due to poor morale as a result of insensitivity on the part of top management to the human needs for status, recognition, etc., of the executives. Attention to these human factors on the part of top management may lead to improved morale and a decline in turnover of executives.

Similarly, relations with government and the general public may be more important to a company than short-run profitability. A company may gain more profits in the short-term by dumping waste in a nearby river. The result of such dumping may lead to public hostility toward the entire industry and the imposition of regulations that may be more costly to the firm (and all firms) in the long run than if the wastes were carted to a safe disposal area at a higher price in the short-term.

The skills of good management discussed throughout this text may be more important to the success of the enterprise than financial controls or other direct controls. The higher the level of quality of the managers, the less direct controls will be needed. Indirect controls, through a higher quality of management, may obviate the need for many direct controls. Qualified managers may make fewer errors than less qualified managers. Study of management will help managers become more qualified and will help these managers better evaluate the performance of their subordinates. Managers who exact self control will check what is going on and correct errors before they are revealed by financial controls. Thus, the informed judgment by good managers is a key part of a successful control system. Financial controls, control of human factors, and indirect controls are all important to the organization to ensure that plans are properly carried out or that changes are made as soon as possible if conditions change.

13

Techniques of Control

There are many different techniques of control used in business and in not-for-profit organizations. The most basic control technique is the budget. Basically, a budget is a plan that spells out the allocation of resources in the future to different activities in the organization for a certain period of time. Usually budgets are expressed in terms of dollars. Budgets can also be set up to utilize floor space, labor, materials, or other items, as expressed in any quantitative terms. For example, a floor space budget will allocate use of floor space in a factory to various departments for a stated period of time in the future.

As stated above, a budget is a plan. The budget states in numerical terms how we intend to allocate our resources to carry out plans of the organization. Budgets are techniques of control as well as being plans since they may be used to specify and, therefore, limit the amount of resources (dollars or some other measure of resources) used by the organization or one of its departments or divisions. Budgets also serve as a control benchmark by setting standards against which actual performance can be compared and measured.

In many organizations, the budget is the main method of exercising control over operations. Sometimes budgets are referred to as profit plans. Later in this chapter, other methods of control will be described to expand an organization's control beyond budgeting or profit planning.

Budgets all have certain characteristics. First of all, budgets are always expressed in numerical terms — dollars or some other numerical measure.

Second, budgets are always created for a specific period of time — a month, a quarter, a year, a biennium. Third, they are approved in advance by top management, often after consultation with other levels of management. Finally, budgets are generally binding upon the organization — any change in the use of resources requires approval as per an agreed upon process. In most government organizations and many not-for-profit organizations, items in the budget for personnel usually cannot be used even in the same department for other purposes, and other items cannot be transferred to use for hiring or paying personnel.

Budgets notably define plans on a numerical basis. They also divide these plans into categories based on the structure of the organization. Thus, a company organized on a functional basis will have a budget for the sales department, one for the finance department, and one for the manufacturing department. Those budgets in turn will be broken down into subunits. The sales departments might have a budget for advertising, one for direct sales, and one for special projects. Each of these budgets may again be broken down into smaller budgets for smaller units. Budgeting thus helps management delegate authority and responsibility down to the appropriate units with control being retained as needed. Management can tell, via the budget, what number of dollars can be allocated at which level of the organization and under whose authority to spend these allocated dollars.

Budgets are designed to preserve and promote the effectiveness of financial and physical resources of the organization by careful allocation. They are a key planning and control device to help the organization achieve its goals and objectives.

Budgets have a number of decided benefits for an organization. Budgeting requires management to establish its objectives in numbers and to communicate these objectives to other levels of the organization. Budget review on a regular basis means that activities and objectives of the organization will be reviewed on a regular basis. Lastly, the use of budgets makes clear many of the major responsibilities of the departments and their managers.

There are a number of types of budgets. The most common budget found in most organizations is an operating budget based on the revenues and expenses for a period. In a for-profit firm, this budget begins with the sales forecast. In a government organization, such as a state or a province, forecasted tax revenues may be used instead of sales. A not-for-profit organization may forecast both sales of services (such as revenue from patients in a hospital) and donations. The sales or revenue forecast is then used to build a sales budget. Other direct and indirect expenses may then be budgeted by department and for the organization as a whole. The manufacturing budget, for example, would include expenses for such categories as labor, materials, utilities, rent (or other cost of space), supplies, administration, travel, and entertainment.

Once an operating budget has been devised for the organization as a whole and for its various departments and divisions, other budgets for special purposes can be devised.

A cash budget can be devised to forecast cash receipts and expenses based on the proposed operating budget. The cash budget is essential for almost every organization to ensure that enough cash is available to meet requirements when due. For example, enough cash must be available to pay all employees on the regular pay days. Failure to meet the payroll may lead to rapid bankruptcy for the organization. If the cash budget shows extra cash as being available at certain times, this information can be used to plan short-term investment of the cash to maximize income for the organization.

Many organizations set up a separate budget for capital expenditures. Capital expenditures are for items for plant, machinery, and equipment that will be in use for periods longer than one year. Investment in capital equipment and plant is usually for a long period of time and often for substantial amounts of money. A separate capital expenditure budget highlights this use for management. A decision — for example, to build a new plant to make ice cream in California — commits the firm and limits other alternatives as total capital available to the firm is limited. Obviously, capital expenditures budgeting should be based upon the long-range plans of the organization. Once a firm has built an ice cream plant, for example, it may find little alternative use for this plant if it discontinues manufacturing ice cream and there may be few buyers for a specialized facility.

Some organizations also set up specialized expense budgets for some particular category, such as a budget for engineering to highlight the total cost of this item on a company-wide basis. Not-for-profit and governmental organizations may have an organization-wide personnel budget with a limit on the total number of employees imposed by the legislature or some other controlling body. A number of items on the balance sheet may be highlighted with separate budgets. A budget for accounts payable, for example, may help an organization focus attention on the amount of those obligations and help the organization establish procedures for payment. Inventory and accounts receivable are also often singled out for special budgets due to their importance to many organizations.

A budget for the entire organization can be made up by including both the operating budget and capital expenditure budgets and other specialized budgets. This can help the organization develop a projected profit and loss or income statement and a pro forma balance sheet. The projected profit and loss statement can be completed in detail or can be completed showing only major items, depending on the need in the organization for this information. The pro forma statements may be very helpful to the organization for planning and control purposes and in the event the organization needs credit from a financial institution or additional capital from the stock market, the legislature, or donors.

The budget process varies from organization to organization. Often the process begins at the department level.

The process begins when management has agreed on the objectives of the organization for the time period to be considered (usually the year ahead). A large organization may have a central budgeting staff to help each department prepare its budget in light of those objectives. Forms and advice may be available from this central staff. In a smaller organization, the chief financial officer may perform this function or the head of each department will be fully responsible.

In many organizations, a first draft of a department budget will begin after looking at the present budget and adjusting it for actual changes in revenue and expenses for the present period as compared with the budget, and further adjusting for expected changes in the future. Estimates are made by managers to cover unexpected events — role of competitors, increased/decreased government regulation, etc. This draft may then be submitted to the central budget office for their review. After this input, a formal budget for the department will be submitted to higher management for its consideration. This part of the process may then involve negotiations and trade-offs subject to review of the total division budget by top management.

After a budget has been approved, actual performance can be reviewed on a periodic basis. Reports are generally submitted by the department explaining why there are positive and/or negative variances from the budget and what steps the department is taking to correct variances or adjust plans in light of the new circumstances. The budget itself may need to be revised, subject to the approval of whoever is responsible for the budgeting process, in the event of a major change of circumstances.

Large firms may group departments or units into profit centers or centers based on some other category, such as expense centers or investment centers, if such grouping helps the firm in planning or control. A profit center may highlight the profit (revenues minus expenses) for a particular group or for manufacturing or some other basis of importance to the company.

Budgeting, like other techniques used in management, is not a perfect tool. Some firms overbudget — they have such detail in their budgeting process that it takes too much time or much more accounting than the results are worth. Other budgets may limit widely the flexibility of management in shifting amounts from one category to another in the budget. This is a problem that is particularly common in governmental and not-for-profit organizations where budgetary categories are often narrowly and rigidly circumscribed.

Sometimes the budget becomes more important than the goals of the organization. This is frequently a problem with service departments, such as typing pools and computer centers, that replace the goal of servicing other departments with a goal of cutting costs as a primary objective.

The budgeting process itself may cause problems. Each manager will tend to fight to get a larger budget for his or her department since a loss of resources may cause a loss of personnel or status or both. Competition among departments at budget time may cause disputes and antagonism that can be slow to heal and may affect the organization adversely. These problems cause departments to pad their budget requests. If a department really needs a budget of $9,000, the department may ask for $10,000, expecting that the budget request will be cut by 10 percent or more. There also is a tendency to ask at least for the same amount (plus a factor for inflation and growth) for every item as requested the previous year.

Some organizations have moved toward zero-based budgeting to try to eliminate overstated budgets. Under zero-based budgeting, every item in the budget must be reviewed from scratch — not just the proposed increases. Items are not funded again automatically because funding was received the prior year. Thus, every item in the budget must be defended and reviewed.

Budgets may also lead to other abuses, such as attempts to beat the system. If there is a limit of $1,000 on expenditures that may be approved at a certain level, the manager at that level can often persuade a supplier to submit two bills — each under $1,000. Horse trading can occur. One department might have money in its equipment budget for a typewriter that is really not needed. The typewriter can be purchased and traded to another department for a desired item.

Budgets can also lead to minimum performance and an overemphasis on the short-term. The salesperson may sell just enough to meet his quota to remain on the payroll. If he needs a sale very badly, he may lie to the customer to get the order — even though this would hurt the company in the long-run when, for instance, the customer goes elsewhere after discovering that the product will not do what the salesman claimed.

Some of the negative effects of budgeting can be reduced or eliminated. One way to reduce negative effects is to provide for widespread employee participation in the budgeting process. If employees understand why the process is necessary and have a role in it, they will be less inclined to try to beat or sabotage the system. Employees must know as much information about budgets as is possible — without disclosing information that would be useful to competitors and without disclosing individual salary data — if they are to support the process. Budgets must be seen as fair to all departments if they are to be supported. Rewards for suggestions that will bring useful savings are helpful.

One of the greatest problems in budgeting is inflexibility. Once a budget has been prepared and a specific number of dollars assigned to each department or function, there is a tendency to assume that all will come out as forecast. The sales forecast on which the budget is based may be way off the mark. A sudden change in events or a trend over a long period of time (if the budget is for a long period) may make the budget useless.

One way to avoid the dangers of an inflexible budget is to adopt a variable budget. The budget level may vary depending on changes of some factor, such as level of sales. Over a short period of time, we know that there are some expenses that do not vary with the level of sales. These so-called "fixed costs" are for such items as rent or property maintenance and taxes, depreciation and insurance, the cost of a minimum level of staff, and other similar costs. Whether selling one unit or a million units during the year, these fixed costs will remain part of the budget.

Other costs vary with the level of production or the level of sales. For example, if we own a used car lot and demand for used cars rises, we may have to hire more salespeople. We may also need more personnel to prepare cars for sale.

Under variable budgeting, the sales budget for the used car lot would be adjusted for this need for more personnel. A step approach could be used: as sales increase a certain amount, additional funds are authorized for additional personnel; as sales increase another amount; still more funds are allocated for personnel. If sales decline, the personnel budget steps back down again.

Variable budgeting has its difficulties. If sales are moving upward, it still takes time to find and train new salespeople. If sales are erratic, it is not likely that people will come and go as needed month to month by the used car lot. Five salespeople may be needed in January, 12 in March, and eight in November. Salespeople, like other employees, want more job security than month-to-month employment. Thus, it may not be possible for the used car lot to adjust its number of salespersons to the ideal number required by the level of sales. Some tradeoffs will have to be made; perhaps more salespeople in the winter than desired and fewer in the summer — or people can be added to work longer hours in the summer in exchange for more job security and shorter hours in the winter.

Variable budgets work best when volumes of sales or some other factor (manufacturing volume) can be reasonably well forecast so that levels of employment can be changed without adversely affecting morale.

A variant of variable budgeting can be when where sales forecasting is more difficult. A budget can be approved with a portion impounded until more data is available. For example, a university may adopt a capital equipment budget for its fiscal year beginning July first. No capital expenditures may be made until the students arrive in September. If enrollment is up to expectations, capital expenditures may be made as authorized by the budget. If there is a shortfall in enrollment, some or all capital expenditures can be deferred until enrollment increases or until a revised capital expenditure budget is adopted.

Sometimes an organization approves supplemental budgets to take effect if sales are unusually good or some other eventuality occurs. Budgeting may occur with supplemental budgets on a month-to-month basis if sales or profits reach a certain level.

Government agencies have found program budgeting to be a useful technique in some areas. Program budgeting sets up goals, such as a space program to send persons to the moon, and then resources are allocated to meet the goals as a special program budget. Program budgeting gets away from the normal budgeting concept of looking primarily at a certain time period (a year) and is one way of avoiding government's tendency to budget all items on a line basis — one line for personnel, one line for supplies, etc.

With program budgeting, attention can be focused on the cost of an entire program versus the benefits of the program. How much will it cost NASA to achieve a manned landing on the moon? Will the benefits warrant this cost? How much will it cost to build a new highway or to add a new park? In government, such focused attention on a goal (e.g., land a person on the moon) and the cost of achieving this goal may be highly useful for motivating action on behalf of a program.

Agencies dealing with highly sophisticated programs, such as the Department of Defense in Canada and NASA in the United States, have found program budgeting useful. The planning of an entire weapons system, such as building the B-1 bomber, is made easier by program budgeting. Policy makers in the government can more easily comprehend the total magnitude of such projects when cast in terms of a program budget.

Program budgets do have limitations. The chief problem with program budgeting in government agencies is exemplified by the long tradition of both the U.S. and Canadian governments budgeting on a line basis. National, state, provincial, and local legislators are very reluctant to consider abandoning line item budgeting. Thus, program budgets generally have to be recast in more traditional terms for legislative review. Secondly, legislators in North America are even more reluctant to consider funding programs for longer than a period of one or two years (some legislatures budget for a two-year period). Policy makers at NASA can advocate funding a program to send a person to the moon but the Congress is likely to consider funding such a program on a year-by-year basis.

Program budgeting is less likely to work if the goals are not clear. While a goal of achieving a manned landing on the moon is clear, many governmental programs are not so easily defined — housing the homeless, providing a good education, etc. Therefore, to make program budgeting work, the first step is to develop goals that can be stated in such a way as to be verified by a quantitative measure. For example, instead of housing the homeless as a goal, set a goal of building or rehabilitating 4,000 units of housing for families with net incomes under $10,000 per annum for the next five years. This means more attention to careful planning. Careful and precise planning goals are difficult to achieve in government, particularly since the politics of reelection and the politics of needing to achieve harmony among groups may call for ambiguous versus precise goals to be set by government agencies and legislatures.

If program budgeting is to succeed, voters must be educated to demand that government adopt goals that can be measured and government employees must be trained in the techniques of management by objectives and program budgeting.

Program budgeting is also useful for large private enterprises, particularly when they are considering major new programs. An automobile manufacturer that is planning an entirely new automobile, such as General Motors's Saturn project, may find program budgeting a useful technique. Looking at the development of a new brand of automobile over a long period of time and its cost over this period versus its forecasted benefits to the corporation may be more useful than looking at such a proposed product on a year-by-year basis.

Budgets, under whatever system of budgeting selected by management, all have limits. No device such as a budget or another financial plan can be perfect.

Even a good budget will not work if management lacks the will to adhere to it or lacks the flexibility and capacity to make changes as new data becomes available.

Despite the difficulties in preparing and using budgets, organizations need to have them. Poorly designed budgets can cause many problems. Not preparing and using a budget would be even worse for an organization than trying to administer a poorly designed budget. Use of a cash budget, for example, can help a company avoid the unpleasant surprise of not having enough cash to meet the payroll.

Budgeting can help an organization to better plan its future. It can also help provide adequate control of operations to ensure that plans are being carried out as expected or that information is being generated in time to alter plans in the event that deviations from plans takes place.

There are other useful control systems besides budgets. Many of them are simple devices that have been used in business for long periods of time. One technique often used is breakeven analysis. Breakeven analysis focuses on the point (the breakeven point) at which total fixed and variable expenses exactly equal total revenues. This tells the businessperson what level of sales must be achieved to fully cover all costs, both fixed and variable. If more sales are achieved, the organization will be operating at a profit; if less are achieved, the organization will operate at a loss. Breakeven analysis can be refined by use of a breakeven chart. The chart will not only show the breakeven point of sales, but will show sales at other levels, thereby enabling the businessperson to better understand the magnitude of loss or gain at different levels of sales.

Breakeven analysis is useful to management before deciding to produce a product (or a service) or in considering whether to discontinue a product (or service). It emphasizes the marginal effect of an increase/decrease of sales. That is, breakeven analysis shows management directly how much input additional (reduced) sales will have on profits (losses). Breakeven analysis can show the effect of a change in expenses upon profits at various levels of sales by, for example, the addition of a worker or the purchase of a labor-saving machine that increases fixed costs but may decrease variable costs.

Other statistical information is often used by management as a control device. Statistical reports in a variety of areas helps management understand what is happening and control behavior. Use of charts and graphs of such information is especially helpful in alerting management to changes or trends and statistical techniques, such as probability, can help management make better decisions based on the data and information available.

The use of statistical information, statistical techniques, and other devices, including rapid processing of data by computers and other electronic equipment, has led to the development of sophisticated management information systems that supplement traditional techniques of control. A management information system (MIS) is one which is set up to collect, place in a useful relationship, analyze, and report or disseminate data in the form of information. Data and information have different meanings. *Data* is made up of raw numbers that represent people, objects, money, or concepts. *Information* is data that has been put in a form to become meaningful to a manager for use in decision making. A management information system processes data so that it becomes meaningful or useful information to the manager.

A management information system begins with the gathering of data in one location (a computer, for example, at company headquarters) where it can be processed in a useful way to result in information to help managers make decisions.

Setting up an MIS is not easy. In most organizations, it takes years to establish an effective MIS. The process begins with system planning. Each user of information must be surveyed to determine individual informational needs. These requirements must be written down and compiled for all users of the MIS.

Once the user's requirements have been compiled in written form it is necessary to design and develop a system. System design and development includes design of databases, definition of information flows, and determination of report requirements. After design and development of an appropriate system, it is implemented. This means that appropriate equipment must be purchased or leased, space provided and improved to house the equipment, and personnel experienced in data processing hired and educated to the needs of the organization. Software covering manuals, system documentation, and policies must be developed based on the specific needs of the organization.

After implementation, the MIS must be evaluated on a regular and systematic basis to ensure that it is meeting the goals defined when the system was planned. Modification should, of course, be made to meet changed needs.

MIS can be used in a variety of organizations. A retailer, for example, could use MIS to help forecast when and how many of each item is needed for sale. MIS can help the retailer determine how many salespeople are needed on the sales floor at different times of the day and/or different times of the year. Data can be quickly provided to compare actual sales for each item and for all items per hour or day with budgeted sales. Margins on each item can be shown at actual and budgeted levels of sales.

The manufacturer could use MIS to obtain information on actual costs of manufacturing each product individually and in total, and a comparison with budgeted costs. Information can be provided on product mix and its effect on capacity and labor requirements. Needs for inventory of raw materials and externally supplied components can be furnished by a good MIS. Additionally, a good MIS will provide information at key points. For example, if additional labor will be needed because of a change in product mix, MIS can provide this information to the personnel department so they can advertise for the appropriate personnel.

The MIS may not have to be very sophisticated and may not require use of a computer. A small retailer of paperback books can use a card in the next to last copy of each book to alert him that it is necessary to reorder additional copies of the book. A large company, on the other hand, involved in manufacturing, distributing, and selling many products, may find the use of large computers essential to its MIS.

Complicated management information systems may result in a variety of human problems. Some individuals may input incomplete data into the system or may use the system incorrectly, leading to problems. *Hackers* (computer hobbyists who try to break into systems) may gain entry to the system and learn confidential information or cause damage. The system may be deliberately sabotaged by someone trying to steal from the company or by a disgruntled employee trying to destroy the system. Management must find ways to safeguard the system from theft and prevent unauthorized entry and sabotage.

Some individuals are afraid of computers and data systems. They freeze when seeing a stack of computer printouts or when faced with sitting at a computer terminal. Thus, they avoid the MIS no matter how well it provides the information needed to make good decisions. Systems must be made as user-friendly as possible. Printouts in the form of charts and graphs may be more useful to some users than columns of numbers or large spreadsheets. Personnel can be trained to use systems and equipment. The full participation of all end users during the design of the system will do much to overcome anxiety in the use of systems and computer equipment. The success of MIS depends upon managers who will listen to all and who will be willing to adapt the system to the needs of the organization.

Another problem with electronic data processing systems is the amount of information that is provided. The computer may turn out much more information than is needed. Managers throw out information that is presented in reams of printouts, charts, and graphs that they do not have time to read or do not understand when just a few items are needed. Too much information is almost as bad as too little. MIS should be designed to provide what is needed for the individual manager at each level and position of the organization. This will permit each manager to control what he or she must do and to plan properly. Some companies have a special group of intelligence experts to accomplish this task. They try to discover what information is needed by managers throughout the organization and work with systems designers to provide the information in the form and amount needed.

The same data is often combined in different ways to meet the needs of a number of users. For example, inventory data needed by the factory manager to develop a manufacturing plan is also needed by the treasurer's office to develop a cash budget. MIS provides a way to help manage all those needs for information.

In some organizations there is a need for several major information systems. John Dearden has pointed out ("How to Organize Information Systems," *Harvard Business Review*, March–April 1965, pp. 62–73) that there are three major information systems in most organizations: financial, personnel, and logistics. The financial system deals with the sources and uses of financials, the personnel system deals with data regarding personnel, and the logistics system deals with the input and output of physical goods throughout the company. A good MIS will tie these three major information systems together to best provide the information for planning and controls as needed by the individual organization.

Time–event network analysis is another control technique that has been specifically developed to control special projects in an enterprise. Bar charts — often called Gantt charts because they were first developed by Henry L. Gantt, an early twentieth century scientific management expert — chart various activities over time.

The Gantt chart shows the relationship in time of activities performed in a production process, such as constructing a house. Some bars on the chart may overlap. These represent activities that can take place over the same period of time, when they overlap. Others that do not overlap must be performed in sequence. The chart is helpful in showing what steps must be accomplished, when they must be started, and how long each activity takes. A simple Gantt chart is most useful in production scheduling of activities that are unrelated. Thus, the foundation of a house must be completed before the frame can be built and the frame must be completed before the siding can be installed.

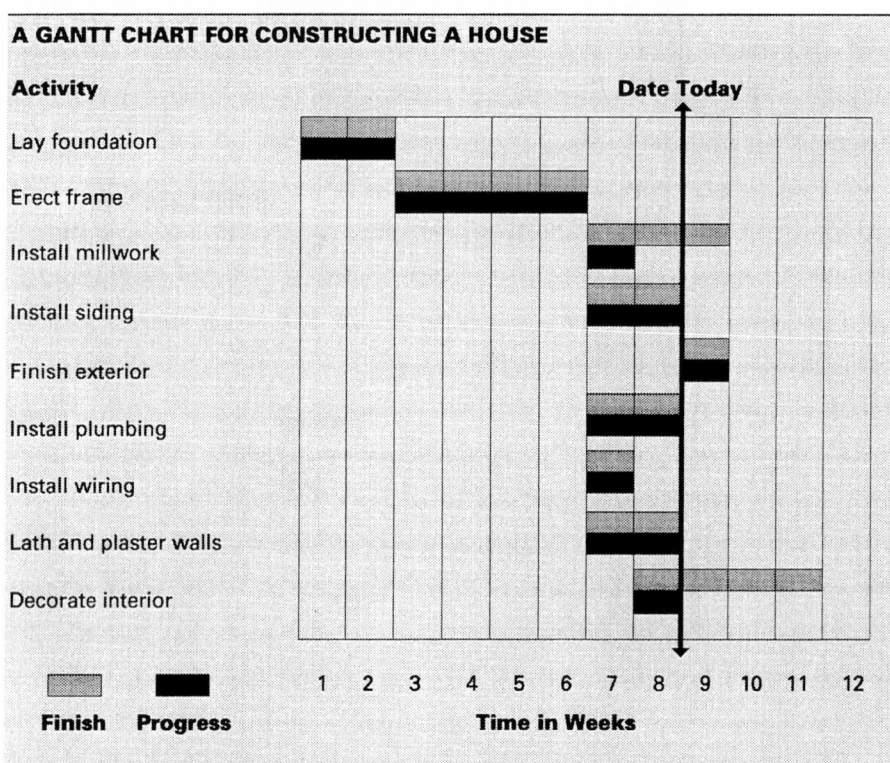

A GANTT CHART FOR CONSTRUCTING A HOUSE

Activity   **Date Today**

Lay foundation

Erect frame

Install millwork

Install siding

Finish exterior

Install plumbing

Install wiring

Lath and plaster walls

Decorate interior

Finish   Progress   1   2   3   4   5   6   7   8   9   10   11   12

Time in Weeks

(SOURCE: Adapted from Kenneth L. Dean, *Fundamentals of Network Planning and Analysis.* St. Paul, Minn.: Military Department, UNIVAC Division, Sperry Rand Corporation, 1962, p. 67.)

For more complicated production scheduling, other techniques have been developed to supplement the Gantt chart.

Milestone budgeting is used to break a project down to pieces and help in following each piece. A milestone is a portion of a project that is significant for cost or other purposes. To take a simple example, building the foundation of a house is a discrete part of building a house. The cost of building the foundation can be budgeted, the time for building the foundation can be budgeted, and the personnel and material needed to build the foundation can be estimated and obtained. Each part of building a house can be broken down into a milestone for planning and control purposes. Milestone budgeting enables a production manager to plan, schedule, and control each part of a production process. The Gantt chart can help the production manager by showing these major milestones in a visual fashion for time. This chart can be supplemented by written records that show the cost of each milestone and inputs of labor and materials needed.

PERT, or program evaluation and review techniques, and CPM, or critical path method, are other more sophisticated production control systems. PERT diagrams the relationship among the events and activities in a production project. Each event starting an activity is shown as a circle. An arrow shows the beginning and end of any one activity. Arrows represent the time necessary to complete the activity (in order to reach the next event). The critical path is the longest path in the network. This path shows which activities must be monitored most closely. Overtime may be justified for activities on the critical path.

A PERT chart requires six steps:

1. Prepare a list of each event, in chronological order, that must be accomplished to finish a project.

2. Plot a chart showing each event in chronological order. A number of events may occur at the same time. Each event can be connected with arrows to show the desired sequence of activities.

3. Estimate time in weeks required to complete each activity after the previous activity has been completed.

4. Total the time for each activity along each path of activities on the PERT chart. The critical path will represent the longest time in which the entire project can be completed.

5. Various paths can be calculated for total time. By reviewing these times, slack time, or extra time for some segments can be shown that would not delay the completion of the project. Slack time would permit the deployment of labor to other projects.

6. Review the production process to see if the process can be altered to shorten the critical path or to permit several operations to occur in an order to better utilize labor or material.

PERT charts can be developed for a variety of time sequences: expected, optimistic, and pessimistic. PERT analysis for complicated production processes, such as production of a space vehicle, may chart thousands of events. Use of the computer has made use of PERT charts more feasible for such complicated production processes.

PERT charts are useful to managers of a production process because they aid planning. PERT charts focus attention on critical areas of the production process, including the critical elements of time to accomplish each event. PERT charts are less valuable where time cannot be estimated very precisely. PERT is most useful for construction projects and large aerospace projects and weapons systems. It is less useful for repetitive assembly projects since such projects generally follow a single critical path.

Specific control techniques may or may not be appropriate to any one organization. Management must select those techniques of control that can best help accomplish the goals and objectives of the organization with the fewest negative side effects.

14

Managing Not-for-Profit Organizations

There are three major categories of organizations:

1. **Private for-Profit Business Organizations.** Such organizations are generally set up as corporations in the United States or private limited companies in Europe, partnerships, or sole proprietorships. The goal of all private enterprise is to earn a profit for the owner(s) of the business.

2. **Government Agencies and Departments.** In North America, government organizations or departments are set up at the federal, state or provincial, and local levels. Some government bodies are authorized to levy and collect taxes (such as the City of Montreal or the State of California). Government bodies authorized to levy taxes are generally elected democratically by the public. Another kind of government organization, often called an authority or a government corporation, is set up to perform a specific function or group of functions, such as the Port Authority of New York and New Jersey, the Canadian National Railway, or the University of Wisconsin. The authority or government corporation type of government agency usually has a control group selected by public officials. The authority or government corporation may be permitted to charge user fees (a public power authority's electric bill or a state university's tuition

charge) but generally cannot levy or collect taxes as can democratically elected government organizations.

3. **Independent Not-for-Profit Organizations.** These organizations usually are controlled by independent boards chosen by members of the organization or on a self-perpetuating basis. They operate through contributions, grants from corporations, foundations, and government and user fees (e.g., college tuitions). Not-for-profit hospitals, nongovernmentally-controlled universities and colleges, and many organized charities and religious bodies as well as labor unions and co-operative organizations are examples of the not-for-profit private organizations. This sector is often called the independent sector. Unlike private for profit businesses, both government departments and agencies and not-for-profit private organizations do not have the goal of earning a profit as their main purpose for being.

Management is important in all organizations, whether private for-profit businesses, government organizations, or independent not-for-profit organizations. In general, much less attention has been given to the management problems of governmental and independent not-for-profit organizations than to for-profit businesses. In recent years, the interest in applying the principles of management to government and independent not-for-profit organizations has increased greatly. This increased interest in management of not-for-profit organizations has occurred because of the growth in importance of the government and independent sectors and the need to achieve efficiencies in such organizations for a variety of reasons. More than a third of the total GNP in the United States and Canada is in the government and independent sectors. In western Europe, the percentage is even higher since many enterprises privately owned in North America are owned and operated by government departments or government corporations in Europe, although there is a trend toward privatization in a number of these countries. In North America there are almost 4,000 independent and government-owned not-for-profit hospitals, 3,000 independent and government-owned colleges and universities, and hundreds of thousands of houses of worship and other organized charities.

Economists categorize some goods as "public goods" — goods from which people receive benefit without paying for them directly. For example, most highways, schools, national defense (armed) forces, and fire and police services are generally provided by government or by independent not-for-profit organizations. No charge can be made for public goods, like national defense or law and order since users cannot be excluded if payment for use is refused. Fees can be charged for merit goods, like education, parks, and highways, but the government provides them free or below cost as a desirable social service.

Government corporations and independent not-for-profit organizations generally are given exemption from income and sales taxes. They may also receive preferential rates for some services, such as postal services or electric rates. In addition, gifts to some charities may be spurred by tax incentives for the donors. These benefits are generally given since both governmental and independent not-for-profit organizations exist to provide a service, not to make a profit. If the not-for-profit organization does show an excess of income over expenses, such funds are generally used to improve service or lower the price of services to whatever group is served.

The profit-making business depends on sales of goods or services for its entire revenue. Not-for-profit organizations, on the other hand, may receive revenue from a variety of sources, from furnishing of goods or services, donations, and funding from government and private foundations. The source of revenue for an organization has a lot to do with how the organization works. The profit-making business has a high priority in trying to please its customers as the customer is usually the only source of sales and revenue. The not-for-profit corporation may have a very different relationship with its customers. For example, the customers of a soup kitchen operated for the homeless do not pay for the soup. The ingredients in the soup may be donated by local merchants or may be purchased from funds given to the soup kitchen by a government agency or individual donors. Since the soup kitchen is dependent for funding on these sources, its management needs to be responsive to the donors as well as to the customers of the soup kitchen. Some not-for-profit organizations are fully funded by donors. Others have some or almost all funding provided by users (often referred to as clients rather than customers). When a not-for-profit organization is heavily dependent on outside donors for funding, the donors will have an important role in the decision making. Users of the service provided by the organization may be in a position to influence the organization indirectly by talking to the donors, as well as directly by contacting the management.

The lack of a profit motive and the complex relationship between the not-for-profit organizations, its donors, and its users make not-for-profit management more complex than management of a profit-making business.

Donors may interfere with the management of the not-for-profit enterprise. For example, alumni donors to a university may cause the university to change its building priorities so as to build a new football stadium rather than a new library since the alumni may be more receptive to giving for better football although the management of the university would prefer to build the library first. In such a situation, the users (the students in this case) and the professional staff (faculty of the university) may have little influence on the decision. Similarly, a trustee of a museum who gives a large donation each year may have great influence on the selection of new paintings. The museum curator (professional staff) and the visitor to the museum (the user or client) may have much less influence than the large donor to the museum. In government agencies, the providers of the funds (such as the state legislature) may interfere with management in setting priorities for use of funds.

The varying roles of providers of funds in not-for-profit organizations make it difficult for managers to set goals and plan. Some donors to the Girl Scouts, for example, may be interested in camping, others in crafts. The scout executives must be conscious of the desires of the donors in setting the goals for each troop of scouts. Thus, it is likely that goals will be set broadly or even with deliberate fuzziness so as not to lose potential donors. The girls who are participating in scouting may have less to say about the scouting services offered than would customers of a service in a profit-making business who pay for the service. The clients' influence may be weak also because there are not often local monopolies in not-for-profit services — there is likely to be only one soup kitchen or one shelter for the homeless in a particular neighborhood or town.

The influence of donors may also make it difficult for not-for-profit organizations to use decentralization. Management may not be willing to risk decentralization to avoid activities that some donors may object to.

Another difficulty in managing a not-for-profit organization is that the exact service provided may be difficult to measure. For example, how does the college basketball team fit into the goal of providing a good college education? Is the service offered by the college the provision of a good education or is the service something broader that would include the morale boosting and identification provided by the basketball team as well as its entertainment value?

The need to constantly seek resources, the lack of a profit motive, and the difficulty in measuring the service provided tends to make managers of not-for-profit enterprises concentrate on raising funds rather than on the needs of the users of the service provided.

This lack of focus on the user is often enhanced in some not-for-profit organizations with strong professional staffs where professional traditions may resist changes in how things are done irrespective of changing needs of users. Thus, doctors and nurses in a hospital may resist changes from traditional hospital care where the patient stays overnight to ambulatory care where the patient is treated and released the same day. Professionalism may also lead to rigid job specifications. Although the needs of the organization and its users may be for more flexibility, the university professor, for example, may resist broadening his or her job title to include advising students on career planning as well as teaching and research.

The lack of the profit motive and the difficulty in setting precise goals also has an impact on the evaluation of performance. How can performance be fairly judged when there are only vague goals and performance measures? This tends to lead to use of impressions to make judgments or making judgments on those factors (however unimportant) that can be measured: Does the employee look neat? Are all forms properly submitted?

One way to try and get around some of the difficulties arising from the nature of not-for-profit organizations is through establishing a system. The Department of Defense in the United States established a Planning, Programming, Budgeting System (PPBS). PPBS, as used in the Department of Defense, requires the following:

1. Objectives are to be specified in measured quantitative terms.

2. The performance of the organization is to be analyzed in terms of the stated objectives at specified periods of time.

3. The actual cost of each program will be measured and compared with the budget cost.

4. Alternatives that will be the most effective in achieving the objectives should be chosen after careful search and analysis of all alternatives.

Once the PPBS process is used, it should become regular procedure and continued over time as new objectives are set.

Zero-based budgeting, discussed in a previous chapter, is another planning process that was developed in government agencies. This process requires that all budget requests be justified each year from scratch rather than taking the previous year's budget and adding something extra for inflation and growth. Every budget item must be reviewed and justified each year. The major benefit of zero-based budgeting is trying to tie input of funds with output of services.

Both PPBS and zero-based budgeting try to emphasize rational decision making. In some cases it works that way. In others, it is just window dressing for making decisions already arrived at look better in writing. Management by objective (MBO) is also being used more in not-for-profit organizations as familiarity with this technique increases.

The board of trustees (sometimes known by other names) of a not-for-profit organization often plays a key role. The function of the board is to ensure that the organization is functioning effectively in following its board-set objectives. The board hires and fires the chief executive officer. It sets his or her compensation and often that of other key executives as well. The board either sets or approves the mission and objectives of the organization. Often, a major function of a not-for-profit organization's board is fundraising. Members of the board very often provide needed skills and professional advice to the organization (lawyers, bankers, businesspersons, etc.).

Management in a not-for-profit organization must work to help improve the quality of the board. Sometimes an organization will seek board members who lend prestige or give funds. Others want "working board members" who will actively help manage the organization. Often the CEO helps recruit new board members even though the board may select its membership or it may be selected by an outside authority (election by alumni, appointment by mayor or governor, etc.). Some managers desire boards that provide public visibility but leave all the major decisions to the management. Some boards take a more active role and help stimulate management to better performance. In some cases, the board interferes with management, making effective performance by the CEO impossible. Sometimes the board or some member of it (usually the chairperson) effectively becomes the top management of the organization — the real CEO may be a volunteer board member rather than the paid executive director.

One of the weaknesses of a not-for-profit organization is how to change a self-perpetuating board (one where the board picks its own members) when the board is ineffective or too conservative to permit the changes needed to keep the organization viable. Sometimes the CEO can bring in consultants to help the board recognize it needs change. In other cases, change does not occur and the organization gradually (or quickly) loses its viability and, ultimately, is merged with a more effective organization or ceases to exist.

Working for the board of a not-for-profit organization is the paid professional management and staff (professional and nonmanagerial) employees. A hospital, for example, will have an administrator or chief executive officer who is in charge of the entire hospital. A professional staff of doctors and nurses handles the medical and health services provided by the hospital. Other staff would include the hospital business administrator and other managers of departments, various office workers, dieticians and kitchen workers, maintenance personnel, and a myriad of others necessary to support the medical and health services offered.

As in for-profit businesses, an effective staff is necessary in not-for-profit organizations and government agencies. Positions must be established, staff must be recruited, trained, motivated, evaluated, and paid. Training may be very important. The telephone operator's courtesy may affect donations to the local United Way, for example. Staff motivation may be especially important in not-for-profit organizations where compensation may be lower than in for-profit business or government agencies.

A unique component of not-for-profit organizations is the use of volunteers. Some not-for-profit organizations are staffed completely by volunteers. Others use volunteers to supplement services offered by paid staff (docents in museums, candy stripers in hospitals) or to manage particular areas, particularly in fundraising (e.g., alumni telethons in colleges). Volunteers also need to be motivated. They are harder to manage since they work for no compensation and often at whatever time is convenient for them. It may be difficult to successfully impose deadlines for when work is due on volunteers.

Recognition is very important in motivating volunteers. Awards, recognition dinners, letters of appreciation, honorary degrees, and special organization titles all are helpful in motivating volunteers to work hard and effectively for the organization.

For-profit businesses have customers. Customers are usually referred to as clients or users, or by some other name in not-for-profit enterprises. The patient in a hospital, the client in a welfare agency, the student in a college, the citizen dealing with a government agency are all users of the service provided by the not-for-profit organization. Unlike a for-profit organization's customers, the user or client in a not-for-profit organization may not pay for the services or may pay only a small user fee. This makes measuring the value of the service more difficult as the normal price mechanism in a marketplace may be absent. For example, the child who participates in scouting does not pay for the cost of the services provided by the troop's scout leader. That cost may be paid by donors to the scouts, by funds from a United Way, and by time volunteered by scout masters, den leaders, etc. How valuable is the service to the user? Not-for-profit organizations tend to value this service by how much it is used. The child who is involved in scouting may attend troop meetings regularly or seldom. If attendance at a particular scout troop is poor, then perhaps the service provided is worth little to children. Another way of measuring performance is to compare competing not-for-profit organizations. For example, what is the percentage of beds occupied in Hospital A compared with other hospitals in the area?

In addition to users of services provided, not-for-profit organizations, like other organizations, must pay attention to the general public, to press and broadcasters, and to government. These groups may all impact on what is offered or may affect donations, availability of volunteers, or lead to government regulation or even more competition. For example, the Buckley Amendment was passed by Congress to regulate access to student records in colleges as a result of perceived abuses of student files in some colleges. Recreation departments in a city may add services if, for example, the local YMCA/YWCA or the local Boys Club is perceived as not providing adequate service to youth in the area.

Philip Kotler, in *Marketing for Non-profit Organizations* (Second Edition, p. 62), states that: "A responsive organization is one that makes every effort to sense, serve, and satisfy the needs and wants of its focal clients and publics. Each organization must determine how responsive it wants to be and the appropriate system for measuring and improving its satisfaction creation ability." According to Kotler, some organizations are unresponsive. They do not encourage inquiries, complaints, suggestions, or opinions from users. They do not measure current user satisfaction or needs nor do they train staff to be user-minded. Others are fully responsive to the needs of the users. Most organizations may be somewhere in between these alternatives. The goal of the management of a not-for-profit organization should be to become fully responsive to the needs of its users, within the limits of the resources (human, physical, and financial) available. Where more than one group of users are served (for example, adult evening students and traditional day undergraduates in a college), the management of the organization must make choices as to how much response can be given to each group of users, given the resources available. Responsive organizations utilize surveys of users, complaint systems, comparisons with competing organizations, and other devices to measure the satisfaction of users with the services provided. The not-for-profit organization must rely on such measures, due to the partial or complete lack of the price mechanism available to measure the success (profits) in for-profit businesses.

Not-for-profit management may be more complex than management in for-profit businesses. Who controls the organization may be unclear or may shift as the board changes. What is to be accomplished and how it is to be measured also may be unclear. Nevertheless, there is a challenge to managing a not-for-profit enterprise. There are also rewards for success beyond the compensation provided. The president of a college may experience real pleasure in seeing a student graduate; a manager of a soup kitchen will derive satisfaction in seeing clients fed; a hospital administrator enjoys tremendous satisfaction in seeing a patient cured and released; a police chief will find satisfaction in seeing crime reduced in the area served by the police department.

Because of the complexity of not-for-profit organizations and lack of clarity of their goals, there seems to be a trend toward substitution of for-profit enterprises for some not-for-profit services. For example, proprietary hospitals are taking over voluntary or government-owned hospitals in a number of cities and for-profit hospitals are being set up in a number of locations throughout North America. Proprietary colleges and technical schools compete with independent and government-operated colleges with success in a number of states and provinces. Increasingly, proprietary schools have been allowed to award students with bachelors degrees and even graduate degrees. There also has been a trend toward privatization of some government-owned enterprises in a number of countries in Europe and North America. Railroads, communications companies, and industrial plants have been sold to profit-making enterprises by government in the belief that the profit motive will lead to more efficiency and greater user satisfaction. Some cities even have privatized fire departments. There are experts in management who believe that not-for-profit organizations will adopt more of the incentives and measurements used by profit-making businesses in order to continue to operate in the future. Thus, the not-for-profit hospital may offer a bonus to the hospital administrator who keeps the beds full and produces a surplus from operations. Others are concerned that this trend may lead to a diminution of needed service by applying the wrong measurements to the operation of not-for-profit organizations. The challenges of managing a not-for-profit organization are likely to be exciting in the years ahead.

Some writers distinguish the not-for-profit from the nonprofit organization. In a not-for-profit firm, the excess of income over expense is a profit in accounting terms, but the profit is not the motivating force. In a nonprofit firm, income may arise primarily from donations which are not necessarily generated by the services offered. A donor does not pay for the art exhibit or the concert; he or she makes a donation without regard to the benefit enjoyed. Thus, in a real sense, the "bottom line," the difference between income (not directly related to the expenses of the firm) and expense (not incurred to gain income) cannot be called profit.

15

Comparative Management: Japanese Management

While American management has been striking out in world markets, until recently Japanese management has been hitting home runs. The score is evident from the number of Japanese cars sold in the United States, or in the popularity of Japanese appliances. Japanese cars, radios, microwave ovens, and electronic toys have a reputation for high quality at competitive prices. The reasons for Japanese success are many, but they can be reduced to two major explanations: the Japanese work ethic and good management. The work ethic, as part of the Japanese culture, is hard to teach to American workers, but American managers have much to learn from Japanese management.

Much attention has been paid, for many years, to the cultural environment of Japanese business. Technical management innovations have attracted attention only in more recent years. Both are important. There is no doubt that the new technical innovations can be copied and modified by western firms, but cultural factors are not easily transportable. American managers lament the lack of loyal and devoted workers, while western labor unions reject a seemingly servile posture. Nevertheless, the cultural milieu of Japanese industry should be examined before the innovative management systems are discussed.

CULTURAL INFLUENCES ON JAPANESE MANAGEMENT

By western standards, Japanese workers seem obedient, complacent, and cooperative. They are also highly productive and prideful. The results are good products at good prices. The source of their productive attitude is their culture.

Japanese culture is closely associated with the philosophy of Confucius. Confuciusism is less a religion than an ethical system of precepts for the management of society. It puts great emphasis on the social order. While recognizing the hierarchical nature of society, the power of the rules is derived from ethical concepts, so that authority rests on moral law, just as the bureaucracy in a government agency is based on rules.

The Japanese worker appears to subordinate his selfish interests to the interests of the group; he accepts his role as a member of the industrial organization ungrudgingly. But the Japanese manager also accepts the ethical concepts of Confucius. He respects his subordinates and seeks their help in decisions. This explains the success of the Japanese quality control circles — the secret of success is that the managers really rely on the input of the workers, and the workers know it.

The attitude of the Japanese manager is very different from his American counterpart. The American manager would not dream of leaving his plush, carpeted office for the noise and discomfort of the factory floor for long periods. In case of serious problems on the Japanese production line, no one would be surprised to find the Japanese manager moving his desk to the floor of the factory in order to become totally immersed in the problem. As in the United States, Japanese organizations are hierarchical; the Japanese manager has clear authority. However, decisions are made by consensus, and those closest to the problem, regardless of rank, are likely to be key players in the decision process.

The attitude of the Japanese worker can be seen in external displays which American workers would find offensive, or possibly even ludicrous. For example, picture hundreds of Japanese workers, clad in uniforms, assembling in the factory courtyard before the work day begins to take part in exercises and singing the company song in unison. If the cumulative production for the day passes the established norm, the workers break out in cheers.

LIFELONG EMPLOYMENT

The attitude of the workers is not merely a matter of social philosophy. It is reflected in common industrial practices. One such practice in many Japanese firms has been lifelong employment. The typical worker in Japanese industry, at least in the recent past, can expect to remain at his job until the day he retires, not unlike the American professor who enjoys tenure. During periods of recession, when a production line may be closed down, the nonessential worker may not be laid off. In the past, he or she has been retrained and sent out on another job. Examples include workers in a firm producing appliances who were trained as salespersons and sent throughout Japan to sell the appliances door-to-door during a recession. In this case, their success led to the reopening of the factory.

With lifelong employment, promotion in a Japanese firm is slow. Staff persons often make lateral moves and careers are typically nonspecialized. The Japanese have a holistic orientation; that is, they seem to see the organic and functional relationships between their specific jobs and the welfare of the whole organization. This organic view of the management process seems to deny clear differences between management functions, such as planning and organizing. Japanese workers identify with their firms and willingly assist each other while on the job, even in job categories not their own.

Other evidence of the effect of the positive work ethic of the Japanese is found in quality control. The first line of assurance of good quality in Japan is found on the assembly line, rather than in the office of quality control engineers. Production defects are rare since workers are concerned about quality and vigilant in finding flaws.

QUALITY CONTROL CIRCLES

It is common for persistent problems of production to be referred to the *Quality Control Circle*. At regular meetings, the workers assigned to a "circle" discuss the reasons for recurrent problems and suggest practical solutions based on direct involvement. Of course, staff engineers will assist when technical problems are encountered. However, the key to the operation is the hands-on knowledge of the members of the circle, their sincere interest in finding solutions, and the respect they enjoy from their supervisors.

The quality control circle was invented in the United States and introduced to Japan in the 1950s by W. Edward Deming. The quality control circle is still more widely used in Japan than in the United States. The quality circle, a small group of workers, meet regularly to discuss problems of quality and productivity in their departments. Benefits of the quality circle include not only the solution to specific quality problems, but increased morale and productivity.

American quality control circles have been less successful than their Japanese counterparts. American managers typically regard the circles as a nuisance, foisted on them by outside academic experts as a human relations ploy. Not unknown in the United States is the quality circle whose members find a way to increase productivity, only to discover that management responds by firing the workers who are no longer needed because of the innovation. Not so in Japan!

The influence of Japanese management culture has been felt in the United States. This influence can be seen in *Theory Z* management, introduced by William Ouchi. Theory Z combines lessons from Japan and the United States, and has been practiced in American firms, such as IBM, Hewlett-Packard, Eastman-Kodak, and Procter & Gamble. It includes selected practices from Japan introduced into the American environment, including group decision making, but maintains individual responsibility. Theory Z includes lifelong employment and slow promotion. It combines less specialized careers with a holistic approach. Its influence in the United States is limited in application.

Of course, we must not exaggerate the effect of Japanese culture on management. There are new indications that Japanese workers, changed by affluence and influenced by contacts with the west, may be moving toward a more modern attitude, one which puts less emphasis on loyalty and devotion to the firm. Will paradise be lost in Japan too? The social harmony of a Japanese firm, however, cannot explain fully the management successes of the Japanese.

MANAGEMENT INNOVATIONS IN JAPAN

In the struggle for survival, the innovator earns a chance for success by scrapping old habits. Western technology, at least in the repetitive manufacturing mode of high volume production, puts great emphasis on keeping the production line moving. In typical assembly line plants, numerous work stations — really individual shops — feed parts to the main line. The work station is expected to produce at top speed. If the assembly line slows down or cannot use all the parts produced by the shops, no matter. Factories are designed with lots of space so that the excess parts are stored as part of the buffer inventory. Buffer inventory, of course, can be used if the individual work station falls behind.

The Japanese reject this approach as wasteful. It is, they argue, the root cause of poor quality. Buffer inventory merely hides problems on the line. The Japanese approach has been *just-in-time* production — stockless production or the "pull" system of inventory. In essence, the individual work station produces only enough to meet the needs of the assembly line; that is, each work operation pulls the parts it needs from the feeder station as it needs them. There is no buffer inventory. Indeed, Japanese factories are designed small so there isn't even room for buffer inventory.

There are many ways to achieve a pull system, or just-in-time production. Many years ago, a primitive pull system was common. As parts were needed, the inventory bins were searched. Empty bins were a signal for additional production. Modern computer systems, in use in technologically advanced factories in the

United States, use a modern push system. Known as material requirements planning (MRP) systems, they are computerized decision centers which compile information on the need for various parts in an inventory system, and order job lots to be produced based on economic order quantities (EOQ).

The Japanese have introduced a new approach to ordering the production of parts, as needed, which is magnificent in its simplicity. There are many ways to accomplish the goal of producing only enough for immediate use, thus avoiding the buffer inventory so common in U.S. factories. For example, a worker at a work station on an assembly line could shout his order to the stations which feed him parts, or telephone the order, or wave a flag, or type the order into a computerized signal system. In one Kawasaki motorcycle plant, workers signal the need for parts by rolling golf balls down a pipe to the work station which produces that part (for example, stamping out a fender). The color of the golf ball tells the producing station which model is desired.

KANBAN

The Japanese have used a system known as *Kanban*. In fact, the Kanban — which means visible record in Japanese — is a card used by a work station to pull parts from the previous station. In Japan it is a triangular metal plate, about 12 inches on each side. The production worker takes parts needed for his operation from a movable bin. The number of parts which can be loaded on the bin are carefully specified. When the bin is empty, the worker takes a "conveyance Kanban," specifying the part number, hangs it on the movable bin, and sends the bin back to the station where the parts are produced. Here a "production Kanban" is placed on the bin. Only then does the worker in this station produce the part. When completed, the "conveyance Kanban" is reattached and the bin is sent back to the station where it is used. Since the number of bins and Kanbans are specifically determined, no parts are produced unless needed immediately.

The American manager will protest that the workers at the production station are idle if no parts are needed. The American view is to produce as fast as possible and spare time is seen as the ultimate sin. In Japanese plants, the spare time is used for routine maintenance, for checking tools, and for helping workers at other stations. This is possible since the Japanese are trained to be flexible and do many jobs, and to cooperate with other stations in need of help.

JIDOKA

Another practice which complements Kanban is known as *Jidoka*. Above every work station are two lights, one yellow and one red. Turn on the yellow light and the production line slows down. Turn on the red light and the production line stops. Every worker has the right to turn on the lights. Indeed, he is expected to do so if there is, in his opinion, a need to do so. The Japanese manager is unhappy if no yellow lights are on. He suspects that the line is not operating at full speed and he pulls workers off the assembly line for reassignment elsewhere. The existence of yellow lights tells him that the line is working as fast as it can. To the American manager, this is heresy. The bible of management teaches us to produce, produce, produce. Surely, time is lost when the line is stopped.

But picture what happens when a yellow or red light is flashed. First of all, the management staff rushes to the station to determine what is wrong, and to take corrective action. Since each worker is trained in many jobs, workers from other stations come over to help. A related matter is that Japanese factories are often U-shaped so that workers at any station are close to other parts of the assembly line where they may be needed in case of a slowdown or stoppage. Here the Japanese culture emphasizing cooperation seems to be at its best. What caused the line to be slowed or stopped? Perhaps the part being installed did not fit perfectly. In an American factory, a defective part would be forced on or, more likely, just discarded. There are lots of other parts in the buffer inventory lining the aisles and so the previous work station will just keep on producing bad parts. No one will know until the goods being produced reach the end of the line and the quality control engineer discovers that there is trouble in the system.

In Japan, the spotlight is immediately put on the worker who produced the faulty part — perhaps his equipment needed a slight adjustment. The correction is made and the defects are eliminated. What about the time lost when the assembly line stopped? The Japanese point to the avoidance of defects in the finished product. American car manufacturers send cars with obvious defects to a special work center where the defects are corrected. The cost is said to be over $700 per car on average. The Japanese avoid that cost and produce better cars.

The system is sometimes called stockless production. The essence of the system is that no parts are made until needed. This system, of course, requires that needed parts can be made quickly. Kanban is not used to supply parts that require extended production time. But even in this case, the Japanese carefully plan that major parts, produced in the plant or purchased elsewhere, are delivered only as needed.

MODEL CHANGEOVER

A major project in modern repetitive production, as in production of automobiles, is the need for different models. In American factories, time is lost in switching from one model to another. In the typical American assembly line, model changes are made as infrequently as possible.

American factories are apt to order large, expensive, multipurpose machines for many tasks. The machine is then adjusted for different models. Presses are reset, dies are replaced in a slow, time-consuming process. In Japan, the focus of attention is on permitting fast changeover from one model to another. It is typical for a factory in Japan to change over to new dies or new drilling patterns in minutes, while American factories take hours to accomplish the same activities. The difference lies in the equipment. The Japanese are likely to purchase several small, cheaper, special purpose machines for a particular operation or to design machines in-house for quick change. If a new model requires a different drilling configuration, the Japanese may simply use a different drill. In other cases, new dies are arranged on special tables, perhaps on rollers, so that they can be slipped into place without delay.

We must concede that Kanban and Jidoka are not merely management devices easily importable into other cultures. They work, in part, because of the Japanese culture. However, the system changes attitudes despite culture. The attitude of workers, American or otherwise, is affected by the system. There is an indissoluble connection between the ideal of producing parts in small numbers, just enough to satisfy the needs of the next station, and the sense of responsibility felt by the Japanese worker for high quality production. It is not only a mechanical system which reminds the worker to check the settings on his drill press with a micrometer. Jidoka reinforces his sense of responsibility. Kanban and Jidoka bring a new attitude to production, quality control, and management in general.

Just-in-time production does more than improve quality. The Japanese system for fast set-up time for equipment has permitted them to make use of mixed model assembly lines that are responsive to demand for particular models. The result is flexibility in production. The factory can turn out models in keeping with demands of the marketing departments. It should be noted that many experts predict that the pattern of production of the future will be based on variety and flexibility, with different models produced in accordance with market demand.

VENDOR RELATIONS

The benefits of Kanban are not limited to reducing internal buffer inventory. Inventory from outside vendors is also tightly controlled. Typically, there is a close relationship between the mother factory and the vendors, both in location and mutual trust. Quality control is an urgent consideration of the Japanese manufacturers. Standards are so high that American suppliers of parts to Japanese owned firms in the United States have been mortified by demands for quality. In Japan, the mother firm may do business with a vendor for years without question. Suppliers are tied to the mother firm not only by long-term contracts, but also by family and personal ties. Quality control inspection is not necessary at the receiving station since the Japanese vendor will follow the same high standards as the mother firm. In fact, the two firms will work together cooperatively to iron out any problems that may exist.

Just as important as personal relationships is the location of the suppliers. Most are located within a few miles of the main firm or at least close enough to be able to deliver parts by truck in a short time.

An example of the system, as compared with the American approach, may be seen in the delivery of tires to an automobile plant. In the United States, a railroad car will deliver thousands of tires to be used over a period of many weeks. In Japan, a truck will deliver enough tires only for an assembly line run of only a few hours. The plant engineer knows how many cars and what models will be produced a few hours later that day. He gives the truck driver a Kanban listing the precise number and size of tires required later. A few hours later, the truck returns with only the specific number and size of tires to be used. There is no place to store any excess tires anyway.

In many ways, the Japanese system flies in the face of modern, mathematically-oriented control, such as material requirements planning and economic order quantity. The Japanese seem to be rejecting this approach. Yet complete rejection is not necessary. It may be possible to put into the equation for the economic order the costs of poor quality which follow from excessive buffer inventory.

American factories are now experimenting with new management techniques. Instead of a Kanban, just-in-time production may be achieved with computerized controls. The last word on efficient management has not yet been written, though it is the Japanese who have set us on a new course.

16
Multinational Management

A multinational corporation (offered referred to as MNC) is an enterprise that conducts business in two or more nations. Some observers define a multinational firm as one with at least a fifth of its sales or employees in a country other than the primary location of the corporation. Regardless of the specific definition, there are now thousands of corporations with significant operations in "foreign" countries.

Often, a firm will begin operations in one country. If a product is successful, the firm will license a foreign firm to produce and/or market the product in a foreign country. Alternatively, the firm will export its product to the foreign country or countries using an export firm which specializes in such activities or setting up its own overseas branch to handle the sales of the firm abroad. For example, BMW has a wholly-owned corporation in the United States with headquarters in New Jersey that imports BMW automobiles from Germany and sells them through independent dealers in North America.

Sometimes a firm will ship parts and components to a foreign subsidiary. The parts are assembled in the foreign country and sold by that foreign subsidiary. Tariff and trade regulations in many countries encourage such a system, particularly for heavy industry and major consumer goods like automobile and electronic products.

An alternative method for expansion into foreign countries is via a joint venture. Xerox expanded its production and sales of copiers to Great Britain through a joint venture with a British company and the joint venture was known as Rank Xerox. There are many creative approaches to joint ventures. Under a unique program, PepsiCo sells Pepsi Cola to Russia in exchange for Stolichnaya Vodka which it imports and sells in the United States.

Some multinational corporations headquartered in one country establish wholly-owned branches or subsidiaries in other countries that engage in the complete manufacture and distribution of products, which may differ from products sold in the headquarters nation. For example, a subsidiary of General Motors produces and sells automobiles in Australia under the brand name Holden.

Some highly advanced multinational firms may treat the whole world as a single entity and produce and sell products on that basis. For example, Ford has produced a truly multinational automobile, the Mondeo, which involves the production of parts in a variety of countries, assembly in a variety of countries, and sales in a number of countries.

As a multinational firm integrates its operations with direct investment, manufacturing plants, and distribution networks in many countries it reduces its risk of being forced out of business in host countries. For example, a firm which sells to a country through a foreign owned sales agent may have its product dropped and replaced by that of another firm if the sales agent believes there is more profit possibility in such a switch.

All corporations, whether engaged in operations in one country or on a multinational basis, have similar objectives. Multinational corporations, like domestic entities, wish to earn a profit, grow in size and profitability, and survive over a long period of time. MNCs look for a good return on invested capital — they invest in projects worldwide according to the expected return on investment, adjusted for risk factors. A firm looking for a 10 percent return on investment in a generally stable country like Canada may require a return of 20 percent in a Central American country where government is less stable and risk of business interruption or even nationalization is higher.

One of the problems facing multinational firms is that the objectives of the company — such as maximizing return and investment over the long run — may conflict with the national political and economic goals of one or more countries it operates in. A country may have a goal of developing a strong manufacturing base. The MNC may be better off economically by manufacturing in another country where labor rates are lower and raw materials are more accessible. The MNC may have to adjust its policies to the goals of the country if it wishes to grow in that country. Some adjustments have resulted in corporations entering businesses in host countries that they would otherwise not enter.

One area for potential conflicts is in staffing the MNC. If the MNC sends nationals from the home office to the foreign country, it may face difficulties with local labor laws and communication. Often, a compromise is reached. One or two persons who are slated for top positions might be sent to the overseas subsidiary and the remainder of the subsidiary is staffed by local nationals, who know the customers and language and can communicate better with the local population. Consultants and technical experts are sent out as needed to train and assist local nationals.

Sometimes well established brand names may not be suitable in some countries. For example, Japan has a popular coffee creamer called CREAP, which probably would not sell well in English-speaking countries. Chevrolet's Nova has had some sales problems in certain areas of Latin America. "No va" in Spanish means "no go." For cultural reasons such as these, it is often helpful to the multinational firm to use local personnel who can help the multinational firm avoid such potentially damaging pitfalls.

With the growth of large multinational firms, such as Royal Dutch Shell and IBM who have extensive operations all over the world, many truly international managers are being developed. As these managers gain experience and perform well, they may move from country to country. Thus, an MNC might have a Nigerian managing a subsidiary in Norway, reporting to a Malaysian who works for the parent company in New York. Expertise in management is scarce. A good manager may be needed for a particular subsidiary and recruited company-wide from anywhere in the world.

The manager in a multinational corporation requires all the skills needed in a corporation operating in one country plus special skills. The multinational manager may need language skills in the host country's language if he or she is to communicate effectively with local employees, customers, government officials, etc. Sensitivity to cultural differences is especially important. The international manager from Scotland working in Boston should not wear an orange tie on St. Patrick's Day. The salesman of machine tools trying to sell his product in Japan should not leave his chopsticks standing in the rice bowl at the end of his meal with the client, as some Japanese regard this as a symbol of death and very inauspicious. Latin Americans maintain a much shorter distance between people while standing and conversing than do North Americans. The North American conversing with a Latin American will keep trying to move further away while the Latin American will continue inching closer. Both will be uncomfortable, if unaware, of this cultural difference and this lack of comfort may make it harder for them to successfully do business. Some multinational corporations have established training programs to make their managers more aware of cultural differences such as those described here.

Because of the growth in trade and multinational enterprises, corporations need to become more and more aware of the international dimension in management. The development of the jet airplane and television by satellite have made the world more familiar and accessible to corporations and individuals. The economies of scale make world markets for some products, such as mainframe computers, very desirable to corporations. United States-based firms are dependent on foreign markets for more than 10 percent of all sales. Canadian-based firms are even more dependent on international markets. Almost half of the GNP of the Netherlands is made up of international trade.

As mentioned above, cultural differences may make multinational management more difficult. The sense of and regard for time may be different in Cuba than that in Germany. To the German businessperson, an appointment at 10:00 A.M. means precisely 10:00 A.M. To the Cuban businessperson, an appointment at 10:00 A.M. may mean anytime between 10:00 A.M. and 12:00 NOON. The attitude toward work may vary from culture to culture, as may the attitude toward permanency of employment. Once a company operating in Mexico has kept an employee through the probationary period, it is expected that the employee will remain with the company until retirement. This may necessitate adjusting the staffing policies of MNCs operating in Mexico from those in countries where it is easier to discharge labor.

The political climate varies from nation to nation. In some countries there is poor security, and kidnappings and hostage-taking may be a real risk to the international manager. In others, there may be discrimination by race, religion, nationality, tribe, or sex. A female manager might meet with great resistance in Iran, for example. The economic climate also varies. Some countries have had rapid inflation, which has led to widely fluctuating values for the local currency. Political and economic theories prevalent in the country may lead to the threat of nationalization or expropriation. Foreign-owned business may be a convenient target for local politicians.

Governmental changes in some countries may occur via coup or military takeover. Some countries have corrupt governments which encourage bribery to do business; such bribery could be illegal and cause problems in the MNC's home country. Other governments may be highly bureaucratic or adhere to rigid ideologies that are hostile to some forms of business. Legal systems vary as well among countries. What may be viewed as a minor drug infraction in one country can be a capital offense in another.

Because of these economic and political factors, the multinational corporation must assess the political and economic risks before deciding whether or not to operate in each country. As mentioned earlier, some MNCs apply such risk assessment to required rate of return on investment before making investment decisions, adjusting the required rate of return for these factors.

Other differences are important. Attitudes toward employees vary country to country. A company with a highly informal management structure, like some of the creative Silicon Valley companies, may find it difficult to implement their management style in countries where relationships between boss and subordinate are much more formal and rigid.

Because of the cultural, economic, and political differences among nations, the organization of the MNC may vary between nations or from that of a corporation doing business only in North America.

Sometimes MNCs organize their subsidiaries on a geographical basis. The basis may be that of a particular country such as National Westminster Bank, USA. This bank is a subsidiary of a large bank based in the United Kingdom. The basis may also be a large geographic region, such as IBM Far East. The geographic organization based on a single country helps an MNC adapt to the local situation and bolsters local pride. It also may permit the subsidiary to trade with a third country which the parent MNC cannot trade with due to rules of its country of domicile. A large geographic region such as the Far East may have enough in common culturally to warrant a subsidiary serving the whole region. The disadvantage of geographical organization is that it may lead to communications difficulties with other units of the corporation or too much concern for one nation's problems or points of view.

MNCs sometimes choose a functional organization. Thus, human resources will be a responsibility for the corporate vice president for human resources in all countries that the MNC operates in. Similarly, such other functions as marketing, finance, and operations will be organized for the corporation as a whole. The advantage of a functionally organized MNC is that each functional area will have good coordination wherever the company operates.

This advantage is most useful when the MNC operates worldwide in a similar pattern and when the MNC has a fairly limited product line. A disadvantage to this form of organization is that functional organization does not permit the flexibility of a decentralized organization like a geographically organized MNC.

Another common form of organization for an MNC is a product line organization. In this form of organization each product line is set up as a separate unit or corporation. This provides good coordination within the product group. On the other hand, a product line organization does not have the advantage of unity of company structure, which may be politically important in some countries.

Obviously, factors regarding the size, goals, type of business, and major countries of operation will be relevant in deciding which form of organization works best for a particular MNC. Some MNCs may compromise with a complex organization that overlays a geographic structure on a functional or product line base using matrix management, as previously described.

Regardless of the form of organization, the MNC needs a variety of controls to ensure proper operation of a firm operating in many areas of the world. Each part of a multinational organization will need the same kinds of financial controls found in a similar size domestic company. Because of currency fluctuations and exchange controls, careful control of the flow of funds must be maintained by MNCs. If a currency is expected to decline in value, the MNC may wish to move funds to a more stable currency or hedge against possible fluctuations in value. Exchange controls, controls on the amount of profits, and tax laws can also be significant factors necessitating special financial controls. Financial manipulations by the MNC to avoid local political controls may cause political criticism in some countries.

Marketing opportunities vary as well from country to country and time to time. Marketing information and intelligence should be reported to the parent company for use in planning and product development. Trends may start in one country and later spread to other countries. For example, fashion trends for a raised hemline on skirts may begin in France, spread to the United States and western Europe, and then later to the Far East and Africa. Competitors may develop a product in one country that the MNC can adapt for sale in other countries. Changes in technology also affect marketing as well as manufacturing and other areas of operation. A new technical development, such as the use of robots to paint cars in Japan, can be studied and adopted elsewhere by multinational automobile companies.

Other information is also often helpful to the parent company. Changes in political trends or economic activity may provide better opportunities for investment or suggest other changes in corporate strategy. The probable coming to office of a government hostile to foreign-owned enterprise may indicate to a company the wisdom of selling the subsidiary to local ownership before potential nationalization drives down the price. On the contrary, the coming to office of a government friendly to business may make possible significant expansion of the enterprise.

In addition to special controls needed because of differences in the political, economic, and cultural environments in multinational operation, the large MNC needs those controls that are normal for a firm in its industry operating in one country. It is imperative that the top management of the MNC have access to the vital statistics on sales, production, finance, human resources, etc., for the entire corporation on a timely basis. The use of the computer should make this possible if proper controls are installed and maintained for management to have this information when needed.

Operating in a multinational environment is complicated by the differences in customs, languages, legal systems, political, and economic factors. Nevertheless, economies of scale and the principle of comparative economic advantage have led to a growing interdependence of many nations of the world for economic prosperity. Corporations are increasingly looking beyond the boundaries of their countries for resources, products, manufacturing, personnel, and sales. Managers must expect to operate in a multinational environment in most fields of business today or in the very near future. The prospect of increased profits and growth make the tradeoff of added complexity worthwhile.

17

Small Business Management: Entrepreneurship

Entrepreneurship is a creative human act. Basically, entrepreneurship is the ability to create and build an enterprise or organization from scratch. The entrepreneur must be willing to take personal, and often financial, risks. He or she must find resources (both human and financial), assemble them for a purpose, and control them carefully. Most new enterprises are small businesses. Most small businesses require entrepreneurial skills on the part of the owners or managers.

There are approximately 15 million nonfarm businesses in the United States and Canada. Most of these enterprises are small. Almost anyone can start a business. Some entrepreneurs have been very successful. Others have failed. Those who fail can, and often do, try again. While it is easy to start a business it is relatively difficult to build a large new enterprise. Of the 15 million nonfarm businesses, fewer than four percent have sales of over one million dollars.

The successful entrepreneur requires many skills: creativity, ability to calculate risks, ability to minimize risks, ability to plan, and ability to work very hard. Almost anyone can try. Age is no barrier: Steve Jobs, creator of Apple Computers was a millionaire before 30; Colonel Sanders launched his fried chicken business after his retirement at age 65.

The biggest problem facing the new business is survival. Approximately a half million new businesses are started up each year in the United States.

Unfortunately, for every three new businesses that open in a year, two others close. Small firms, especially in retailing, construction, and services, show the highest rate of failure. By the end of the first year, 40 percent of all new businesses close their doors. After 10 years, 90 percent of all new businesses have closed. Failure may be a step in the learning process for many entrepreneurs.

There are countless approaches to establishing a new business, however, three elements are key to the process: the entrepreneurs, the business opportunity, and the resources needed for the enterprise. The entrepreneur needs skills and knowledge for the enterprise. Entrepreneurial drive and motivation to succeed are critical factors. Most important is perseverance. New business founders tend to start their enterprises in the same fields that they have been working in. Experience is often important to ensure success.

The business opportunity is also a key element. A good idea in itself is not enough. The idea must be researched to determine its feasibility: Is there a need for the product? Will customers buy it? At what price and quantity? The entrepreneur should prepare a business plan to help adequately research these questions.

Once the business opportunity has been assessed, the entrepreneur must seek the resources to start and operate the new enterprise. Use of a business plan is helpful if outside capital is required from a leader or equity participant. Before someone will lend or participate in founding a new enterprise they would like to see financial, marketing, and operating forecasts for the new venture.

Once a new enterprise has been started, it requires effective management if it is to succeed. The manager of a new business must know the market, the competition, the product, and the industry in general. Attracting, keeping, and motivating people are key skills for the entrepreneur. Knowledge of business finance and accounting is also helpful. Ability to analyze is important. Equally important is the ability to make a decision and carry it out.

A recent study by McKinsey & Company of growth companies shows that these companies achieved their successes initially with a unique product or a different way of doing business. Product quality and service to the customers were key elements.

Generally, the new enterprise, if successful, will go through a phase of high growth in the early years. At some point in time it will mature. The established, mature company may need very different managerial skills than those required in the start-up and rapid growth phase.

Many times, the new or small business is a family business. People sometimes make the mistake of assuming that because it is a family business, it is not necessary to spell out the specific responsibilities of each family member or financial commitment, including share of equity. Many businesses have been destroyed by family bickering because these details were not spelled out in writing at the beginning. The second or later generation family member who is considering joining a family business must assess whether the family business will meet his or her career goals better than another opportunity. Is the business large enough for more than one family member to have a useful and growing role? Can a son get on with his father? How long will the son have to wait to have real authority in the firm? Sometimes it is useful for the son or daughter to acquire experience at another company before joining the family business. This outside experience may help gain acceptance for the younger family member more quickly.

One way the potential entrepreneur can evaluate whether they are suited to entrepreneurship is the use of the *personal strategy assessment*. This assessment enables one to examine goals, aspirations, past performance, strengths, and weaknesses in order to better decide on a long-term personal strategy. As described in Jeffrey A. Timmons's *New Venture Creation*, (Second Edition, Richard D. Irwin, 1985), the personal strategy assessment is divided into four parts: self-assessing entrepreneurial roots; self-assessing entrepreneurial attributes and role requirements; goal setting and goal assessing; and partner, peer, and professional feedback.

Key to success in a new enterprise is planning. Plans often fail because realistic goals that can be measured in a specific period of time are not detailed. The entrepreneur must work with his management team to develop a plan with built-in performance goals spelled out. Plans should be reviewed periodically to take advantage of experience and feedback, however, plans should not be carved in stone. As experience in the new enterprise is gained, the plan must be revised. What is important is having long-term goals and a plan for getting there.

One of the key problems in small business is obtaining the resources (physical, monetary, and human) needed to carry out the goals of the new enterprise. Large organizations have access to many resources. The entrepreneur must make do with less. He or she must learn to "bootstrap" resources to achieve the goals of the enterprise. One way to bootstrap is to borrow resources from others — friends, relatives, suppliers, and customers can all lend credit or invest in the new firm. A garage, basement, or an in-home office can be a start for facilities. Use of a friend's copier or telephone line and even bartering can help a company begin its operation. A new enterprise can contract out portions of a project. For example, the firm may use an outside secretarial service to type proposals before cash flow permits hiring a full-time secretary. The new business can call on an accountant, an attorney, and specialized consultants for advice as needed without having an accountant or attorney or other specialist on full-time salary. Such specialists can be very helpful if used wisely. Help can also be obtained by selecting some experienced business people to serve on the board of directors of the new enterprise, often with minimal compensation.

Much information is available to the manager of a new enterprise. Many useful reference books are on shelves at local libraries. The Small Business Administration (SBA) can often supply useful advice. Personal computers and software for many applications are now readily available at moderate prices.

Word processing on a personal computer may significantly reduce secretarial and clerical costs. Use of a spreadsheet for financial data can provide realism for planning. Software is available to help prepare payrolls and corporate income taxes.

Despite bootstrapping, help from relatives, etc., the new enterprise may need additional capital from venture capital sources or sophisticated investors or lenders. In such cases, it is imperative for the entrepreneur to prepare a detailed business plan.

The business plan is a great deal of work. Careful preparations of a business plan can be very beneficial to the entrepreneur preparing to launch a new business venture. A business plan helps the entrepreneur see what resources (human, physical, and monetary) are needed for the proposed venture. The business plan is also a useful tool for seeking financing for the new enterprise if outside funding is necessary from professional investors or lenders. The business plan is a vehicle that outlines why the business venture is a good opportunity for an investor or lender. The business plan must state in writing the key factors in the proposed new venture. The plan should describe succinctly the product or service offered by the new enterprise. Problems as well as prospects should be disclosed.

Generally, it is best to begin the business plan with a section on the proposed product or service, the company, and the industry. The product or service should be described fully in nontechnical language. There should be a brief description of others in the industry and how the new company will fit into this industry.

A second section should be prepared on the management of the proposed new enterprise. This section should include an organization chart for the company and descriptions of the backgrounds of all key members of the management team. It should include information on supporting professional services and outside members (if any) comprising the board of directors.

The third section of the business plan is often a detailed section on market research and analysis. This section describes the current market and projected market trends for the product or service to be entered. A list of all competition and their estimated share of the market is included here.

Following the section on market research and analysis should be a section on the marketing plan for the new enterprise. This section should include details of the marketing channels the new product or service will use (direct selling, use of distributors, etc.), a sales plan, and a service plan. This will include plans for developing new products or applications in the future, if any.

If the new enterprise is involved in manufacturing, a manufacturing plan should be developed as a section of the business plan. This part of the plan would include a production schedule. If the new enterprise provides a service, an operation plan and a schedule for how and when the service is to be performed should be included in this portion of the plan.

A key section of the business plan is one outlining the risks in the proposed new enterprise. This section is important so that potential investors will know the management has recognized the possible risks facing the new enterprise. This area should encompass an evaluation of how serious the risks are and what contingency plans have been established in the event that the risks actually occur. For example, one risk is that sales forecasts are not achieved. An evaluation of this risk will show what margin, if any, exists between breakeven level and sales forecasts to provide a cushion. Contingencies for lower sales than forecast might include a cutback in purchasing or a reduction in staff.

A financial plan for the new enterprise is an important and necessary section of the business plan. A five-year financial forecast based on the marketing outlook should be prepared. Pro formula income statements, balance sheets, and cash flow forecasts for each year can be prepared, listing all assumptions used. Breakeven charts are often helpful.

The final section of the business plan should be a section on funds to be raised and how they are to be raised. For example, a new enterprise may need $300,000 in capital. One hundred thousand dollars may be provided by the entrepreneurs. This should be detailed, along with how many shares each of the entrepreneurs will receive in return. The remaining $200,000 may be provided by investors in exchange for a certain number of shares of stock, or by lenders in exchange for a note, perhaps with stock options.

The business plan is a helpful tool to the entrepreneur in raising money to start up, buy, or expand an enterprise. The entrepreneur must decide between debt and equity (or a combination) and sources include wealthy investors, venture capital firms, public stock offerings, private placements, the Small Business Administration, state government agencies that help develop new business, trade credit, banks, finance companies, factors, and leasing companies. If the new enterprise is to be organized as a partnership, limited partners can be considered as well. Often, the potential investor, after reading the business plan, will call upon the entrepreneur to make a presentation of the plan in person. The entrepreneur may be fortunate enough to have several willing investors and then must make a choice.

Once funding for the new enterprise has been secured, the company can be started up. It is helpful to the entrepreneur to lay out all the steps necessary to start up the new company in advance of actually starting it up. Again, major problems should be anticipated, such as length of time to secure a corporate charter and regulatory approval from government agencies if needed. When will the members of the management team be available to begin work?

The entrepreneur must also think of his or her ultimate goals. If the new enterprise is very successful, what does he or she ultimately seek? They may choose to remain with the business, taking out a good return in salary and dividends. Stock may be sold to employees or other managers through stock option plans or a management buyout. The company may be merged with another company. The assets can be sold or the company may "go public" through a stock offering. Any of these positive alternatives may occur after many years of hard work.

The uncertainties of running one's own business are great. Some may achieve great rewards. Others may achieve moderate success. Still others fail. Some individuals will be happier working for someone else and leaving all the worries to the boss. Others seek the opportunities that are available to the entrepreneur. To be capable of surviving competition means that the entrepreneur must have capability in management, knowledge, and experience in accounting, purchasing, sales, advertising, and financing as well as knowing the technicalities of any particular business.

The art of handling money is important in small business management. In business, money is a working tool like any other commodity. The small business manager must keep business accounts separate from his personal use of money. Every business penny must be kept under strict control at all times. Access to cash should always be restricted to one person who is held accountable. Handling money used in a business is like handling money belonging to a friend — it carries a greater responsibility than personal spending.

The word "capital" is the business term used to distinguish between money that remains permanently in the business from other monies passing through the business. Capital serves a number of purposes in the business. It pays for the furniture, store fixtures, and possibly a building required for the business. Capital also pays for the expenses of starting the business, including the initial inventory of goods to be manufactured or sold. Capital here is used in a revolving fund. As money is received from sales, new goods can be purchased for future sales. Capital also is used to pay initial operating expenses until sales have risen to the level where operating expenses can be paid out of receipts. Capital can be used to carry accounts receivable, money that is tied up in accounts owed to the business by its customers.

In short, money is used to buy a stock of goods to be sold at a profit. When the goods are sold, the manager may take the profit from money received, but he must set aside the money he originally invested as capital to buy more goods if he is to continue in business. Managers of new businesses often overestimate the profits available after operating expenses are paid and underestimate the amount of money the business will keep tied up in working capital.

When proper accounting records are maintained, the manager is able to keep good control of financial affairs. He or she can see what part of the firm's capital is gainfully employed and where it is being wasted, tied up in unused equipment, in inventory that is not being sold, or in overdue customer accounts. The manager must use funds as efficiently as possible — idle funds or funds tied up in unproductive things will not benefit the enterprise.

The new business must have sufficient funds to get it properly started and carry it on until sufficient sales volume has been built up to fully carry the operating expenses. The amount of capital required will vary according to the conditions under which the business operates. In some cases, volume varies by season. In any case, as the business grows and expands it will require more working capital.

The small business manager must learn how to manage credit. When a business buys for cash and sells for cash, the transaction is simple. When a business buys with an intent to pay later or sells with a deferred payment, it is essential to understand the usage of credit. More failures of small businesses are traceable to noncompliance with generally accepted rules of credit than to any other factor.

When a loan is accepted, goods purchased on credit or equipment bought with payment deferred, the manager of a small business obligates the business to comply with the rules of credit, which the manager is expected to know. Before obligating the business, the manager must work out a plan for paying the business debt if incurred, and be reasonably certain that the necessary funds will be on hand to meet each and every payment when they come due. Credit is a sensitive matter. The least infraction of the terms of credit may result in a long-term handicap to the business. Excuses may be listened to and accepted but the future credit of the business can be damaged.

Credit ratings are often based on the three Cs of credit: capacity, character, and capital. Capacity is concerned with the buying record of the business — amounts, punctuality, and regularity of payments. Character pertains to the businessperson's personal reputation for integrity and fair dealing. Capital pertains to the financial worth of the business. Sometimes a fourth "C" — collateral — is used. Collateral consists of assets that are pledged to secure a loan.

A new enterprise may not have a complete credit record. The new business will be able to build up its capacity for buying and paying for what it buys only if some supplier is willing to give the business goods on credit, based on the reputation of the manager or endorsement by a third party. As the new enterprise continues to buy and meet its obligations with regularity, the credit record is built up and more credit will be advanced.

Sometimes a supplier may offer more credit than expected. The manager of the new enterprise may feel flattered and succumb to the temptation to buy more merchandise than was originally planned. This may lead to overstocking of some items and to encumbering the business with unnecessary debt.

Other times goods can be purchased on consignment. Under this arrangement, the business can return unsold items to the supplier. The supplier retains title to goods on consignment until they are sold. The supplier can repossess such goods at any time. Usually a firm needs a good credit record to be able to purchase goods on consignment.

Credit standing is important to every small business. Promptness in meeting financial obligations is essential to building a good credit rating. Salespersons selling to a new firm will often ask the manager to supply credit references — the names of three suppliers who have regularly supplied the firm on open account. Open account means goods are delivered with payment due at a later date. The salesperson may also ask for the statement of the firm's financial condition. The credit manager of the supplier will follow up by asking the references to answer three questions:

1. How long has the customer been sold on open account?
2. What is the highest amount of credit recently given?
3. Does the customer pay promptly and regularly?

Based on replies to these questions and a review of the financial statement, the supplier's credit manager will make a decision on whether or not to grant credit to the firm.

Trade associations provide credit bureaus in various industries with useful information. Dun and Bradstreet and several other firms investigate credit on behalf of suppliers. Dun and Bradstreet, based on its investigations, assigns credit ratings to businesses. Special reports are sometimes made available to supplement Dun and Bradstreet's published directory listing the credit ratings of thousands of firms. Many firms are proud to achieve a good "D&B" credit rating.

The manager of a new enterprise must consider whether the firm should grant credit to its customers in exchange for its goods or services. In this case, the firm becomes a creditor. The manager must now demand the same safeguard from customers that it has been required to supply as a debtor. A customer may come into a store to make a purchase. He wants to "charge it." The manager must be certain that the promise of the customer to pay in the future is sufficiently good that the manager is willing to allow the customer to take something of value from the business. Today, the use of national credit cards makes this decision easier for the manager although a fee (usually a percentage of the value of the sale) must be paid to the credit card company for this service.

Alternatively, the firm could give its own credit. Then the firm has the responsibility of following up with a bill and collection procedures if the bill is not paid. The hazard of loss is always present in any credit transaction. Although it is the customer's obligation to pay for what he buys, the customer may be careless or forgetful or unwilling to pay. Promptness in submitting bills and reminders is often helpful in pursuing collection of the amount due. Use of legal action or a collection agency should only be resorted to if all other efforts at collection fail. Business people should realize that the buying public may not understand the importance of prompt payment of bills.

In addition to the risks of nonpayment, the extension of credit entails costs to the enterprise. The cost of credit includes the cost of capital tied up in the credit, the cost of bookkeeping for the credit transaction, the cost of stationery and postage, and the cost of collection. All of these costs make credit transactions more expensive to the supplier than sales for cash. For this reason, suppliers often give discounts for cash payment at the time of sale or within 10 days. When a customer does not pay on time, the supplier is, in effect, taking on the function of a bank lending money to the customer.

Credit may be of great value to a business. Much of this value may be frittered away if the rules of credit are not followed. A good way to lose a customer is to allow him to owe you money that is past due. Allowing an account to a supplier to become past due is also a good way to lose a good supplier.

Knowledge of purchasing and the ability to buy wisely are very important in the small business. Purchasing management is a skill that is usually acquired through careful study and experience. The manager of a small business must learn how to buy both commodities and services — how to arrive at the right price, from whom it is best to buy, and at what terms — are all key conditions in purchasing. More importantly, the manager must carefully figure out how and when he or she is going to sell that which has been purchased before he or she purchases it. Poor judgment or carelessness in purchasing will penalize the small business. Good judgment in purchasing is a great asset to any business.

Some knowledge of purchasing may be gained through observation and asking a lot of questions as well as seeking competent advice, particularly on "big ticket" or unusual items. A study of available market prices, procuring and comparing competitive bids, and keeping an eye open for sales or liquidations are also helpful. The clever manager is alert to the opportunity of making an added profit through a good purchase. In most cases, competition among suppliers results in the establishment of fair prices. In addition to the price, the purchaser must look at the terms offered. Discount for quantities, free transportation, and return privileges are all important considerations.

The business manager buys to sell quickly at a profit. Therefore, before making a purchase of a good to be resold, the manager must ask some questions:

- Is the quality acceptable?
- How fast can the item be sold?
- What margin of profit can be made on these items?

Suppliers will often give discounts or special services for volume purchases. While such inducements for large quantity buying may be attractive, the manager may be better off in taking a smaller quantity at a higher price if the purchaser cannot see the way to selling the larger quantity of goods in a reasonable length of time. Profit on sales may be wiped out by having to carry inventory for a long period of time. In the ideal situation, the purchaser will always have the goods sold before they are purchased.

Long-term buying contracts and buying for delivery far into the future may be risky. Styles may change, new models may offer better features, and consumers' buying habits or general business conditions may change over time. Some business people may be good at speculating over the long run. Unless the entire business is based on such speculation and the past track record is excellent, the temptation to speculate for a potential windfall should generally be resisted by the purchasing manager.

The manager who is buying furniture and office equipment for a new business must buy wisely. How necessary is each item to the business? Will the purchase contribute to profit? Again, the manager does not purchase unless he or she is convinced that sales at a profit are likely.

All businesses, whether large or small, new or old, have selling as the sustaining and motivating element. Even professional people, such as doctors or lawyers, must sell their services directly or indirectly if they are to carry out their practice successfully.

Some managers of small businesses profess to know little about selling. Many businesses operate without people who are called salespersons. Nevertheless, these businesses are all making sales. Someone must be selling the product or service offered in some fashion.

Every manager does not need to have specific training and experience in sales, however, all managers must realize the selling and applying good sales practices to every detail of the operation of the business. Selling is not the exclusive function of the sales clerk in a store or the salesperson calling upon a customer. Everyone connected with every business who can do anything to help make customers buy is involved in sales. Selling begins with setting up the business and purchasing or making available the goods or services that customers need or want. Selling includes giving customers the opportunity to buy, letting them know what is available, and making it interesting or even fun for them to buy. The purpose of the business is to find customers and make use of whatever is offered for sale. Good selling often begins by studying and analyzing the needs of the customers. The business manager will not be successful in sales management in the long-run if the quality of goods offered is questionable, prices are out of line, or there is laxness in the sales effort.

Competition generally forces sales managers to exert themselves to seek sales. The principles of salesmanship apply to employees as well as to the manager. The values of personality, neatness, courtesy, and orderliness in business help in salesmanship. Having a product that will fill a need is essential in salesmanship.

A particularly important form of communication in business is advertising. Advertising is anything and everything the firm may do to let prospective customers know the name and address of the business and what it offers for sale. Everything that helps build up the business is good advertising and good salesmanship. Whatever is done to hurt the business is bad advertising and bad salesmanship. Everything the customer sees, hears, or knows about the business is advertising and salesmanship, whether good or bad.

The purpose of advertising is to sell, to bring in new customers, and to hold onto and bring back old customers. Some managers, in their efforts to attract new customers, forget about taking care of current customers. Retaining existing customers whose patronage has been clearly earned may be more valuable than gaining new customers. Advertising is important in business today as is evidenced by the billions of dollars spent on it each year to aid the selling process.

Every manager cannot be an expert on all forms of advertising. Nevertheless, the business manager must be able to let customers know who they are, where they are located, and what is for sale. The manager of a small business must plan his or her own advertising as they are unlikely to be able to afford the use of an advertising agency.

Observations and study of what is being done by others in advertising is useful to the manager of the small business. Study of what has been successful for others is likely to be helpful. It is good business practice to observe and learn everything possible that is helping other businesses and adopting what works to one's own business.

Good advertising includes the signs and appearance of the business premises, the attractiveness, cleanliness and order of the interior, the freshness and quality of merchandise offered, the appearance of employees, and the promptness and reliability of service.

Advertising of a new business may be mainly by word of mouth where one customer tells another. It may be by a printed business card, a painted sign, or a small ad in the local paper. These may appear to be simple things but every detail is worthy of careful study and planning. Advertising is continually essential to business. Planning and use of advertising and salesmanship are important for business success and growth.

Managing a new enterprise or a small business often will require leading and directing others. Perhaps the foremost qualification for being a good boss in a small business is being deserving of the respect of employees. A good boss primarily is one who has complete mastery over all elements of the enterprise and has the respect of employees because they realize that the boss knows the business and can intelligently direct the employees. Good personal character, fair and square dealing, courtesy, economy, and efficiency in business are other traits of a good boss.

People enjoy doing interesting things, but an employee's work in a small business may be monotonous and repetitive. Employees may not have the benefit of incentives the boss has in pride of accomplishment and profit from the enterprise. It is up to the boss to lead by example and create a business atmosphere conducive to accomplishing the goals of the enterprise. The good manager in a small business leads and inspires employees by his or her example and by instilling a spirit of teamwork and cooperation.

Small businesses need organization just as large enterprises do. Our definition of organization is "to bring into systematic relation as parts of a whole." Managers use the words "organize" and "organization" in a variety of ways, always associated with the bringing together in a systematic relationship the various elements and functions of business, as follows:

1. In starting a business, an entrepreneur organizes it by bringing together his or her ideas with ways and means of putting them into operation, in preparation for opening the business.

2. If other people are to be involved in the enterprise, the entrepreneur brings them together as the nucleus of his or her business organization.

3. The business relationship, the duties, responsibilities, and authority that each person is to exercise, along with the detailed work routine that each is to perform, is laid out by organizing the business operation.

4. The manager also organizes the work he or she is to do personally and schedules his or her time.

5. The manager may also reorganize from time to time elements of the business based on experience as a going concern or based on plans for growth into new lines of business.

Some managers of small businesses are gifted with the ability to organize. They have well ordered minds with the facility of readily fitting into a smooth working plan the elements of their business.

The manager needs the assistance of employees who have been properly instructed and trained. The employees need to be prepared with all the necessary materials, supplies, or tools needed to carry out the functioning of the business.

The manager of a small business, inundated with a multitude of details, often is reluctant to take the time to properly train employees. The manager may trust to verbal instructions that are perhaps given hurriedly and incompletely. In such a case, much of the manager's time may be taken up correcting mistakes or repeatedly explaining what needs to be done. The efficient manager gets this job of training and supervising of employees properly organized and reduced to a systematic procedure, thus saving time and improving the efficiency of the organization.

Employees generally appreciate having the opportunity to work where all details of business operation are governed by systematic procedures and routines. Such organization gives promise of job security and advancement and is an incentive for the best effort from the employees. When new employees are started off with an explanation of the business and a clear understanding of their duties, the chances are more favorable that these employees will prove to be satisfactory and reliable.

Organization permits the manager of a small business to run the business. Without such organization, the business will run the manager. Picking the right person for the job is important but perhaps is not so difficult when the work routine and training procedures have been properly set up by the manager. A written job description is helpful and saves misunderstandings as to lines of authority.

The manager of a small business must organize the functions to be carried out. Additionally, a qualified person must be selected and deputized to assume responsibility for a particular department or area. The manager must then supervise the person in charge of this area. No business other than the very smallest can succeed without division of work, delegation of authority, and appropriate supervision.

A small business may be well organized, treat employees well, have a good product, and good marketing. All of these are essential elements but a business requires more. The making of a profit is the incentive that keeps businesses going. Profit does not come by happenstance or luck. Successful managers know that profit must be planned for and earned by performing the right actions at the right time.

Errors are often made by novices in small business by figuring profit as the difference between initial cost and selling price without deducting the operating expenses and overhead involved. Gross profit is never the net profit. The net profit can only be approximated until all true expenses for any given period of time are deducted from the gross profit for such period.

Managers try to estimate the amount of business they expect to do within a certain period of time and establish their operating expenses and overhead (rent, payroll, etc.). They try to keep expenses to a minimum to ensure at least breaking even if sales do not come up to expectations. The objective is not only to achieve their sales estimates but to beat that figure and derive more profit.

"Never pass up an opportunity to make a profit" is a common saying in business and generally good advice, but not always. Eager to build a large sales volume, a manager may reach out for new business, knowing that the profit will be small, but under the delusion that the larger enterprise must somehow make more money. Unless the results of the expansion are figured carefully, the manager may find that the new business was costly, wearing out the firm's equipment and employees and earning less than a smaller volume of business.

For the manager to know how profitable a business is, accounting records must be kept. Maintenance of accounting records is definitely the responsibility of the manager of a small business. In many instances, such records must be kept by requirement of law or for tax purposes. The manager must know the facts pertaining to the business in order to operate it successfully.

A manager may hire staff to do the bookkeeping and accounting for the firm. Nevertheless, it is the responsibility of the manager to direct the bookkeeper or accountant — to determine what records should be kept, how they are to be kept, and how to use the information generated to the firm's best advantage.

The correct and proper system of accounting for a small business is the simplest system that will give the proprietor complete and accurate information whenever it is needed.

The time to start making written records of a new business is when the first money transaction is made for starting the business. A record of the financial facts at the beginning is important to any business. Continuing with each day's record thereafter is equally important. This daily "chore" is not generally relished by the manager of the new business. Procrastination or carelessness in keeping these records may result in running the business at a loss.

The first and most important record to be kept is the cash account. This account is maintained to keep the manager informed as to all monies paid out and received — also to or from whom and for what. There are other major accounts. The *Capital Account* records the money put into the business by the owners. *Notes Payable* is an account to keep a record of loans contracted when due or when paid. *Organizational Expenses* is an account set up to record money spent when a business is started — this is not a normal expense of operation. *Furniture, Fixtures and Equipment* is an account to keep a record of the funds invested for business use that will have monetary value beyond a year. *Operating Expenses* is a record of the cost of doing business, including such things as rent, light, heat, telephone, and payroll. *Purchases* is an account of stock of merchandise or material to be sold. *Accounts Payable* is a record of what is owed to suppliers. *Sales Account* is a daily record of sales to customers. *Accounts Receivable* shows what customers owe the business. *Inventory* is a record of the monetary value of the salable stock on hand. *Profit and Loss* is the account that shows whether or not the business has been profitable over a certain period of time.

Whatever system is adopted, the main principle is that some record be made of each transaction at the time it takes place. The manager should not trust his or her memory or that of an employee. Whenever possible, bills should be paid by check to keep a record of the expenditure. A petty cash fund may be useful for minor purchases and receipts here should be retained.

There are a good many things on the mind of the manager of a small business. Keeping up the accounting records should be high in priority. This will enable the manager to know quickly if inventory is growing too large, if accounts receivable need a more vigorous collection effort, when the bank loan must be paid, etc. Analysis of the accounting records of the firm on a monthly basis will help the manager know what areas of the business need priority attention so that results will improve in the future.

Managing a small business can be a great challenge to an individual or to a team of compatible managers. The manager of a small business must be adaptable to the many challenges. He or she must often perform many tasks that may not be enjoyed to get the job done (such as sweeping the floor at the close of business) and to ensure the smooth functioning of the business. To survive the vicissitude of competition in an uncertain economy means that the manager of the small business must have knowledge and experience in many areas, ranging from accounting to production to marketing to financing to managing others, and must master the special techniques and knowledge base of a particular industry. A career in small business or in the creation of a new enterprise can be very satisfying to those who are happy in this environment of hard work and multifaceted challenges, and for those who relish responsibility and leadership.

18

Managerial Economics

While the hard-headed CEO deals with practical problems, the economist is given to theory, abstraction, and speculation. Yet the keen manager will pay close attention to the theories of economics, for therein may lie the path to greater profits. The story is told of the tailor who gave up his $20,000 a year job and opened his own tailor shop with an investment of $100,000. At the end of the year his accountant reported that the bottom line of the financial report showed a gain of $25,000. "I made a $25,000 profit," he crowed, "25 percent on my investment!"

But his son had just taken a course in economics. "No, Dad," he said, "your profit is only $5,000, or five percent on your investment. In the financial report, you didn't charge your salary to the business. You could have earned $20,000 anyhow for working as a tailor, or you could have hired a tailor to do the tailoring work. Your real profit is the return over all your costs, including the cost of labor, whether you choose to count your own labor or not."

This story illustrates one difference between the way an accountant figures costs and profit and the way an economist does the same thing. If a manager wants to make a decision to invest, it is important to know whether the return on the investment is five percent or 25 percent. In this case, there is a question about what costs to include. The economist has a different view of costs than the businessperson or the accountant. Managerial economists have other insights as well. They engage in forecasting rather than merely reporting. For future-oriented decisions, the foresight of the economist may be more important than the ledger of the accountant.

Managerial economics provides a framework for analyzing management decisions. While broad economic principles deal with universal conditions, managerial economics is concerned with the efficient use of specific resources for decision making in a particular situation. The method it uses is to examine incremental changes in costs, revenues, output, and other relevant quantities — a process known as marginal analysis — to find optimal solutions for management problems. For example, the incremental method focuses on questions such as what happens to profit as output is increased in successive, microscopic units.

General economics is concerned with the principles affecting the efficient use of resources. Managerial economics uses these broad principles in individual cases in which a manager must decide between the use of limited resources in one situation as compared with alternative possibilities. Managers are accustomed to analyzing in accounting terms. Accounting is standardized, exact, and rooted in historical records. Managerial economics, in contrast, is conceptual, speculative, and approximate. We do not know precisely how to measure income and costs which have not yet occurred. However, decisions concerning the future cannot be precise; speculation is a necessary ingredient of forecasting.

Both accounting and managerial economics accept the primacy of profit in business operations, and both approaches do measure profit as a residual element, subtracting costs from income. The differences between them lie in the measurement of costs, the way depreciation is handled, and the valuation of assets. These differences are crucial to the management decisions that will greatly affect profit in the future.

Businesspersons often use the reports of accountants to support decisions. However, exclusive dependence on such reports may be misleading. The accountant's report is historically-oriented. It tells what has happened. A business decision, however, is future-oriented. Past history may or may not be relevant.

The past may reflect on the future, but is not a certain guide. An economist is accustomed to predictions and projections, much needed for future-oriented decision making. His broader interests take the entire environment into consideration, including current trends in costs and prices, and expectations for the future.

Managerial economics is often quantitative. It deals with the application of statistics and mathematical techniques to management problems, as in inventory control or investment decisions. Mathematics, of course, does not necessarily yield exact results; statistical analysis is based on probabilities rather than certainties. However, the mathematical formulae are derived from economic concepts. These concepts explain the underlying behavior of the rational businessman attempting to maximize profit. The concepts are basic to the rational functioning of the decision maker since they focus, more than the principles of accounting, on future quantities, such as the expected value of inventory and prospective investment returns.

Business managers assume that the ultimate purpose of the firm is to earn the maximum profit possible. Some economists have suggested that other factors are at work in the motivation of the executives who control the modern business corporation, such as security, hopes for renown and respect, salaries and bonuses, maintaining market share, or the avoidance of competition and government regulation. Some writers argue that firms accept satisfactory profits, and do not necessarily seek maximum profits. We call this "satisficing," rather than maximizing behavior. However, it is generally accepted that the single, most important motivating force in business firms is profit. Profit maximizing may not be an absolutely certain rule for all management behavior, but it is a reasonable assumption in analyzing the way most managers act. For this reason, managerial economics is based on profit maximizing behavior, despite questions asked by some theoretical economists.

Economists have developed a technique for explaining how a firm combines the various factors of production, continuously adjusting the prices, costs, revenues, and the quantities that can be produced in the quest for maximum profits. The technique involves the use of models, which are simplified cases, omitting much of the detail of the real world situation. An example of a model is a map which ignores hills, small turns and other topographical features, but which is useful in getting from one place to another, despite the omissions.

Basic to the economic model of the firm is the idea that certain costs and revenues vary in some regular, systematic, orderly way as output rises slowly in small steps. With this assumption, we can draw diagrams or use mathematical formulae to examine the changes in these costs and revenues as output rises incrementally, and determine at what point profit (the difference between costs and revenues) is maximized. The process is called marginal analysis. We generally assume in typical models that in order to sell a greater quantity of a given commodity, the prices must drop. If a businessman wants to move his inventory, he or she cuts prices in a special sale. This principle can be illustrated with a diagram showing prices, also known as average revenues, as a curve sloping down as output goes up.

Costs, too, can be illustrated with a curve on a diagram which compares costs and output. We refer to these cost curves as U-shaped because in many industries, they go down initially and then go up. Average costs (the cost per unit produced) drop at first because the firm enjoys the benefits of mass production. At some point, perhaps at extremely high output in the typical assembly line plant, costs rise because of bottlenecks, shortages of labor, materials, space, power, or managerial expertise.

For example, aluminum can be produced cheaply only in a gigantic plant. Vast amounts of electricity are needed to process the bauxite from which aluminum is produced. With a great hydroelectric plant nearby, the average cost of production drops as output rises. However, when the capacity of the hydroelectric plant is reached, the benefits of large scale production are exhausted. Perhaps a less efficient fossil fuel electric generating plant must be added to the manufacturing complex if a higher output of aluminum is to be reached. A higher electric cost means that additional output can be achieved only at a higher cost of production per pound of aluminum. The average cost of aluminum was lowered as output increased till an optimal point was reached, and then costs started up. That is why we say that cost curves are U-shaped.

Given these factors, which vary in a regular fashion with output, it is possible to determine at what output the difference between revenue and costs (i.e., profit) is greatest. We merely develop mathematical formulae that can deal with functions which vary regularly, or show the changes on a diagram.

The trick is to know what to include in revenue and costs, and how to measure them in a way that reflects on future profits. We learn that the maximum profit occurs, as we expand output by infinitesimal units, when the added costs rise to equal the added revenue. With one more tiny unit of output, the added cost will exceed the added revenue. Economists call this the point where marginal cost equals marginal revenue. (NOTE: Marginal means the little extra or additional amount.) The reason that we discuss revenue and costs instead of income and expenses is that the latter terms have specific meaning in accounting terminology. The meaning of revenue and costs are different from income and expense mainly in the treatment of depreciation and inflation. But we will consider these factors later.

Managers are seldom aware of the economic analysis which underlies the market decisions they make. Yet the practical decisions which increase profit or create losses are based on the application of this theory, whether the manager knows it or not. An example is the manager of a firm producing ties. He wants to expand sales by cutting his prices. This involves raising output, but in this hypothetical case he cannot hire more workers in the restricted space of his small loft. Moreover, he cannot rent more space at the same cost per square foot as at present. So he decides to ask the employees to work overtime, but that makes it more expensive to produce each additional tie. He then decides not to increase output and to forego the increased sales since they would not raise his profit.

An economist would have told him that he faced a situation in which the extra (marginal) output pushed the marginal cost over the marginal revenue. The manager may not have known the theory, but he did know that his profit began to drop when he had to increase variable costs (pay overtime to labor) as the only way to push output past the optimal point. A number of other economic concepts differentiate the measurement of profit by economists from that of accountants.

One economic concept of importance to management is opportunity cost, sometimes known as the alternative cost. This is the cost of anything measured, not in the historical record of the actual expense, but in terms of the value of the benefit that is sacrificed by choosing one alternative over the next best one, i.e., the value of the good you give up in order to enjoy another. In the story of the tailor, the alternative cost ignored was the sacrificed opportunity to earn a salary of $20,000 by working for wages. The accountant recognizes only those costs which are recorded in the books of the firm. Alternative possibilities, or opportunity costs, are not recorded. However, a manager can make better decisions by recognizing all costs, even those which are not written down in the ledgers.

Managers consider profitability in decision making, but the measurement of profit presents some difficulties. To an accountant, profit is the difference between income and expenses. However, accounting conventions and tax considerations affect the particular figure shown on the bottom line. The particular number the accountant shows on the bottom line is not sacred, even with standardized accounting conventions. Profit can be made to look larger or smaller, depending on the goals of the businessman. Accelerated depreciation may reduce the taxable profit without making the firm less desirable to the owner. In fact, with the reduced, recorded, taxable profit in this case, the firm is more valuable to the owner. The economist makes judgments about the profitability of a firm on a slightly different basis than the accountant. In many ways, this judgment provides a more rational basis for the manager to make business decisions about the future.

For example, accountants use historical costs in preparing a balance sheet. This approach may be satisfactory in stable times but is misleading during severe inflation. Managerial economics might suggest the use of replacement costs in weighing the value of the assets of a firm. The economist might suggest to the businessman that the value of an asset is better measured by the disposal cost of that asset, or its value in an alternative use. To the typical, practical manager, the replacement cost probably makes most sense. Certainly, replacement cost is more meaningful during high inflation, or when the manager is considering selling the firm. In this case, the accounting report would probably be ignored by the rational businessman, or at least supplemented with managerial economic analysis.

Another example of the approach of the managerial economist is in the valuation of windfalls. Unanticipated capital gains and losses, known as windfalls, are not recorded by accountants until actually turned into cash. The value of a new patent held by a firm does not show up as an asset on the corporate books unless sold. More likely, the value of a patent will be reflected in standard financial reports by increased profits for years to come. An economist, however, would not wait for the value of the asset to show up in future financial reports, but would acknowledge the windfall at once. The manager who evaluates a company, perhaps for acquisition, would be wise to consider the value of the unrecorded asset.

Depreciation is another area in which economic ideas may be better than accounting conventions in reaching decisions about investment. Depreciation is historically rooted. In many cases, however, the historical costs are irrelevant. An economic approach would consider opportunity or replacement costs in a more realistic evaluation of depreciation. The wise manager would supplement accounting reports with an economic analysis of the business before making important decisions affecting the future.

Perhaps the central contribution of the economic understanding that underlies managerial economics is the incremental approach. Economists argue that profit is maximized at an output where marginal cost rises to be equal to marginal revenue. The idea is that as the output of a firm rises, the cost of one tiny, additional unit of goods produced will eventually rise as bottlenecks are encountered, while the extra revenue from the sale of that additional tiny unit will drop as sales resistance is encountered. As long as the extra revenue is more than the extra cost, it pays to increase the scale of output in very small increments. Once the two quantities are equal, the manager stops increasing output. At a higher level of output, however small the increase may be, the extra cost would exceed the extra revenue. The major benefit of the use of incremental change is that it permits quantitative methods of analysis.

A relatively simple quantitative model, based on economic analysis, is breakeven analysis. The question it answers is how high output must rise before losses turn into profits. With very limited output, costs per unit are very high because of the impact of fixed costs. There are costs which exist without regard to the level of output, such as the cost of building the plant in the first place. As sales rise, revenue rises. At some point, revenue will be sufficient to cover all costs. This is the breakeven point.

The breakeven analysis can be found by the use of mathematical formulae or diagramatically with a breakeven chart. In a breakeven chart, dollars are plotted on the vertical axis and the number of units produced on the horizontal axis. The diagonal line shows total costs (fixed plus variable) rising as output increases. Revenues are assumed to be fixed per unit sold, i.e., prices do not change in this model. Total revenue rises at a 45 degree angle, starting from zero revenue for zero units, but average revenue (the price) is shown as a horizontal line.

The analysis is weak for a number of reasons. It is a static analysis assuming that costs and revenues vary in a direct and predictable way. A more realistic assumption is that costs vary in a more complex pattern, perhaps as represented by a curve rather than a straight line. Moreover, average revenue may decline given a fixed demand in a competitive society. However, in many cases, the breakeven analysis is reasonably accurate for small changes in output, and is helpful in decisions about plant capacity and the introduction of new products.

A more sophisticated analysis is known as linear programming. Linear programming permits a manager to determine the best mix of a number of limited resources to maximize profit or to minimize costs. By linear, we mean examples in which the relationships between the factors involved are proportional; that is, they vary directly, in equal or correlated amounts.

Managers require a still broader analysis of the environment for a true understanding. Lest we exaggerate the importance of managerial economics, we should remember that the future of a business firm can be affected by the general condition of the nation, government actions, the policy of foreign nations, union activities, competition, new technology, public perceptions, political problems, environmental concerns, unexpected disasters, drought and other natural phenomena, and a host of uncertainties impossible to assess. Thus, managerial economics offers an improved view, not a panacea.

19

Managing the Environment

Every manager must carry out his or her organization's activities in an environment that is external to the organization. There are a number of environmental factors that must be considered by every manager. These environmental factors can be divided into six key areas:

1. governmental, political, and legal factors
2. economic factors
3. geographic and demographic factors
4. social and cultural factors
5. technological factors
6. competition

As these environmental factors change, the demand for the products and services provided by the organization will change. Hence, managers must reshape their organizations to take changes in environmental factors into account if their organizations are to survive in the long-run. This chapter will look at each of the six key environmental areas in detail.

Governmental, political, and legal factors affect all organizations wherever in the world they are located. In Canada and the United States, federal, state and provincial, and local governments are major environmental factors for every organization. Some firms may rely on government contracts for all or most of their business. Government agencies may be major suppliers or customers to many organizations. Hospitals, universities, agricultural organizations, and others may rely on governmental subsidies for much of their revenues. Government regulations and taxation affect virtually every organization. Changes in the legal system, such as changes in antitrust laws, can affect organizations. Even the manner in which government allows organizations to communicate their needs and fears through lobbying and access to executive functions of government may be important to organizations.

As business becomes more multinational, managers of organizations must become more cognizant of activities of foreign governments, of other international organizations (such as the Organization of Petroleum Exporting Countries and the European Common Market), and of interrelationships among sovereign nations.

Organizations may need to raise capital on a worldwide basis in today's multinational economy in which changes in currency values and trade balances may cause firms to switch where they raise their capital from one nation to another. Organizations that operate in many areas of the world may wish to divide some of their functions based on the economic principle of comparative advantage, if governments permit it. For example, a firm making television sets may wish to take advantage of the relatively low cost of labor in such countries as South Korea or Taiwan to assemble components if high tariffs and quotas are not imposed by nations, such as the United States and Canada, on television sets. The television set maker may, at the same time, prefer to have the marketing part of its organization located in a country with many potential purchasers of the television sets, unless governments require otherwise. Changes in the labor market can be skewed by actions of governments to protect local employers or local industries. Thus, actions of one or more governments may complicate decisions that are normally made on economic factors as government actions may distort the functioning of markets for commodities, raw materials, manufactured goods, labor, and flows of capital.

Political factors may even be more important than economic factors to some organizations. For example, a pharmaceutical firm that has developed a new wonder drug and wishes to sell it worldwide might be more concerned with the patent laws of every country in the world than with the current or forecasted level of economic activity for the world.

Government actions may favor some industries and cripple or destroy others. Sometimes actions of governments can be inconsistent. For example, the U.S. Government Department of Agriculture encourages the growing of tobacco by a system of price supports. At the same time, the Surgeon General of the United States encourages people to stop smoking and warning labels are placed on all cigarette packages as a result of federal legislation. Some state governments try to discourage smoking by imposing high excise taxes on cigarettes, while others try to encourage sales of locally grown tobacco with low excise taxes on cigarettes and promotion of their tobacco. Local governments may also get involved by regulating smoking in restaurants, movie theaters, etc.

Sometimes an industry may be politically unpopular and its activities hampered as a result. For example, no one likes to have the rent on their apartment raised. Therefore, rent control and rent stabilization laws are often popular with politicians and voters even though the long-term effect of such laws tends to be to discourage construction of rental housing with consequent housing shortages and pressures to raise rents and housing prices higher than would occur if there was no rent control or rent stabilization.

Some projects may make economic sense but may be politically impossible. For example, a number of nuclear power projects have been abandoned in North America because of fears for safety, with the result that industry dependence on low cost power locates or relocates to areas of the world which do not have such strong public fears against nuclear power or whose governments are less responsive to such fears.

Government regulations can encourage or discourage an industry or favor some firms at the expense of others. For example, a new secretarial school might find it difficult to meet regulations for access to handicapped persons that may require it to install an elevator at high cost and still charge a low enough tuition to compete with better known, established schools that are likely to have more students per class. Access to the handicapped may be a worthy government policy but it also may discourage new entrants to a particular industry through high cost of compliance. Firms that wish to discourage competition could favor the imposition of regulations to reduce the number of entrants to their industry. Barbers, for example, may promote licensing rules that prevent beauty parlor operators from becoming unisex haircutters by requiring the beauty parlor operators to take a separate apprenticeship and exam for men's haircuts.

An industry or company can even use the government to clobber competition. For example, soft drink manufacturers might promote the sales of their products by sponsoring legislation or regulations to prevent the sale of beer at supermarkets, where it may be more convenient to shoppers than package stores.

Automobile companies may pressure their governments to limit imports of foreign produced automobiles to benefit their companies. For example, the French automobile manufacturers successfully pressured the French government to limit the import of Japanese automobiles through imposition of a quota. Japanese manufacturers of baseball bats successfully limited the import of American baseball bats for many years through rigorous customs regulations requiring lengthy and complicated procedures for safety testing of each lot of bats imported. American baseball bat manufacturers then petitioned the U.S. government to protest these procedures to the Japanese government so as to open the Japanese market to American baseball bats.

Sometimes governments prevent some products from being sold at all. Sale of liquor is prohibited in many Moslem countries. Marijuana and narcotic drugs cannot be sold in many countries. Fur coats made from rare animal species cannot be imported to the United States.

Some countries require citizenship before certain activities can be conducted. For example, ownership of newspapers in Canada and television stations in the United States are generally restricted to their respective citizens. In Mexico, land can only be owned by Mexican citizens.

Sometimes government maintains a monopoly for sale of certain products or services to itself. Sale of salt, tobacco, liquor, and telephone service are government monopolies in a number of countries. The United States prohibits competition with its postal service for certain types of mail. The Canadian government has reserved airline routes for its government-owned airline. Radio and television broadcasting are government monopolies in a number of countries.

The legal system may vary greatly among countries. The North American company doing business in some Moslem countries may have to learn about Sharia — religious law that regulates secular activities in some Moslem countries. After the chemical accident at Bhopal in India, Union Carbide had to decide whether it preferred to face litigation in India — where monetary damages for a loss of life tend to be low — or in the United States — where damages tend to be high but where Union Carbide would be viewed as a local company rather than as one seen as controlled by "foreigners." In Japan there are few lawyers and little litigation, while the opposite is true in the United States. Some companies may benefit through legal systems that have many levels of appeal and long periods of time before damages have to be paid. In such legal systems, the delays of going to trial may enable companies to negotiate better settlements than in others in which court action is swift. Organizations might wish to avoid doing business in nations where the courts are corrupt or biased against foreign companies.

The legal system, government laws, regulations, and activities, and politics are important to all organizations. Sometimes the system can be used to benefit the organization. Other times, governmental or political activity may be a major threat to the organization.

Economic factors are also of major importance in managing an organization. Inflation, for example, may be a significant factor in what consumers buy and what manufacturers decide to produce. If consumers expect rapid inflation, they may wish to spend their money as quickly as they earn it. In countries with hyperinflation, no one wants to hold cash. More moderate levels of inflation can permit some savings for future expenditures. Stable prices (no inflation) may encourage even higher levels of savings and investment.

Government monetary policies may affect investment decisions of organizations. If the government's central bank follows a policy of "tight" money (higher interest rates, restrictions on credit), then firms could find it economically disadvantageous to borrow to build a new plant or expand a product line. Higher interest rates also cause the price of common stock to decline, thus making it even more unlikely that firms will expand. Conversely, "easier" money (lower interest rates, fewer restrictions on credit) will encourage firms to expand through sale of common stock at higher prices or through borrowing at lower cost.

The business cycle affects every organization. Some firms may benefit in a recession. Others may do better when the economy is expanding. Managers or organizations must carefully study economic trends. Economic forecasting can help the manager make better decisions for his or her organization.

The internationalization of capital markets and the greater interdependency of economies makes forecasting more difficult and economic cycles more complicated. Economic fluctuation may bring great opportunities or threats to an organization. Economic factors will always be of great importance to organizations and their strategies of management.

Geographic and demographic factors are also of great importance to organizations. Any child knows that you do not sell refrigerators to Eskimos living in igloos. Climate affects the opportunities that are available to organizations. Air conditioning and central heating have moderated the effects of climate somewhat, although the cost of fuel to take advantage of heating or air conditioning is a limitation. One factory in the Philippines found that production was limited because workers could not work very fast in the hot and humid climate. Air conditioning the factory was prohibitive in cost. An innovative manager overcame these limitations by shifting operation of the factory to the night time when temperatures were lower and there was less humidity because of evening breezes.

Geographic location is an important factor to many organizations. Being located in or near a large city has advantages to many industrial organizations — skilled and trained workers are more available, materials and parts can be more easily purchased, more sales can be made to other companies in the area (lower transportation costs), and managers and other workers prefer being near the cultural, intellectual, and recreational advantages of large agglomerations of people, resources, and institutions. As population has shifted to the suburbs, industry has followed.

Shifts in population are important. Population in the United States has shifted toward the sunbelt states of the south and west. Equally important, both the United States and Canada have become more suburban. Despite often heralded (in city media) back-to-cities movements, people continue to move out of the cities to suburban locations in both the United States and Canada. Changes in location from cities and rural areas to suburbs and from the frostbelt to the sunbelt are important to managers in deciding where to locate plants, distribution facilities, and retail outlets, and even in determining what to produce. Bergdorf-Goodman is a very successful upscale store in Manhattan. Its branch in suburban White Plains, New York did not meet the needs of suburban women as well. The store was replaced by a Neiman-Marcus branch, which has been very successful in this suburban location.

Other demographic changes are important as well. The United States, for example, is moving toward an older population — the decline of the birth rate, focus on better nutrition and health care, and prevention of illness have led to longer lives. The aging population means changes in products needed — fewer diapers and more nursing homes, for example. An older population also is likely to lead to more intergenerational conflict as fewer workers will have to support more retired persons on social security.

Changes in ethnic composition also carry influence for managers of organizations. With the relative growth in the numbers of Hispanics and other minorities as a percentage of the U.S. population, for example, or the growth in the numbers of Asians in Great Britain, managers will have to work harder to prevent discrimination (actual or perceived) in hiring and promoting managers and workers. As the population changes in ethnic composition there will be opportunities for firms producing, for example, ethnic foods desired by growing ethnic groups.

Social and cultural factors are also of great importance to the manager. One great change since World War II in North America has been the women's movement. More women have entered the work force than in any other period in history. They are more conscious of their rights for equal treatment as employees and citizens. The women's movement has helped improve the quality of the work force, as more promotions are made on merit and more human resources are better utilized for productive activities. However, the greater number of women in the work force has led to need for additional child care services and to the rapid growth of the fast food and convenience food industries. Dual income families have also had greater affluence. These families have more discretionary income to spend on housing, education, and other goods and services than a single income family. A contrary trend has been the increased level of divorce (almost half of all marriages in the United States end in divorce), more illegitimate births and, consequently, more households headed by a single parent — often with little or no income, thus necessitating more welfare payments and leading to continued high rates of crime despite fewer young people.

More North Americans have benefited from higher education since World War II. Since there seems to be some correlation between the level of education and affluence, this trend has helped increase affluence. More education and more affluence have led to changes in lifestyles, including more diversity and more leisure time and activities.

There seems to be a decline in the work ethic in North America. More employees seem to have a smaller commitment to their organizations, job turnover and absenteeism have increased, and there is more questioning of organizational procedures and values. Recent legislative changes regarding retirement ages and pensions (encouraging or permitting people to remain employed beyond the age of 65) may lead to diminished opportunities for younger employees to move ahead in their firms. This could lead to worker dissatisfaction in the future.

The development of the electronic media (especially television and the videocassette recorder) and increased rapid transportation by air at comparatively lower prices has brought about both major and more rapid changes in society. The discovery of a new fashion in Hong Kong, such as a new miniskirt, and its publicity on television all over the world, coupled with automated production, rapid distribution through air freight, and intensive marketing can lead to changes in style in just a few months. Styles, tastes, and preferences have become more internationalized through television and rapid transportation. More information is transmitted all over the world and so is information overload.

Managers today must be aware of social and cultural factors in the environment. These factors will be of increasing importance to organizations in the future.

Technological factors are also of major importance to the manager of today. We live in an era of increasingly rapid technological change. New fields, such as robotics, videocassette recorders, laser surgery, computer-aided design and manufacturing (CAD/CAM), strategic defense initiatives ("Star Wars"), electronic funds transfer banking via automated teller machines engineering, and a host of other developments create new opportunities and threats for managers and their organizations.

A single technological change can rapidly affect an organization's products or services, its supplies, customers, regulators, competitors, employees, etc. For example, the development of xerographic copying by Xerox Corporation rapidly changed the duplicating industry. Companies that made mimeograph machines and supplies, such as stencils, lost most of their market in just a few years. Industry rapidly converted to the newer, cleaner, and more convenient copying process. Today, the xerographic copier is available in compact form with few technical problems even to the small office at a cost of less than a thousand dollars. Large machines that will generate hundreds of copies in a very short period of time using varieties of color, and which collate and staple automatically, service the needs of large users. As a result, Xerox has grown rapidly as a corporation and other companies — new to the copying industry — have successfully entered this industry. Suppliers of xerographic copy paper and allied products have also benefited greatly from the successful development of xerographic copying.

Thus, a technological advancement like xerographic copying can create new competitive advantage that can completely alter a market. Some companies, like Xerox, can benefit greatly by the change in technology. Others, like the producers of the mimeograph machine, can be devastated. No company is immune to the threat of sudden technological change.

Technological change can quickly alter an industry in a number of ways. A new product, such as xerographic copiers, can render old products obsolete. A new process for making an existing product can reduce the cost of manufacturing a product or shorten its production time. Modular housing, for example, is both a quicker and a lower cost way to build housing than the standard process of building a "stick built" house.

Patent laws are a big incentive for companies to engage in research and development of new technology. Patent laws provide a period of protection for new inventions. During this period of protection, other companies may not use the invention in their products unless such use has been licensed by the owner of the patent. Polaroid, for example, gained a tremendous marketing advantage because of its patent on several areas of instant photography. A century ago, Alexander Graham Bell gained a similar advantage for his Bell telephone companies because of his patent on the telephone.

Large companies today often have sizable research and development departments trying to keep up with or stay ahead of technological change. One reason that AT&T was willing to agree to divestiture of its local telephone operating companies in settlement of an antitrust suit was that it was able to retain ownership of its famous Bell Laboratories, which developed the transistor and many other new technological products.

Governments often subsidize new technology in order to help industry in their nations. In Japan, the Ministry of International Trade and Industry (MITI) helps Japanese companies fund new technology in such areas as computer chips by providing capital from Japanese financial institutions at low rates of interest. MITI targets certain fields for its support based on future market potential, what development will do to provide employment in Japan, and favorable balances of trade. The Department of Defense in the United States helps fund substantial research and development efforts for American defense contractors. For example, Department of Defense funding of a new bomber provides technological developments that also benefit civilian aviation. NASA funding of research in space has developed technology that benefits many industries in addition to space research — miniaturization of components and equipment needed because of the limitations on a rocket's payload has been applied to many other fields by NASA contractors or their licensees.

The pace of technological change seems to be quickening. Whether something is developed in an industrial R&D center like Bell Laboratories, or it is developed in a university, or as a spin-off from defense or space research, or research from government or industry, new technology will continue to be developed rapidly. Managers need to constantly think about technological change and how it may affect their organizations. Management of technological change today is a major responsibility of top management. Failure to deal with technological change effectively may be disastrous for an organization.

Some industries in the past have had more technological changes than others. Such fields as computers, electronics, aviation, and pharmaceuticals are often referred to as "high tech" industries. But other industries, such as the steel industry and even agriculture, have been affected greatly by technological change. New processes for making steel developed in Europe and Japan have made many steel plants in North America obsolete, causing their abandonment before their normal economic lives were completed. The "green revolution" in agriculture, consisting of new types of crops that are more hardy and can be grown in different environments, often with the help of new fertilizers, has revolutionized agriculture to the benefit of many people in underdeveloped nations that can now grow more of their own food or can import more food at lower prices from agricultural exporting areas of the world.

Every top manager must continually ask questions about his or her organization's technology. A technological audit can be used to help in this effort. Such an audit begins by surveying what technologies are used in the organization's business, products, production processes, purchased parts, etc. The technology audit focuses on how critical each of these technologies is to each business, product, etc. For critical technologies, the source of technology is examined in more detail. Who produces this technology? What will happen if it is no longer available to our organization, or a new and better technology is developed outside our organization? Should our organization invest in the research and development of new technology for these critical areas? If so, how much should we invest? Should we be prepared to phase out this part of our business if new technology is developed elsewhere? The technology audit should also focus on whether our organization's level of technology is appropriate to our firms' goals and objectives.

A major environmental factor affecting virtually every organization is competition. Sometimes it appears to be simple to find out who the competition is. For example, competitors for General Motors in the automobile industry would seem to include Ford, Chrysler, Toyota, Nissan, and other automobile producers. Actually, competition for GM is much broader. The consumer living in a city may not buy any automobile. He or she may depend on the subway, bus, train, taxicab, or walking for transportation. The consumer may decide to keep his "old clunker" for an extra year or two and use the money instead to take a vacation trip to Tahiti or buy a fur coat for his wife. Thus, GM must compete with a wide variety of alternative purchases extending far beyond automotive producers. A large company like GM has a number of divisions that operate in different industries. GM's direct competition in the bus manufacturing industry is likely to be different than in the automotive industry.

Despite these difficulties, it is very useful for an organization to try to identify its competitors. Facts and information about competitors will be helpful in developing objectives and strategies for each organization. If competitors are weak in certain areas, there may be special opportunities for the organization. If competitors are strong in certain areas, a decision must be made as to whether to compete head-to-head with them or avoid such areas. Both strategies can be successful — Ford and GM compete head-to-head on a wide variety of automobiles and both have been successful. Mercedes-Benz, on the other hand, sells only luxury cars and is very successful in this specialized niche.

It is often useful for an organization to try to uncover its competitors' objectives and strategies. Their past performances may be a good indicator of their future strategies. Some organizations go to great lengths to learn what competitors do. Some industrial intelligence activities seem to come out of a James Bond spy novel. Competitors' garbage has been known to be analyzed, competitors' plants photographed from the air or by hidden cameras carried into the plants, and similar such activities have been undertaken. More commonly, however, companies read sales literature and annual reports provided by competitors and other information provided by the news media. Additionally, they often buy a competitor's product for benchmarking and field testing and, where legal, for copying useful features.

As mentioned previously, virtually every organization has competition. This applies to nonprofit organizations as well as profit-oriented businesses. Harvard competes with Yale and many other colleges and universities. One hospital can compete with another on the opposite side of town. Charities compete with each other to gain donor support. The Boy Scouts may compete with a city-operated youth bureau for membership of boys in their cities. One church may compete with another for parishioners. Even governments compete. One state or province competes with another for locating new industry. One nation may compete with another in economic areas or in military strength.

Competition has many benefits. It spurs innovation and tends to produce more economic efficiency through lower prices or better products or both. Sometimes, however, competition can be destructive. Either way, competition is a fact of the environment of every organization.

Every manager must consider all the environmental factors — governmental, political and legal factors, economic factors, geographic and demographic factors, social and cultural factors, technological factors, and the competition. Because these factors are so complex, it is often necessary for the organization to divide up the monitoring of each of these areas to ensure that each one is being researched and considered by management as it develops its objectives and strategies.

A great deal of information is available on the environment. Newspapers, magazines, annual reports, and other printed information is available on competitors, governmental factors, technological factors, etc. Larger organizations may maintain careful files on each factor. Individual employees may be assigned to scan particular sources of information to ensure that the organization remains current on the environment.

Once an adequate database has been developed on the environment, an organization is in a position to use it in planning activities. Forecasting is a useful device to help a company better predict future trends. Sometimes forecasts are available in published form. Stock market analysts forecast the future of the market, economists forecast the future of the economy, technologists forecast the future of technology. Sometimes organizations need to make their own forecasts. Quantitative forecasts can be made on the basis of statistical data. Qualitative forecasts can also be made using information from sales forces, market surveys, and techniques such as scenarios, brainstorming, and Delphi forecasts.

Estimates made by each salesperson about future sales, competitors' activities, and customer reactions can be aggregated into a sales force forecast of the future. Such a forecast is based on those who have the most direct relationship with the external environment — the salesperson. Sometimes organizations balance these sales forecasts with estimates made by the functional top executives (marketing, operations, finance, research and development). These later forecasts are called juries of executive opinion. Scenarios are forecasts of alternate future developments. The late Herman Kahn, founder of the Hudson Institute, made scenarios popular with his forecasts of scenarios depicting what would happen in a war using nuclear weapons. Dephi forecasts are joint forecasts of a panel of experts. Brainstorming is a method whereby a group gets together to try to generate new ideas.

All forecasting, whether quantitative or qualitative, is subject to error and inaccuracy. Some forecasters engage in wishful thinking. Others are either pessimistic or too optimistic. Despite these problems, forecasting remains a useful tool for helping organizations consider the environment when developing objectives and strategies.

The external environment will continue to be very important to organizations. Managers must deal with environmental factors in planning objectives and strategies for their organizations. Analysis of the environmental factors is a continuous process for the manager. Careful analysis of the environment on a continuous basis will help managers face the changes that will occur in the environment in the future.

20

Management Under Adversity

The vision of a composed and thoughtful manager, dispassionately engaged in planning, organizing, directing, and controlling, is a myth. Managers, like taxi drivers in New York City, get caught in disabling traffic, encounter ruinous potholes, battle ruthless competitors, and arrive at their destinations unscathed only if blessed by luck and skill.

Management strategies to avoid disaster are many; we are concerned here with two major ones — corporate turnabout to avoid bankruptcy and management conduct to avoid hostile takeovers.

CORPORATE TURNAROUND

Bankruptcy does not creep up on little cat feet. Usually, alarms of imminent failure are clearly heard in advance: slowing sales, rising costs, decreasing working capital, declining earnings, shrinking cash flow. Good management should react to these signs well before bankruptcy becomes unavoidable.

The manager active in a firm is seldom aware of his own poor management practices, but is more likely to be sensitive to major changes in the climate of operations, at least if he or she is alert. The good manager is aware of increased competition, technological innovation elsewhere, changes in public taste, the emergence of new products, and inflationary pressures. The complacent manager, enjoying a satisfactory return, secure in his control of the firm, buoyed by remembrance of profits past, tends to ignore danger signals. He may believe his firm can withstand new competition as it had in the past, ignore technological changes in his affection for old ways, and deny management weakness in his ebullient self-assurance.

In the past, we believed that all managers maximized profits. Any return below the maximum, if managers could recognize that ideal, would trigger corrective action. Today, we teach that managers satisfice, i.e., they seek satisfactory profits. This concept, probably closer to actual behavior in the real realm of business, permits a less rigorous reaction to intimations of adversity. The best assurance for prompt action to avoid decline is an alert manager and a vigilant board, but practical steps to recognize danger can be outlined.

A prerequisite is to make certain that danger signals are visible. Even the most elementary information system will reveal that sales are dropping, costs rising, and bank balances declining. Chapter 12 on *Controlling* discusses a number of specific measures of business results. One such measure is the Z-score as a predictor of bankruptcy. Statistical analysis can be made of various financial relationships in the operating statement and balance sheet to reveal danger points.

Edward Altman (Edward I. Altman, *Corporate Financial Distress*, New York: John Wiley & Sons, 1983) advises managers to use the Z-score or ZETA model, not merely for information, but as a guide to action. As soon as the Z-score drops below a satisfactory level, and well before it reaches a dangerous level, the turnaround program can be introduced.

INITIATING TURNAROUND

There are times when existing managers recognize danger and act in time. Unfortunately, many managers do not react until it is too late for ordinary corrective action. In such cases, there may be little else that the sleepy board can do than to call for a "doctor," the "turnaround" expert. The management doctor must have absolute authority to act. Probably, as an outsider, he will be more likely to prescribe strong medicine, since the focus of his job is to save a corporate life. Often this desperate step is not taken till after bankruptcy is declared and there is no way to revive the patient.

Action must be decisive. While a total program to turn around the ailing firm is necessary, the first step is to stop the cash bleeding. This is more important in the short-run than profitability. Simultaneously, major creditors, including the bank, must be informed. The firm may want to halt the trading of stock on the Exchange.

RESTORING CASH FLOW

The urgent first step for the new manager is to restore a proper cash flow. Collections must be sped up. Inventories must be cut. Purchasing must be curtailed. Staff must be reduced, including the staff in corporate headquarters. Perks must be sacrificed. Programs of repair and replacement and especially new construction must be stopped, at least temporarily. Only repairs which are absolutely necessary for the operation of the firm can be continued. The accounts payable should be closely managed; a judgment should be made as to which accounts must be paid and which can be delayed.

It should be noted that cutting the size of staffs, or reducing the payroll, may be difficult because of contracts. A number of firms in recent years were able to abrogate union contracts after declaring bankruptcy. An example is Continental Airlines. In 1984, Continental laid off 12,000 workers and rehired 4,200 at pay cuts of 50 percent after declaring bankruptcy.

In the United States solvent firms are permitted to file Chapter 11 of the Federal Bankruptcy Act of 1978. Under the provisions of the revised act, the executives of the firm may be permitted to continue running the impoverished business as "debtors-in-possession" with some court supervision. Section 365(a) of the Bankruptcy Code authorizes the firm to reject executory contracts (such as a labor contract), with certain exceptions, on the approval of the court after notice and hearing. Though the National Labor Relations Act makes it an unfair labor practice for a trustee in a bankruptcy reorganization to refuse to bargain in good faith, the courts have not permitted the NLRA to supersede the Bankruptcy Code. In a number of cases where breaking union contracts took place after declaring bankruptcy, the union has charged that the purpose of bankruptcy was precisely to void the contracts. It is not the purpose of this chapter to argue the merits of the case, but only to indicate that such action by management may be possible under certain circumstances.

One way to stop cash bleeding is to sell major assets. However, assets considered for sale and plants scheduled for closing may be necessary for the long-term survival of the firm. A rational decision must be reached as to whether the immediate sale of assets is unavoidable or a hasty action which should not be taken. There is no firm guide for such decisions other than rationality or good intuitive perceptions.

THE WRITTEN PLAN

If stopping the cash bleeding is a first step, it is not sufficient. As a second step, a written plan must be prepared to convince creditors that better times lie ahead. The management must buy time to put the full turnaround program into operation. Planners will argue that an early step must be a careful evaluation of the situation. Logic tells us this is correct. Unfortunately, in the face of actual bankruptcy, there may be little time for deliberate action. We will assume that the surgery to stop the cash bleeding was undertaken by knowledgeable administrators with at least a strong intuitive grasp of the situation. But eventually, careful analysis will be an absolute requirement. A thorough evaluation of the firm must be undertaken as soon as possible. Projections should be prepared, based on conservative expectations about the P&L, the balance sheet, and cash flow. The analysis must also include comparisons of product lines, locations and their comparative operating costs. A matrix of these costs could be a guide for decisions on which products and locations to continue, expand, or eliminate.

Questions must be asked about each product and each location. Is there an adequate market for the product? Are new products available for the firm? Can units be eliminated? Can groups be consolidated? Are new locations feasible? Is the poor showing of a profit center short-term, an intermediate-term problem, or a permanent disability? Should better systems be introduced? Can the management structure and staff be improved?

Once answers are found to these questions, a plan of action must be designed. A schedule, showing the timing of planned activities, should be included. Since relationships with creditors and the banks are of utmost importance, it may be well to communicate without delay with those who have the option of crushing you at once, or giving you time. However, aside from this urgent communication, the plan must be put in writing.

BRIDGE FINANCING

A key third step in the turnaround process is to secure "bridge," or temporary financing, but no bank will throw money to a dying firm. The written plan may well be the crucial step in convincing the bank, or other lenders, that the interim financing will improve the chances of survival and assure repayment of debt. The possibility of private placement of a loan must be considered, but a written plan will be needed for this alternative as well.

To obtain bridge financing the written plan must be a rational statement of steps to be taken as well as a persuasive declaration of faith. It is a plan of action as well as an assurance that the firm is viable. Without seeming to be a sales pitch, it must show enthusiasm, a positive attitude and a reasonable chance of success.

Financing is more likely if the plan not only outlines management changes, but also changes in the underlying business of the firm, if needed. Management must demonstrate a "hands-on" attitude, concern for tight control and an understanding of the competition, as well as an intuitive feel for the future.

The plan may demonstrate reasonability by the elimination of major production lines and the acquisition of others for which funds are needed. It can include changes in production methods, marketing approaches, and will certainly include a new financial structure. A detailed outline of how the debt will be restructured is critical. Financing will be contingent on new systems of control and projections of business activities in the years to come. It must be a multiyear projection, not merely a short-term statement.

THE PLAN IN OPERATION

Once the cash crisis is over, the written plan completed, bridge financing becomes available, and creditors indicate a willingness to wait, step four begins. This is the urgent business of conforming to the plan. This is the time to make permanent changes in the management team and structure, in contractual obligations, and in the financial structure. This is the time to reach the goals of the reorganized company and to take steps to achieve objectives. This is the time to sell off major divisions of the firm, or to dispose of plants that cannot be profitable. Once the bankrupt firm has won time for the reorganization, decisions to sell off major assets can be made more rationally than in the initial excitement of failure. Moreover, once the worst crisis is past, sales of major assets may be achieved at better terms. Finally, we note that in the early stage of the turnaround process, profitability was secondary to cash flow. Now the manager can pay attention to profits as well as long-term growth.

If the firm is able to survive and return to normal operations, it must avoid the mistakes of the past. In a sense, the entire turnaround operation is a reminder of previous poor management. Good management would require that the manager must be alert to the elimination of unprofitable lines and locations at all times, and not merely in times of crisis. Tight controls should have been in place before bankruptcy loomed. It can be said that a good manager should always act as if there is impending disaster ahead.

THE HOSTILE TAKEOVER

In the good old days, before the 1980s, corporate managers could feel relatively secure in the control of their firm. Berle and Means (Adolph A. Berle and Gardiner C. Means, *The Modern Corporation and Private Property*, New York: The Macmillan Company, 1933) had pointed out that boards of directors did not need substantial ownership to maintain control. Boards of directors were largely self-perpetuating, with directors even holding small percentages of the common stock of the firm. Battles for directorships and control of giant firms were not unknown, but with the incumbents controlling the corporate election apparatus, the odds were on the side of the insiders.

Times have changed. The once secure CEO seems to be involved in a game of invisible chairs; his seat as chairman is up for grabs. The culprit is the raider or "shark" seeking control of a firm or a target for financial manipulation, and perhaps for the excitement of the hunt. The response of the management is to apply "shark repellent" activities to repulse the invader.

The new game in town is the corporate takeover, hostile or friendly. An investor finds a company that seems to be undervalued on the stock market. But other reasons may attract an investor. The management of an oil company may find that it is safer to buy a firm with great oil reserves than to drill for oil. A calculating financial manager could believe that the assets of a corporation would be worth more if sold separately than as part of a going concern. The potential raider may not even want to acquire his victim; his real goal may be to wrest a profit by threatening to take control of the firm and collecting "greenmail" from the victim. That is, the corporation will buy back the raider's shares at a profit to the raider.

In any case, the raider buys shares of stock in the target firm. Under SEC rules, when ownership reaches five percent, the investor must notify the target firm and the SEC as to his or her plans. The problem for management is what to do about it.

THE "HIRED GUN"

A first step, in many cases, is to retain a "hired gun," often an attorney or a banker with expertise in takeovers. A knowledgeable management team could fight with internal staff, but this option involves risks since the technicalities are great. Strategies available to the "hired gun," or existing management, include the following:

1. Go private.
2. Resort to "greenmail."
3. Increase the number of shares outstanding.
4. Increase debt.
5. Sell off assets.
6. Buy the potential raider.
7. Buy a small firm in a highly regulated industry.
8. Encourage a friendly takeover.
9. Get a "golden parachute."

GOING PRIVATE

If funds are available, an entrenched management may take the firm off the market, giving up public trading of its shares and buying out other shareholders. An objection may be the loss of access to the public for funds by selling additional shares. The typical approach is the leveraged buyout. The management often owns only a small percentage of the total shares outstanding, while tremendous funds may be needed to buy all outstanding shares from the public. Few groups have the necessary money on hand.

The management borrows the funds from a bank or private investor, putting up the assets of the firm as collateral. This is the leveraged buyout. Many bankers are wary of such activities. However, an investment banker may be the author of the plan, earning an advisory fee plus a commission on the sale of any securities. With funds assured, management is able to make a public offer to repurchase the stock at a price above the market price, buying shares of stock until a specified date.

The manager should know that this process is not without danger. The potential raider, or a new one, may make a better public offer. Of course, if a substantially better offer is made, the management has the option of accepting the offer itself and retiring with a nest-egg for a future effort elsewhere.

The raider must also have the funds for the takeover. A new approach avoids a simple bank loan. Raiders form a new corporation which offers unsecured securities at high interest, usually to insurance companies, wealthy individuals, or savings and loan associations in order to quickly gather the funds necessary for a raid. Since the securities bear a great risk, this approach is known as "junk financing" and the securities sold are known as "junk bonds."

A consequence of the leveraged buyout is that the premium paid to purchase shares may have sharply increased the debt of the firm. In the case of the successful defense, security from the clutches of the raider has been purchased with the insecurity of being hostage to the lenders. If the raider wins, he may have bought control of a weakened firm. The bankers may have wrested control in exchange for the loan. Future profits may be dedicated to paying off the debt, rather than paying dividends, investing in new productive assets, or increasing the value of the firm.

Another problem is that takeover bids have been marred by lawsuits from unsuccessful suitors, ousted directors, or stockholders who believe the parties to the struggle may have damaged the firm for their personal benefit and not for the benefit of the firm itself. The entire transaction may be overturned in the courts if the liabilities of the new firm exceed its assets.

GREENMAIL

Greenmail is another route for managers to escape the raider. It is a new twist in which the raider alone of all stockholders is offered a special high price for his recently purchased stock, in excess of what he paid. The raider wins a substantial bonus for his recent acquisitions in exchange for a promise to give up his takeover attempt. Other stockholders are not given this privilege. The victim of the takeover has depleted his firm for the right to continue in control.

Successful greenmail does raise problems for the manager, since the firm has depleted its cash reserves or borrowed heavily on its assets. The firm may have been forced to sell off existing assets or to have incurred substantial debts, only to find, after the raider has gone, that another raider appears on the scene. Other options can be considered by management.

OTHER "SHARK REPELLENTS"

Management strategies to ward off raids include staggered terms for board members, or the issuance of warrants and other opportunities to purchase additional shares in the target firm if the raider buys more than a certain percentage of the stock of the target firm under the terms of a formal tender offer. The plan to increase the number of shares outstanding if the raider acquires a certain number of shares is known as the "poison pill." The manager of a firm under attack may increase the number of shares outstanding in order to dilute the holdings of the raider. For example, The Walt Disney Corporation, facing a takeover attempt by a major investor, purchased stock in Arvida Corporation (a real estate development firm) and Gibson Greetings, Inc. (a greeting card firm), issuing $525 million in new shares of common stock. In this case, the dilution succeeded, and the attacking investor failed. However, it should be noted that Disney also resorted to greenmail, giving the raider a profit of $31.9 million on the sale.

Even if successful in putting off a raider temporarily, the increase in shares of stock outstanding creates problems. Expansion and issuing new shares for new business activities is a basic way of life for growing companies. The problem is that the deals are often rushed, forced by the activities of the raider, rather than by a long-range analysis in which the firm decides on price and timing in a rational manner. This is a case in which management planning takes a back seat to current pressures.

THE POISON PILL

Increasing debt is another form of shark repellent, a powerful form of the poison pill. The manager may acquire new assets for his firm not by issuing additional shares, but by borrowing additional funds at high interest rates. Such an expansion, while possibly desirable in itself, makes the firm a less attractive partner. It is nicer to marry a rich widow than one who is hopelessly in debt. Unfortunately, the present owners, as well as the potential raider, must suffer the new embarrassment.

A target of takeover may sell off assets in order to secure needed funds or in order to appear less attractive to the suitor. Perhaps the raider is really interested in a particular division. In such case, the incumbent management may keep its control by divorcing the favorite. More generally, a firm may sell off divisions in order to secure the funds to fight the takeover. The disposed division may be one which offers good prospects in the future, but which must be given up because of the short-term goal. This type of poison pill defense, painful to managers, is known as the "scorched earth policy."

A strange reflection of the scorched earth policy is the action of the successful corporate raider. Once the shark acquires his victim, he may sell off divisions anyhow, since his interest is often the short-term cash that can be accumulated by the sale. It appears that the sum of the parts may be greater than the total value of the entire firm as a going concern, at least in the short-run. This sale of the prime divisions of a large firm is known as the sale of the "crown jewels."

All these tactics are orchestrated by law firms and investment bankers who reap high fees for their services. The lawyers who make a practice of takeover strategy are sometimes known as "killer bees." Since their fees for directing or stopping a takeover attempt run in the tens of millions of dollars and more, the fees have been dubbed "feemail," a counterpart of the better known greenmail. Feemail, too, contributes to the cost of fighting a hostile takeover and weakens the target.

A sophisticated tactic is to heed military strategy. Attack is the best defense. The target firm can buy the raider. A prime example was the 1982 battle between Bendix Corporation and Martin Marietta. Each tried to buy stock in the other until Allied Corporation stepped in and purchased Bendix. One lesson is that no firm is so large that it is immune to takeover fever.

A more frequently used strategy is to buy up small firms in severely regulated industries, including banking and broadcasting. Investors are generally advocates of free enterprise, entrepreneurs, individuals unwilling to be shackled by government restraints. Buying a highly regulated business may discourage the raider who does not want to become involved in the complex legal regulations of the Federal Reserve Board or the Federal Communications Commission required when changes are made in ownership. This approach may not be unlike that of the young men in Czarist Russia who starved themselves in order to avoid the draft.

THE WHITE KNIGHT

An option for management is to find another firm that is willing to acquire control of the target firm. This is the friendly takeover. Often the understanding is that the new owners of a controlling interest will retain the old management team. Since the new stockholder has come to the rescue of the distressed managers, he or she is known as a white knight.

THE GOLDEN PARACHUTE

The golden parachute is another solution for managers who may want to bail out of a takeover target. The wise manager must consider his future should the hostile takeover attempt succeed. A favorite way to assure a healthy personal future, is to set up a munificent retirement pension. In the Bendix–Martin Marietta–Allied struggle, William M. Agee, chairman of Bendix, convinced the board to award him a $4 million pension in case he was ousted.

Pensions for top management are normal, but special pensions, passed by the board during a takeover battle, are new. There is a danger, however, that angry minority stockholders will initiate lawsuits to set aside such contracts, but most courts have refused to interfere with the business judgment of boards. In the case of Chairman Agee, the parachute opened.

A variation of the golden parachute is the tin parachute. This is a pension for all employees, triggered by a hostile takeover. In the case of Herman Miller, Inc., a Michigan furniture manufacturer, each of the 3,300 employees will receive a pension payment of amounts up to two-and-one-half times the annual pay for those who have worked for more than five years. While the cost of golden parachutes for a dozen top officers may not be a large enough sum to deter a takeover costing hundreds of millions of dollars, a bonus for thousands of employees can amount to a substantial sum. The tin parachute may be a poison pill too expensive to swallow. It should be noted that tin parachutes are triggered by a takeover deemed hostile, and do not become effective if the board of directors agrees to the takeover as friendly or in the case of a leveraged buyout by management. The tin parachute may be an extremely effective defense for beleaguered management.

The new role of hostile takeover attempts and the shark repellents used by the targets are hotly disputed. Many economists, lawyers, and businessmen are seeking ways to limit these tactics, particularly greenmail and golden parachutes.

It is generally argued that American business is too much focused on financial gimmicks and not enough on the fundamentals of production.

Managers must be concerned with innovation, productivity, efficiency, and effectiveness. However, the manager cannot pay full attention to these basics of good management when faced with the possibility of a hostile takeover. He cannot ignore the field of defense against the hostile takeover.

MANAGEMENT IN THE FACE OF A STRIKE

Steering through the Persian Gulf, many a ship hit a mine. Steering a firm through labor problems can be just as dangerous. Make a miscalculation and you end up a wreck. The best strategy in dealing with a labor union strike may be to avoid it in the first place. If avoidance is impossible, then a sophisticated defense is needed, not an angry, thoughtless response.

It may not be possible for a firm to remain nonunion; in some industries, unions are deeply entrenched. However, an alert management can take steps to reduce the likelihood that a union can organize the employees successfully. Basically, this means providing pay and working conditions comparable to those in firms with unions. It also means an attitude which considers employees as human beings essential to the success of the firm. In narrow, practical terms, in some cases there may be little benefit to the firm in terms of the total payroll. The advantage of keeping the union out of the firm could be in management flexibility.

To stay nonunion, the manager must follow practices associated with the human relations approach. It is urgent for the manager to communicate with employees regularly. The manager should make certain that working conditions are pleasant. Most important is building a sense of trust and credibility. One way to do this is with grievance and disciplinary procedures that are fair. As part of such a plan, it is desirable to issue an employee handbook so that employees understand their rights, and can see that all members of the work force are treated alike. The handbook would list management and employee rights, rules and regulations, benefits, including holidays, overtime, rates of pay, absenteeism, lateness, pensions, as well as grievance and disciplinary procedures. A corollary is that all supervisory employees must be trained to understand and carry out the policy of the firm as set forth in the employee handbook.

A part of this approach is the open-door policy of management. A worker who can walk into the office of the boss to air his or her complaint is less likely to seek union support. In general, a participative management culture, job enrichment, profit sharing, opportunities for growth within the firm, and other similar practices are helpful in avoiding unions. Of course, these management approaches have other justifications. Moreover, they cannot work in certain types of industries. However, an extra benefit of a management style derived from ideas of the human relations school may be labor peace.

Despite an attitude of appreciation for the employees, the alert manager may discover that a union is conducting an organizing drive in the plant. In such case, a prerequisite to any action is thorough knowledge of employee and union rights under the National Labor Relations Act. The manager may not interfere with the right of the worker to join the union. The manager may not discriminate between union and nonunion workers. For example, it is not legal to give higher pay or other benefits to employees who refuse to join the union.

What to do in the face of an organizing drive by a union? Management can argue its case. It can issue written material. It will have to depend on the front line supervisors to maintain a friendly relationship with the workers. It can remind workers of the costs of a strike, union dues, and the advantages of working for a strong and successful nonunion firm.

Despite all efforts, the drive to form a union may succeed. The law requires the management to bargain collectively, that is to deal with the union on issues affecting the workers. Indeed, there are excellent management opportunities for specialists in personnel, sometimes known as human relations managers, who deal with trade unions. Collective bargaining is both a technical skill and an art. The person heading personnel activities must work closely with top management to establish the boundary line between compromise and capitulation. Labor peace is worth a lot, but union demands may be more than the firm can sustain.

Management has many options. One might be to close the plant. Another is to outsource many of the inputs, though this option can itself trigger a strike. Perhaps a plant can be established overseas or another section of the country might be more conducive to profitable operations. No formula can be provided to make decisions about relocation easy. The job of the manager is to examine options and make choices.

It may come to pass that despite all efforts, a strike is unavoidable. Then management must have a plan readied. An urgent step in such a plan is to appoint one person with full authority to handle the strike. This is a time when unified command is necessary. During a strike, the manager may work through a committee composed of department heads. Since strike arrangements might include publicity, security, and options for continued operation, the skills and specialized knowledge of the various department heads are essential.

Members of the committee can help answer a number of vital questions. The strike activities manager must know if the firm will be able to continue operations, for what length of time, and at what level. What is the possibility of nonunion employees carrying out operations? What about the delivery of material during a strike? How big are inventories, especially of vital parts? What is the status of the security force? The strike activities manager, with the advice of the committee, prepares a recommendation as to whether the firm should attempt to remain in operation. While the strike activities manager must have full responsibility, this decision is so basic that it must be presented to top management. In fact, such a decision is often made before the strike activities manager is appointed.

The decision may be based on factors that are not purely economic, such as a desire to demonstrate control of the firm, to make a stand and maintain power, or because of extremely strong feelings of anger. In the real world, the decision to close the plant or continue operations may or may not have a rational basis. Rational factors to consider include the costs of the strike, its effect on future sales, and the likelihood of winning. Major factors in assessing the likelihood of winning a strike are the strength of the union and the strength of the firm. If the purpose of the firm is to earn a profit, these economic factors should be controlling.

Another urgent matter to be established concerns public relations. The office of the strike activities manager should supervise all public statements to be made to the press or to employees concerning the strike. Marketing divisions should be prepared in advance to deal with customers in a unified manner under the centralized leadership.

Once a strike is in progress, all activities should be coordinated by the strike activities manager. Of course, a crucial activity is continued collective bargaining. The firm cannot give concessions that will destroy it. If it appears that the firm is in imminent danger, it may be necessary to file for bankruptcy. One advantage of filing for bankruptcy is that it may permit the firm to set aside previous labor union contracts.

21

Career Planning

Planning careers is important to both individuals and organizations. Career planning can help the individual take full advantage of his or her talents, interests, education, and experience. Career planning can help an organization develop people to their maximum potential, thus improving the quality, efficiency, and productivity of the management of the organization.

Thinking about careers begins early in life. Even three year old children talk about careers: "Daddy, I want to be a firefighter when I grow up." Serious career decisions may be made by late adolescence — the high school dropout may have foreclosed many career options. The high school graduate who decides to go on to college may do so out of a desire to have a career in a white collar profession a desire for a managerial job. Others who decide to enter the world of business after high school may prepare for a managerial career by planning to work their way up the ladder. Many who decide to enter the business world after high school do not plan on a career in management or a white collar profession.

College students who are thinking about careers face a more competitive situation in the job market than students of 25 years ago. First of all, a higher percentage of youngsters attend college today than did a generation ago. The baby boom of the 1950s and 1960s has increased the number of college graduates in the 1980s and 1990s. In addition, a higher percentage of female college graduates are entering and remaining in the work force as attitudes about female workers and child rearing have changed in response to the women's liberation movement.

Economic growth has also slowed down somewhat in recent years. These trends have combined to make more analysts believe that there may be an oversupply of college graduates in the late 1990s, when about 65 million workers will be in the 25 to 45 age range in North America, as opposed to approximately half that number of workers 20 years earlier. If creation of new jobs does not increase, this larger number of workers in the prime age range of 25 to 45 may make finding a good job more difficult for the college graduate.

The college student must think not only of a first job after graduation, but also about lifelong career objectives and plans. In the short run, a first job must be found. In the long run, career objectives and planning are important. The choice of a first job after college may or may not be significant in terms of a career. Career planning is a process by which a person hopes to find a career that will best utilize his or her talents, interests, education, and experience. Career planning is not a once-in-a-lifetime process, engaged in only during college. Like other planning, career planning takes place over time. Career plans are adjusted depending upon opportunities, experience, change in lifestyles, and changes in circumstances (such as marriage, children, changing health).

For many individuals, work is an important part of life. Some people work only for financial gain but most find meaningful work to be a satisfying part of life. By working, people gain satisfaction through achievement. ("I sold more cars than anyone else in the salesroom this month.") People may also derive satisfaction in work through recognition or approval from others, such as a boss or fellow worker, or from status accorded to their job or profession.

A career must begin with a first job. The college student who finds summer work with a potential for a job after graduation has an edge over the student who spends the summer partying or at a job that is unlikely to lead to long-range employment after graduation (such as a lifeguard job). Nevertheless, any work experience is likely to be given some value by employers. Work that may enable a student to see whether he or she will like a career in that field may also benefit the student by giving them additional job knowledge and professional contacts, which may be helpful towards the first rung on a career leader.

As a first step, the college student looking for a job should begin with a self-assessment of his or her assets and liabilities. Many individuals find it helpful to list these assets and liabilities in writing.

The assets might begin with the student's educational background. What activities engaged in at college will be transferable to the world of work? For example, the student who has been an officer of the management club in college may have had an opportunity to learn some "hands-on" leadership skills. The student who has written for the college newspaper or taken courses in writing may be able to offer a firm some experience and skills in written communication. Other courses may be of value to employers in a wide range of fields.

In addition to educational background, the student may have some work experience that can be valuable to a future employer. The entrepreneurial student who sells pizza in the college dorm to help pay expenses may have marketing experience of value to many organizations or entrepreneurial talents useful in a variety of industries.

Experience as a volunteer is also typically an asset. The church volunteer who has worked with young people may find such experience useful in a store catering to youth. The volunteer in a hospital may have gained "on-the-job" experience that would be useful in a variety of organizations in the health care industry. Other experience, such as a hobby, might be of value to some organizations. Participation in sports while in college is also an area that might be of value in some careers.

In addition to a person's educational background and his or her experience, a person may have other assets. Someone who has the ability to work long hours without a break has an advantage in a career that requires a great deal of stamina under difficult conditions, such as a floor trader on the stock exchange. An outgoing, friendly personality may be a useful asset for a career in sales. An ability to work with numbers may be useful to someone hoping to enter a career in financial services.

Liabilities should also be assessed. The very shy person who is happy doing research may have little affinity for a career dealing directly with the public. A liability in one field may prove to be an asset in another.

After one has assessed his or her assets and liabilities, it is helpful to assess interests and preferred lifestyle. For example, the person who desires to live near the ocean in a resort area may be unable to seek a career in fields where the action is likely to be in the heart of a large metropolitan city.

Once this self-assessment has been completed, the next step is to assess the opportunities for a career that will take full advantage of one's assets and personal preferences. This requires an assessment of opportunities. One might begin such an assessment by looking at long-range trends. As the population moves toward the sunbelt, will there be more opportunities in that area or will skills possessed be more useful in the long-term in the frostbelt despite projected changes? Various career fields can then be assessed in light of these long-range trends. The current status of career fields that might have long-range promise can then be assessed. Are opportunities better now for profit in business? government? not-for-profit institutions? What competition would I face in an industry? in an organization?

The individual may also wish to consider the likes and dislikes of parents, spouse, children, and friends as well as general views of certain fields. College professors may have a great deal of prestige but truck drivers may have higher incomes. Is prestige more important to you than money? One's expectations about work are also important. Is it more important for you to be your own boss in a small organization than to have the greater security and support that may exist in a larger organization where you will not be the boss?

Again, it is helpful to write down the major career fields that are of interest and the pros and cons of each of those fields. The priorities can then be decided on. Once a long-range career plan has been decided on, strategies are developed for both the long- and short-term. At this point, it is necessary to begin a job search. One must work diligently and actively to get the job that is desired. Finding a specific job in a desirable career is 99 percent perspiration and one percent inspiration. The job seeker must plan a job campaign and carry it out.

The first step will generally be to prepare a resume covering one's background. Such a resume would include name, home address, and telephone number(s). Many resume writers recommend listing a job objective on the resume (such as becoming a marketing representative for a branded products company selling to supermarkets). If more than one job or career is being considered, multiple resumes can be structured for the different fields being considered. The resume usually will include educational background, activities, honors and recognitions, and previous work experience. Some people list their references on the resume. Others submit a separate list of references when required by a potential employer. Resumes are often used by employers to exclude people quickly so they must be carefully written. Long resumes often wind up in wastebaskets or dead files. The resume should be no longer than two pages unless one is very senior and has many significant accomplishments to list. Resumes should always be carefully typed on white paper with no errors. Some employers discard resumes if there are gaps in the time of work experience listed. If a year is missing, the employer might wonder as to the candidate's activities during that time period. Resumes are most valuable to quickly show one's qualifications for an available position.

A second step in the job campaign is to seek interviews. The college student or graduate should take advantage of the career planning or placement office on campus. Some good jobs are listed and interviews given at professional meetings and meetings of academic societies, such as the Academy of Management. Some industries hold job fairs where applicants can talk to many employers in one place.

Networking is a process that can help one get interviews. Networking involves talking with your friends, professors, employers, neighbors, etc., telling them you are looking for a job and seeking their assistance in providing leads or contacts or other information.

The secret to finding a job is to be able to convince the employer to hire you over someone else. Sometimes bold tactics like carrying a sign on the street listing your qualifications and walking in front of the office of the advertising agency you would like to work for will attract attention and lead to an interview and the desired job. However, such bold tactics might backfire in more traditional and conservative fields.

Once you have succeeded in being scheduled for an interview, the next step is to learn whatever you can about the organization that is considering you so you can demonstrate to the interviewer that you care enough about the job to be thoroughly prepared. The job interview for an entry level position may be 15 to 30 minutes long. A more senior position may involve a series of interviews with executive search firms and key company executives. Information on major companies can be found in annual reports of the company, investment manuals such as Moody's or Standard & Poors, which can be found in libraries with business reference sections, or over the Internet. The job applicant should know what an organization does, its size, its profitability, its history, its future plans and prospects, and who its key owners and managers are.

Before going to the interview, the applicant should make sure that he or she is clean and well groomed. Extreme hair styles, such as purple mohawks, very long hair on men, or frazzled unkempt hair on women may be useful if one is planning on a career in rock music but will not help land a job in most business organizations. Business suits with white shirt and tie still are the safest dress for men although sport jackets with white shirt and tie are acceptable in a growing number of companies. Women can safely choose from conservative dresses, business suits (with skirt versus slacks), or skirts and blazers. Again, extremes in dress or excessive informality (shorts, polyester pantsuits, sneakers) should be avoided except in the entertainment industry.

Punctuality is important. If one is not sure where the interview will be held, it is helpful to arrive early so you can find the interview room on time.

Courtesy is very important at all times in the job search process. Being friendly to the receptionist and other employees at the interview site along with a pleasant smile are helpful in most settings. Following the interview, it is courteous to send a thank you note to the interviewer. This gives you an opportunity to remind the interviewer of your interest and qualifications.

Sometimes an applicant is fortunate enough to receive more than one job offer. In such cases, the pros and cons of each job and its potential for the short-term and the long-term can be listed on paper and compared. Advice from peers, mentors, and others can be helpful before making a choice among a number of jobs in different companies and/or industries.

Once a candidate has accepted an offer, the initial weeks of employment may be crucial for long-term success on the job. The new employee can experience anxiety or fear about success. Asking questions whenever possible will help the new employee overcome these anxieties or fears and will help the new employee do a better job with fewer errors.

Many jobs for recent college graduates may be routine and deal with mundane problems. Firms often expect the new employee to build up a record of performance of several years before major responsibility or raises and promotions are given.

In addition to offering good performance on the job, it is important to participate in work-related social activities on the job. Having coffee or a snack with one's associates, getting involved with in-house athletics and other company social events, and participating in company-sponsored charitable drives will all increase your visibility and help to give you informal channels, building friendships that can be critical to your career. Civic participation outside your company in service groups, church work, charitable groups, and professional and alumni associations are all likely to be helpful.

Once a job has begun, you can start analyzing how it can become a career and begin preparing a career development plan. If one begins at a bottom level job, plans can be initiated for the next level — perhaps lower middle management. What additional education will be required to achieve the next level in your career? Is other experience needed? Can you get this education and/or experience with company assistance?

One can set career goals as part of a career development program. In five years where could you be? In 10? Goals can be adjusted over time based on experience. Often, the new employee will have unrealistically high expectations about their first job. The career development plan may have to be modified due to changes in the external economic environment, changes in the environment of the corporation (such as a major decline in sales), and changes in personal goals as a result of gaining experience in the real world. As mentioned earlier, one's preferences, abilities, and experience should be considered in building this career development plan.

Some career planners begin by setting their ultimate career goal. They then work backward in preparing their career development plan, showing different stages that must be achieved.

As one moves up a career ladder, there will be choices: Do you take a position at a branch plant with more diverse managerial duties and greater responsibilities or can you progress faster toward your career goals by staying in your functional area at headquarters? Such decisions are difficult when more than one area of opportunity opens up.

It is important to periodically review your career development plan. Perhaps one has come to a "dead end" job in the organization. It may be necessary to find another company or transfer to another division of the company if career progress is to continue. Sometimes a new career may be a better option. People today increasingly have two, three, and even four careers during their working lives. Luck and happenstance may play a role. Do not let success in a present job derail your career development plan. Even though your job is enjoyable, you must continue to look toward your long-term career plans.

Failure in a job is not the end of the world either. Some people have failed in a number of jobs and careers until they found the right career at the right time. A less than desirable job may lead to stress on the job. If job-related stress seems to be heavy, perhaps one should consider seeking another job or field. Alternatively, sometimes job-related stress can be handled through exercise and relaxation or by talking about job problems with co-workers, friends, spouse, or professional counseling. Off the job stress in one's personal life can also affect performance on the job. A sick child, a pending divorce, death of a friend or relative, the problems of a dual career marriage can all induce stress.

As one gets older, other problems can occur. Some people face a midlife crisis in their forties. They may seek a new spouse, a new career, or a new lifestyle as a result of such a crisis. A midlife crisis usually occurs due to aging — one's mortality is felt more deeply due to death of parents, less good health, gray hair, or some similar age-induced factor. One may also suffer a midlife crisis as a result of career disappointment and/or increased rivalry and competition for promotions as one moves up the career ladder.

One may also suffer a crisis when reaching a plateau in their career. It may not be possible to move any higher within the organization. This may cause a crisis for some. Others will cope by spending more time with family or friends or with hobbies and other interests.

Women in business often face even greater burdens. Some traditionalists still do not approve of careers for women, although most women must work today to help provide a decent standard of living for themselves and their families. Women who have been well educated usually have similar needs for work-related achievement as do men with the same backgrounds.

As a result of more women working, there are now more two-career households. Such dual income families may face difficult choices. Suppose a promotion for one spouse requires a move to a distant city or state? Does the other spouse have to suffer abandonment of his or her career plans to accommodate this change? Sometimes such choices lead to long distance commuting by one or both spouses, a breakup of the family, or a refusal of the promotion.

The choice of having children especially affects two-career families. Can a sitter be found if both spouses must work during the same hours? Who will drive the child to school and pick the child up when school lets out (usually the school or daycare schedule will not fully accommodate parents who must work until 5:00 P.M. and then commute from work in the city to a residential suburb). Such difficulties add to stress but also have led to changes in the workplace and family life. For example, some daycare centers remain open until 6:00 P.M. Work rules have been changed in many companies to permit maternity (and, in some cases, paternity) leave to employees who wish to remain employed after having a child. "Flex time" may permit better scheduling for employees who can thus better meet the needs of both the workplace and parenting. Fathers now take on more responsibilities for nurturing and caring for children. Nevertheless, the problems of two-career families are often great due to conflicts between job and family responsibilities.

Even with legislation extending the retirement age, at some point in time most individuals will retire from their jobs. Retirement planning is part of career planning. One must plan for retirement not only for financial reasons, but there is life after retirement. One can still be active in their field as a volunteer or a consultant or can pick a new field to either work for remuneration or for personal gratification as a volunteer. As in planning a job campaign, one should plan for retirement while working. One should begin developing interests outside their organization while still working so that there will not be an abrupt transition away from activity and involvement at the time of retirement. Retirement can provide satisfaction if one keeps busy with family, friends, and volunteer activities while beginning this phase of their career. For example, Colonel Sanders started Kentucky Fried Chicken after retiring from other employment and collecting Social Security for a time. One should plan on continued involvement in some activity after retirement. Career planning should continue as long as one's health permits useful activity.

MELLEN STUDIES IN BUSINESS